Indo-US Strategic Partnership
Roadmap Ahead under Trump

Indo-US Strategic Partnership Roadmap Ahead under Trump

Sanjay K. Singh

PRASHANT PUBLISHING HOUSE
DELHI-110094

Published by :
Prashant Publishing House
C-34, 28 Foota Road, Gali-3,
West Karwal Nagar, Delhi-110094
Phone : 011-22963970, Mob. : 9810396373
e-mail.: prashantpublishinghouse@gmail.com

Indo-US Strategic Partnership Roadmap Ahead under Trump
Reserved
First Published 2017

ISBN 978-93-80565-9-10

PRINTED IN INDIA
Published by Mr. R.K. Jha M/s Prashant Publishing House and Published at H.S. Offset House Press, Delhi.

Contents

Preface

India-US partnership has been one of the few areas that has been non-controversial and a bright spot for the USA on the foreign policy front in recent years. It can be confidently asserted that India-US relations enjoy bipartisan support in the US Congress and across the board among the US citizens. Starting with Bill Clinton's visit to India in March, 2000, the state of partnership today is the highest ever between the two countries.

Donald Trump has hence inherited a vigorous and vibrant relationship between India and the USA. It is expected that Trump will do all that is necessary to take the bilateral partnership to newer heights. This was clearly evident from the fact that Prime Minister Narendra Modi was the fifth world leader, after Presidents of Mexico and Egypt and Prime Ministers of Canada and Israel, whom Trump called after his inauguration on January 20, 2017.

The Modi-Trump conversation on January 24 was marked by cordiality and warmth which cannot be said about some other conversations that Trump had with some other leaders. Official statements issued by the two sides did not go into specifics but Trump's early phone call is evidence of the priority that Trump attaches to Indo-US ties. According to a White House statement, Trump emphasised that Washington considers India a "true friend and partner in addressing challenges around the world." Both leaders were said to have discussed opportunities to strengthen their partnership on the economy and defence. They also discussed security in south and central Asia and resolved to "stand shoulder to shoulder in the global fight against terrorism." Modi tweeted that he had a "warm conversation" with the President and said the pair had "agreed to work closely in the coming days to further strengthen our bilateral ties." Both Modi and Trump invited each other for state visits. This telephonic conversation could set the tone for the future of Indo-US relationship under a Republican administration.

The nature, intensity and direction of the US' relations with friends, foes, partners and the marginalised countries entered a period of unprecedented uncertainty with Donald Trump's victory in the 2016 US presidential election.

That Trump's foreign policy approach would be drastically different from that of his predecessors' was amply clear from the days of the election campaign. Trump fought the election on a platform that raised questions about the relevance of long-standing alliances; portrayed possibility of redefining the country's adversaries; and held mere hopes of continuity of policy as far as Washington's emerging strategic partnerships with some countries are concerned. All the matter is just compiled and edited in nature. Taken from the various sources which are in public domain.

This book contains the fundamental and basic information of the subject and useful for teachers, students and researchers.

—*Editor*

resources from around the world, so he would be keeping good ties with China in economic ties even as he would rework terms of engagement with Beijing", said M K Bhadrakumar, former diplomat and commentator.

For New Delhi one worry is US withdrawing from global affairs considerably - there was no mention of Asia, China or even Europe in his speech - could make China more aggressive on issues of territorial disputes such as the South China Sea.

The US President has generally spoken positively about India. But he has also consistently denounced job outsourcing to India, even making fun of the accents of Indian call centre workers. If there was one leitmotif of Trump's campaign, it was his constant barrage against immigrants. It has been pointed out Trump wants a freeze on new green cards and a restructuring of the H-1B visa programme to make it harder for US firms to hire skilled workers from abroad. Indians are the primary recipients of H-1B visa.

"The free movement of people is something which is taken for granted in the free world of free trade. So let's see how it goes", said an Indian official as New Delhi plans to engage more for with the Trump administration. Foreign secretary S Jaishankar had extensively interacted with the transition team. Nirupama Rao, a former Indian envoy to Washington, said, "India should not waste time in reaching out to Trump and his team in order to establish a durable understanding that will take the relationship forwards in all sectors of relevance."

But India will be relieved if Trump's admiration for Russian President Vladimir Putin softens US diplomacy. Indian officials often complain that the West's economic sanctions drove Russia into the arms of China. Strategic affairs experts like Brahma Chellany believe that Trump will be more firm on Pakistan. But some other experts see this wouldn't actually happen in a manner, India would like it to.

Another area of concern is climate change, which Prime Minister Narendra Modi sees as an almost existential threat to India. Trump denies such a problem even exists.

India developed a large number of collaborations with the US in climate change, especially in clean energy. Modi's idea is to use these platforms to channel US private investment and technology to help India reach its ambitious climate targets, says Arunabha Ghosh, head of the Council for Environment, Energy and Water.

THE INDIA-US TIES WILL PAN OUT UNDER TRUMP

It appears highly likely that relations between India and the US will continue their upward trajectory under President Trump. But, with every passing day it is becoming more obvious that Russia is getting increasingly clasped in a Russia-China-Pakistan nexus, which will have to be accepted by India and managed in the best way possible.

It is possible to make some prudent postulations on the future course of India-US relations. Some clues and indications are discernible on the direction that Trump and his cabinet might take, particularly on ties with India, over the next four years.

At the outset, it needs to be recognised that no matter what we might have been led to believe or think, ties with India do not fall in the top rung of priority for the United States. That place is occupied by China, Russia, Middle East, jobs, economy, immigration, terrorism etc.

At the same time, it needs to be recognised that the India-US partnership has been one of the few spheres that has been a bright spot and successful area for the USA on the foreign policy front in recent years.

It can be clearly stated without much fear of contradiction that India-US relations enjoy bipartisan support in the US Congress and across the board among US citizens as well as among Indian political parties and people. India has the largest Caucus comprising more than 300 members in the US House of Representatives which promotes relations between the two countries.

The three most recent presidents viz Bill Clinton and Barack Obama (Democrats) and George W Bush (Republican) have all worked assiduously to take the relationship to ever newer heights. On the Indian side also, if former prime minister Atal Behari Vajpayee had characterised the two countries as "natural allies" and Prime Minister Narendra Modi termed the connect as an "indispensable partnership," Manmohan Singh had staked the survival of his government on the India-US civil nuclear deal and termed this as the biggest achievement of his 10-year rule.

President Obama termed India-US ties as the "defining partnership of the 21st century". Both Obama and Modi invested considerable energy and political will and capital in the relationship by meeting nine times and holding three summits during the two and a half years since Modi came to power in May 2014.

Today, the India-US bilateral cooperation is broad-based and multi-sectoral, covering trade and investment, defence and security, education, science and technology, cyber security, high-technology, civil nuclear energy, space technology and applications, clean energy, environment, agriculture and health. Vibrant people-to-people interaction and support across the political spectrum in both countries nurture the bilateral partnership.

Donald Trump will hence be inheriting a vigorous, vibrant and multi-faceted relationship between India and the US. To get a feel of how he will approach it and take it forward, it will be useful to browse through some of the comments made by him during his election campaign.

While reading these statements it should, of course, be kept in mind that oratory and rhetorics resorted to by candidates during election campaigning cannot be taken as policy. Candidates competing for victory are prone to make rather extreme proclamations during campaigning, but they tend to revert to somewhat centrist positions after assuming office.

Another complication in assessing what President Trump is likely to do arises from the fact that he is a business tycoon who has never held a public office in his life before. Nothing much is hence known about his views on major international issues as there are no official statements made by him on the floor of either the Senate or the House or votes on any contentious or polarising issues that he has participated in. In addition, Trump has been seen to change his statements and position rather frequently and tailor his responses to the audience that he is addressing.

With the above caveats and reservations in mind, let us look at some of his more significant statements on India:

Indian and Hindu community will have a true friend in the White House.

I have great respect for Hindus. I have so many friends that are Hindu and they are amazing entrepreneurs. I have jobs going up in India right now. I have great respect for India. It's an amazing country.

I look forward to working with Prime Minister Narendra Modi who has been very energetic in reforming India's bureaucracy. Great man. I applaud him for doing so.

I am a big fan of Hindu. I am a big fan of India.

I'm involved in two massive developments in India...and that is because I have great confidence in India. Generations of Indian and Hindu Americans have strengthened our country...your values of hard work, education and enterprise have truly enriched our nation.

I presume everywhere in the speech Trump said "Hindu," he really implied "India."

It would be clear from the above that he has not had a foul word or adverse remark to make against India during all of his campaigning.

The issue of job losses in the United States has consistently surfaced as a contentious and divisive issue in previous US presidential elections. In the current elections also, factory closures and "stealing" of American jobs has featured extensively. Trump has however trained his guns mostly at

China and Mexico for taking away American manufacturing jobs and blamed them for shutdown of industries. Very rarely has he criticised the off-shoring of software and IT jobs to India.

He has referred to the issue of H1B visas on a few occasions. Indian industry, particularly in the IT sector like Infosys, Wipro, TCS etc who are active in the USA has already started taking additional measures to employ more Americans in view of some comments by Trump in recent days. Jeff Sessions, Trump's nominee for US Attorney General (AG) told a Senate committee at his confirmation hearing on 10 January 2017 that he would take measures to curtail the "misuse" of H-1B visas. This could impact Indian IT companies that use these visas in large numbers. As a senator, Sessions has been in the forefront of a campaign against the H-1B programme, and as AG, he will be able to interfere with it in several ways. It is however expected that as in the past the issue of H1B visas will recede into the background after the din and fury of the election subsides.

I feel reasonably assured that in the near future, the US government will be persuaded by its industry and will realise that the competitiveness of the US industry is critically dependent on the presence of experts and professionals in the US on H1B visas.

If however Trump acts on his promise of bringing down the corporate tax rate in US from 35 per cent to 15 per cent, it could encourage and attract some US companies currently based in India (and elsewhere) to relocate to the US. This could have an adverse impact on the "Make in India" initiative of the Indian government.

There are other trade issues like IPRs, pharmaceuticals, immigration etc on which India and the US differ, and which are being discussed in separate international fora. These issues could also come under the gaze of Trump. He is a businessman. He is a deal-maker. He could feel tempted to apply pressure on India (and other countries) to get a better business deal for America. This approach might yield dividends in the short term but in the medium and long term, such a transactional attitude is bound to be counter-productive.

Modi is reported to have said at a meeting just after the US presidential election that he is looking forward to working with Trump with whom he has good relations and feels that the Republican administration will be well inclined towards India. Modi said that there was no reason to be apprehensive about any dramatic change in bilateral relations. He is also reported to have remarked that Republican Administrations on the whole have been friendlier to India. Most recently, speaking at the Raisina Dialogue in New Delhi on 17 January 2017, Modi remarked: "In my conversation with President-elect Donald Trump, we agreed to keep building on these gains in our strategic partnership."

Trump's relations with Pakistan are also likely to have a strong impact on India. His strong statements against terrorism make it likely that he will apply additional pressure on Pakistan to stop supporting and providing sanctuaries to terrorists. He referred to this in his inaugural address when he said: "We will reinforce old alliances and form new ones - and unite the civilised world against radical Islamic terrorism, which we will eradicate completely from the face of the Earth." Pakistan being the epicentre of terrorism could come under significant pressure. This could be beneficial for India.

Several of Trump's statements like the one made after Osama bin Laden's killing in 2011 were highly condemnatory of Pakistan saying that it is no friend of the USA as it took billions of dollars from America while it continued to help its enemies and got US soldiers killed. He has also commented adversely against nuclear weapons in Pakistan. He stated at one of his election rallies that he would like to get the help and support of India to deal with the problem of a "semi-stable, nuclear armed Pakistan".

As far as Trump's ties with China are concerned, the beginning has not been reassuring or encouraging. Even before assuming office, a spat between China and Trump and his transition team has taken place on the issue of Trump's telephonic conversation with the Taiwanese President Tsai Ing-Wen, the first time since 1979 that a US president has spoken to a Taiwanese leader. It is not clear whether this interaction took place as a result of ignorance on the part of Trump on the sensitivity of China on the one-China Policy or it was a well thought through move to apply pressure on China to get a better trade deal.

During the campaign, Trump had called China a "currency manipulator" and a "thief" for stealing American jobs. In trade and economic terms, the US and China are joined at the hip with total bilateral trade standing at $680 billion with an adverse balance of trade for the USA being around $380 billion. In addition, China has invested $1.25 trillion of its foreign exchange reserves in US government bonds. Because of this deep and close economic partnership, it will be difficult for the US to take any precipitate action against China. However, "America First" and "Making America Great Again" are slogans on which Trump has been voted to power and he will not be able to open factories and create jobs in the US without applying significant pressure on China.

Trump's move out of Trans-Pacific Partnership (TPP) on the first day of his presidency could prove to be a mixed bag for India. US jettisoning the TPP could make available more strategic space to China, which would be to India's detriment, particularly if China decides to replace the US in that agreement.

Also TPP is not a purely economic agreement. It has wide-ranging geo-strategic implications. Moreover, if Obama's Pivot to Asia is dumped, it will be a shot in the arm for China and will result in making China even more aggressive in Asia and elsewhere. Thereafter China will face no opposition to extend its unrivalled sway over the South China Sea (SCS). Trump has stated that he will invest more in building a stronger and more powerful navy. If so, it will have to be placed in the Pacific and in the vicinity of SCS. More clarity would need to emerge on these opposing assertions, hopefully within the coming days.

At the moment, there are a large number of imponderables as far as US relations with China under the Trump Presidency are concerned. It will be prudent to wait and watch rather than come to any hasty conclusion, which might need to be revised in a hurry in the near future.

If relations between USA and Russia improve, it could have the (un) intended effect of loosening the Chinese grip on Russia. Over the last two years, Russia has been forced into the arms of China as a result of sanctions following developments in Ukraine and Crimea. However, notwithstanding improvement in US-Russia ties, it is possible that Russia may have gone too far in its economic, security and strategic linkages with China that it might be well nigh impossible for it to extricate itself from China's vice even if it wants to.

It was earlier being thought that Russia's anticipated proximity to the US could help in strengthening ties between India and Russia as the latter had appeared to drift farther from former because of India's perceived closeness to the US. This now appears increasingly doubtful. With every passing day it is becoming more obvious that Russia is getting increasingly meshed and clasped in a Russia-China-Pakistan nexus, which will have to be accepted by India and managed in the best way possible.In conclusion, it appears highly likely that in strategic, political, security, defence and economic terms, relations between India and the US will continue their upward trajectory under President Trump.

India's ties with the US in the coming years are best captured by the comment of Foreign Secretary S Jaishankar who said at the recently held Raisina Dialogue in New Delhi on 18 January 2017: "Our ties with the United States have been steadily growing and today cover vast areas of collaboration. We established early contact with the Trump transition team and see a strong convergence of interests and concerns."

US UNDER DONALD TRUMP OFFERS A NEW OPPORTUNITY FOR INDIA

A United States that looks at the world differently and tries to create new terms of engagement could offer India new opportunities unafforded by a more orthodox United States, foreign secretary S. Jaishankar said on Tuesday.

On the new administration in the US and the election of real estate tycoon Donald Trump as the 45th president of the United States, Jaishankar said that it was important not to "demonize Trump" but to "analyze Trump".

Indian policy making in the current uncertain global environment would include "some damage control, some risk mitigation" as well as some opportunities, the top diplomat said.

If India were to convince the US that outsourcing—one of the thorny issues threatening to cast a shadow over India-US relations under the new administration—helped the US to become more competitive, it would present India with elbow room to do business with the new administration, Jaishankar said.

The US was only one of the subjects that the foreign secretary spoke about at an event on the geo-political situation in the world organised by the Mumbai-based think tank, Gateway House.Jaishankar also spoke on relations with China and Pakistan, two countries with which India has tense relations.

On Trump, Jaishankar said that the US President represented "a thought process. It is not a caprice or a monentary expression of feelings", the foreign secretary said.

Noting that offshoring and outsourcing were two issues on Trump's domestic reform agenda, Jaishankar said the difference between the two was stark.

Offshoring damaged the tax base leading to revenue losses for the exchequer whereas outsourcing helped sharpen the competitiveness of US companies, the foreign secretary said. "If we can distinguish ourselves from the basic problem Trump is attacking, my sense is that we will be differently perceived," he said.

India's multi-billion dollar IT industry is unnerved by new legislations that the US Congress and administration are mulling over that include cutting the number of H1B and L1 visas—used mainly by Indian techies. The new legislations include cuts in the numbers of visas in both categories as well as doubling the minimum pay requirements to obtain the visa.

In his very first speech as US president, minutes after his inauguration on 20 January, Trump stressed on the need to "buy American and hire American" as well as pledged to stick to his election promise of putting "America first".

"We must protect our borders from the ravages of other countries making our products, stealing our companies, and destroying our jobs. Protection will lead to great prosperity and strength," Trump, in his first speech as president, said. China, Mexico and Japan are some of the countries that have come in for scathing criticism from Trump for alleged unfair trade and currency practices as well as taking businesses awy from the US.

According to Jaishankar, India was, so far not seen as part of the problem but was instead seen as a "credible" partner. But "that does not mean we wont get affected by the downstream impact of decisions made," he warned.

"A US that looks at the world differently and tries to create new terms of engagement might actually offer us opportunities which a more orthodox America might have been timid about," he said.

Given that a number of countries—like the US and Britain—were looking inwards, Jaishankar said "when horizons of a lot of major countries are getting narrower ... If the major (countries) are pulling back there is a space out there and it is in our interest to use that space. In my views, we should be looking at more powered position in international forum," he said.

On India's engagement with the other great powers, Jaishankar said, "if there is one relationship that we need to work on, it's the China one."

India-China ties have been on a see-saw lately with Beijing upsetting the Indian government by opposing New Delhi's bid to join the elite Nuclear Suppliers Group of countries controlling global nuclear commerce and refusing to designate Pakistan-based militant Masood Azhar as an international terrorist under UN norms.

In a humanitarian gesture, India last week permitted a Chinese army surveyor, Wang Qi, who is said to have accidentally crossed over the border in India in 1963, to visit his family in China.

Wang, now in his eighties, was unable to leave because he had not been given the correct exit visa.

Jaishankar said "it does not help to duck issues" when it came to China and admitted that there was a need to invest more to manage the relationship better.

On Pakistan, Jaishankar said Islamabad needed to shut down "terrorism factory" in the country. "Western countries may not be open about Pakistan and terrorism problem but they have concerns. The issue really here is whether Pakistan is willing to take fundamental steps. They need to shut down terrorism factory," he said.

He also said that India has not given up on a South Asian grouping but it will keep looking for other opportunities for regional integration "since SAARC (South Asian Association for Regional Cooperation) is stuck".

2

India-US Strategic Partnership

The nature, intensity and direction of the US' relations with friends, foes, partners and the marginalised countries entered a period of unprecedented uncertainty with Donald Trump's victory in the 2016 US presidential election.

That Trump's foreign policy approach would be drastically different from that of his predecessors' was amply clear from the days of the election campaign. Trump fought the election on a platform that raised questions about the relevance of long-standing alliances; portrayed possibility of redefining the country's adversaries; and held mere hopes of continuity of policy as far as Washington's emerging strategic partnerships with some countries are concerned.

India fits in the last category of nations. Since the post-World War II era, US-India relations have always been marked by highs and lows, and convergences and divergences. The Cold War calculations - and not the merits of bilateral relations - shaped the US' policy towards India during the approximately four decades of the Cold War era. However, the end of the Cold War too witnessed ups and downs in the relationship.

It was only in the early years of the 20th Century, with the then US President Bill Clinton's visit to India that a new paradigm of US-India relations began to emerge. Months after Clinton's India visit, the Democratic Party lost the 2000 presidential election and George W. Bush of the Republican Party became the US' president. For a brief while, it appeared that the new paradigm of US-India ties would die in its inception.

However, such apprehensions were misplaced and short-lived. Eight years of the Bush White House witnessed a carefully nurtured US relationship with India that cemented a strategic partnership with the conclusion of the Indo-US civil nuclear cooperation agreement. Defence and security cooperation between the two countries too tremendously improved with bilateral military exercises, trade in sophisticated arms and ammunitions, and defense technology transfer from the US to India.

The Obama Administration picked up the thread where his predecessor had left and the Indo-US strategic partnership witnessed vertical growth and horizontal expansion. There were several hiccups in the process but those were deftly handled and the strategic relationship did not get derailed.

Significantly, there was no indication at all during the 2016 election campaign that the outcome of the election would in any way negatively affect US-India ties. After all, bipartisan consensus on sustaining and improving Washington's relationship with India has existed in the US for years.

While Trump was by and large an outsider to the beltway foreign policy consensus and was not a mainstream Republican Party leader, even his statements and remarks displayed no sign that a Trump Administration would alter the US' policy towards India in any significant way. In fact, candidate Trump had aired many views against Pakistan, China and many other countries, but not against India.

Soon after Trump's victory, the Indian government led by Prime Minister Narendra Modi demonstrated activism to engage with the new US Administration. India's National Security Advisor Ajit Doval landed in Washington to connect with the Trump transition team. While Prime Minister Modi and President Trump exchanged views over a phone call, news leaked that they invited each other to visit their respective countries. More recently, India's Foreign Secretary S. Jaishankar visited Washington to exchange notes with various branches of the US government with a view to further strengthen the India-US bilateral. Despite all these efforts, there are critical issues that may adversely shake the India-US strategic partnership, unless handled dexterously and in a timely manner.

First, the economic nationalism of the Trump White House should not come on the way of Prime Minister Modi's "Make in India" initiative. Second, the Trump Administration's job creation and retention measures should not excessively hit the Indian workforce employed by American and Indian IT companies. Third, the Trump Administration's Afghanistan policy should not clash with India's core interests in that country. Fourth, the Trump Administration should keep the Kashmir issue outside his political bargaining with Pakistan. Fifth, the Trump Administration's disproportionate confrontation or measured cooperation with China should not outshine or overshadow Washington's policy towards this region. Last but not least, Trump's immigration policy should in no way hamper the interests of the Indian-American community. A series of attacks on the Indian-Americans in the US threatens to weaken the very constituency that has become a social bridge linking peoples of both the countries.

It must be noted that the above menu of issues is for both the US Administration and Indian policymakers to work on to manage the difficult political and bureaucratic transition in Washington and ensure that the India-US strategic relationship does not get negatively impacted.

INDIA-US TIES IN A TRUMP PRESIDENCY

On 9 November, Prime Minister Narendra Modi spoke with US president-elect Donald Trump to congratulate him on his victory. In no previous change of administration—either in the US or in India—did India rise to the next-day call list. For that matter, in no previous US election did a major party candidate release a campaign ad in Hindi. Or attend a Bollywood-and-anti-terrorism-themed jubilee in Edison, New Jersey.

The Trump administration thus heads into office positively disposed towards India, and will likely continue to pursue stronger ties with the world's largest democracy, in keeping with a general bipartisan consensus on India. But Trump has signalled throughout his campaign that he will focus on "America First". The direction the US takes will affect US-India ties as a result. India will likely benefit from impending geopolitical shifts, but will likely find itself at odds with a balance-sheet approach to trade and economic policies.

From the George W. Bush administration forward, the US has actively supported India's rise towards great power status and a larger role in the world. While it remains unclear how actively a Trump administration would champion a permanent seat for India in the UN security council—in fact, he has said little about his approach to the UN—it seems clear that in their approach to global security concerns, Trump and Modi will find commonality on the urgent threat Islamist terrorism poses.

The Trump administration will need to develop its approach to the US effort in Afghanistan—its longest war, where the Islamic State has now spread. Based on his promise to crush the IS and to calibrate a limited but strong role for the US military abroad, we can anticipate a more counter-terrorism focused approach to Afghanistan than a larger, full-scope governance and democratization assistance effort.

This has direct implications for Pakistan, provider of safe havens for the Afghan Taliban and other terrorist groups like the Haqqani network, and groups focused on India. The Obama administration and the US Congress have grown weary of Pakistan's insufficient actions to counter terrorist groups, and we are likely to see a Trump administration flatly tell Pakistan that the American well of patience has run dry. New Delhi will find this firmer approach helpful.

The US and India have dramatically strengthened defence ties over the past decade, and naval cooperation in particular has leaped ahead. Trump has promised to renew and expand the US navy just at the time India is expanding its navy to ensure its role as the pre-eminent Indian Ocean power. Look for this aspect of India-US ties to develop further.

Trump will enter office with a fully de-hyphenated view of India and Pakistan. He has spoken about India as a land of economic opportunity, has pursued property developments in India, and admiringly cited India's high economic growth rate during the third presidential debate. He has spoken of Pakistan as the most dangerous country in the world, and said that only India can "check" Pakistan.

He is suspicious of the net benefits the US derives from traditional alliances in Europe and Asia, believing that US allies do not carry their own weight in American security cooperation. A US foreign policy approach that places less emphasis on traditional alliance relationships, becoming more focused on ties premised on reciprocity, could open more mental space for India (on the other hand, the pursuit of measurable reciprocity could result in low marks for New Delhi). Trump is suspicious of China, particularly its mercantilist interests and island-building in the South China Sea. India has an opportunity by contrast. And Trump's notable admiration for Vladimir Putin points to a less-adversarial approach to Russia, which may eliminate an occasional source of stress for India.

Trump's campaign contained a seven-point agenda on trade. He has spoken frequently of the damage trade agreements have done to the American economy, and promised to bring jobs back. He has called for immigration reform to limit and better control who crosses into the US. He has said he would end the H-1B high-skilled worker visa programme—a programme with which India has been dissatisfied (although it is the top recipient of all US H-1B visas issued each year); New Delhi filed a trade dispute on these visas in the World Trade Organization against the US this past year. A Trump administration is likely to push back hard on the dispute and in bilateral conversations about visas.

Trump is likely to seek further economic opening on India's part, as all previous US administrations have. A Trump administration will likely continue to perceive India's patent law as insufficiently protective of innovation, so long-running differences, especially over pharmaceutical patents, will likely continue. India can breathe a sigh of relief, however, about the Trans-Pacific Partnership, which many in India saw as an "anti-India," exclusionary trade pact. Trump said he will tear it up.

Trump views climate change dimly and has spoken of cancelling the Paris agreement. He has said little about clean energy, likely not a priority. This means that one of the most successful US-India areas of partnership—clean energy research and development—has just lost its American champion.

Over the past eight years, clean energy collaboration has quietly become a singularly successful technical partnership between Washington and New Delhi, with billions of dollars mobilized with government seed funding and private sector matching funds. Look to see this shift into low gear for Washington, even as clean energy remains a high priority for India due to its lack of domestic oil and gas resources, its tremendous energy needs, and its ample supply of sunlight.

As the Trump team begins to take shape, more clues about the next US administration's approach to India will emerge. For now, it seems clear that broad policy continuity with previous administrations will result (a rarity these days), but the Trump approach to larger geopolitical and geo-economic questions will likely pull ties between Washington and New Delhi in new directions.

AREAS OF OPPORTUNITY FOR THE US-INDIA RELATIONSHIP

The best strategy for U.S.-India relations may be to have no new strategy at all. Whether dealing with an ally or adversary, this White House has been unpredictable to say the least. Yet thus far, India has stood out for being largely unremarkable. This is a good thing. Success in the relationship might be best served by keeping India out of the headlines and just getting down to business. After all, making deals is something that President Donald Trump has touted as his forte.

Following the successive efforts of past administrations, the previous administration doubled down on the relationship with India, bolstered by strong bipartisan Congressional support. Calling it a "defining partnership for the 21st century," former President Barack Obama saw that the United States' future – both strategic and economic – will increasingly rely upon how we interact with the larger Indo-Pacific region. As one of the fastest growing large economies in the world that aligned with our interests and values, India would play a key role in that future.

As a result, the Obama administration (of which I was a part) made a number of strategic overtures, including committing to a Joint Strategic Vision for the Asia-Pacific and Indian Ocean region and calling India a Major Defense Partner, to lay the groundwork for both broadening and deepening our strategic ties. So far, Trump and Prime Minister Narendra Modi have had a good, albeit modest, beginning to their relationship. With an invitation for the prime minister to come to the U.S., there is now an opportunity to identify the priority areas of cooperation that could form the basis of such a visit. In this context, crafting more of a transactional relationship with India to complement the strategic framework already in place would be a welcome approach – at least for the time being.

The following three areas offer a way to focus U.S. efforts in the coming months:

Deepen Defense Cooperation

At a time when international norms and institutions are being tested, the U.S. and India have stood steadfast in supporting an Indo-Pacific region that protects freedom of navigation and the sovereignty of states – large or small. The U.S. has recognized that a defense partnership with India will be critical to safeguarding these values. As India seeks to modernize its defense capabilities, Washington should become India's defense partner of choice by continuing to strengthen bilateral defense cooperation.

It is a good sign that within days of being confirmed, Secretary of Defense Jim Mattis and Minister of Defense Manohar Parrikar have already gotten off to a good start in agreeing to build on the tremendous progress in bilateral defense cooperation, noting for example that continued cooperation in the Defense Technology and Trade Initiative (DTTI) is in both countries' interest. Beyond DTTI, there are additional areas that require robust engagement to give meaning to the label Major Defense Partner, a unique status conferred on India that was even endorsed by the U.S. Congress. From streamlining export procedures to moving forward on the two remaining foundational agreements to continuing joint exercises, there are many more ways to deepen defense cooperation.

Ultimately, these efforts will allow the U.S. and Indian militaries to work more closely together and open the door for increased cooperation on defense platforms and technologies that will enhance mutual security postures. It will also, however, require interagency cooperation and leadership from the highest levels in the U.S. government. Without cabinet-level commitment and engagement across agencies – Defense, State, Commerce, and others – bureaucratic inertia in the system and a reluctant yet persuadable set of Indian counterparts will make changing the status quo extremely difficult.

Pursue Bilateral Economic Deals

In the coming decades, Asia will be the growth engine for the world, and India will be one of the fastest growing large economies contributing to that growth. This presents an immense market for U.S. goods and services, and an opportunity for India to benefit from greater trade and investment – leading to employment and growth for both countries. However, this requires being able to put in place the necessary policy frameworks that give confidence and certainty to the private sector.

The Trump administration has indicated that it is more interested in negotiating bilateral trade and investment relationships than creating large, multilateral trade pacts. This may be well suited for a partner like India, which in the past has been a challenging negotiator in multilateral settings. A first Trump-Modi meeting could announce the start of negotiations for a Bilateral Investment Treaty (BIT), realizing that a bilateral arrangement could be less contentious, though perhaps less ambitious as well. In any case, providing safeguards to U.S. businesses through a BIT could open up new lines of investment, which would be valuable for workers in the U.S. and India.

In addition, there is more that Washington could be doing to focus on the key ingredient that will drive both economies in the coming decades: innovation. Much can be discussed as a part of an innovation agenda, and there is a ready-made platform in the Global Entrepreneurship Summit, which the U.S. and India are co-hosting later this year, to focus on those efforts. Economic negotiations with India are never easy, but given India is poised to surpass the U.S. economy in purchasing power parity terms by 2040, forging greater economic ties and creating a more level playing field for U.S. firms is absolutely in the United States' economic interest.

Invest in Connectivity

It is difficult to find a concept that has such widespread support such as improving connectivity, both within India and across the region. Whether it be improving people-to-people ties, economic and development cooperation, physical infrastructure, energy security and access, or collaboration to address transnational threats, greater connectivity can create tremendous security, economic, and geopolitical value to the United States, India, and countries in the region.

Fortunately, a lot of work has already been done to identify areas where the U.S. could support and benefit from improved connectivity. To name just three opportunities: (1) Strengthen U.S.-India cooperation to address regional challenges that have global repercussions, ranging from transnational terrorism to trafficking-in-persons. (2) Create pathways where U.S.-based innovation and technology can play a critical role in contributing to the region's development. For example, U.S. leadership in the energy sector can have a transformational effect on energy security and access, where India has set an ambitious goal of bringing online 175GW of renewable energy by 2022. Given the leadership the U.S. has shown in this sector, there is an opportunity to unleash the power of U.S. innovation to grow employment and prosperity in both countries. (3) Continue to use the U.S.-India strategic partnership as an anchor to engage others in the region.

Building on the successful trilateral relationship between the U.S., India, and Japan, there are other opportunities to collaborate for peace and prosperity in the region. For example, the U.S. and India should partner with Sri Lanka on maritime domain awareness to help ensure that the Indian Ocean remains an ocean of peace.

For an administration whose foreign policy seems to be focused on getting good deals, no bilateral relationship may be better positioned to take advantage of that mindset than the U.S.-India bilateral. By making tangible progress on transactions that seek to realize the full potential of security and economic cooperation, Washington will bring further meaning to a strategic partnership painstakingly built over the past several years. But it will require a leader-level summit, this year, to put these ideas into motion. Let's get to work.

INDO-US RELATIONS UNDER TRUMP

Donald Trump's infamous rants on countries ripping off the United States have not only included America's major trading partners China and Mexico, but also its close strategic allies Japan and Germany. He doesn't seem to care about the prospect of a resulting trade war or long-term economic and diplomatic interests. The only thing that evidently counts for him is "America first". However, the new president has barely ever mentioned India in this context, which is quite baffling considering India's huge outsourcing industry and the recently launched "Make in India" campaign. Rather, he has called India an "amazing market", maintains close ties with prominent

Indian business figures and holds strong sympathies with right-wing Hindu groups.

Some would point out that this has something to do with Trump's large business interests in the country and his confessed love for Narendra Modi - after all they are both "anti"-establishment with ties to big business, like to see themselves as strong men who can get things done and are extremely good at manipulating the media. According to The Trump Organisation's website, two massive real estate development projects in Mumbai and Pune are currently marketed under the Trump brand. In total he holds financial interests in over 16 projects in India's major cities (such as Gurgaon and Kolkata). NDTV has reported that property prices in Trump buildings have increased significantly since the elections; some sell for more than 30% compared to similar properties. Are they possibly expecting to establish closer ties to the president of the United States? After all the website promises the residents "a host of benefits", such as a "private jet at their disposal" and the "prestige of living" in a Trump Tower.

However, not all of Trump's projects in India have gone too smoothly. His first attempts to "build" a Trump Tower in Mumbai failed in 2013 after the deal with the developer fell apart. The project in Pune has also been proven to be controversial. According to The Guardian, it is subject of two investigations by Pune police surrounding the legality of the land ownership of the Indian developer.

So what does this mean for India? Despite Trump sparingly mentioning India in his campaign, he actually has announced policies that would deeply interfere with existing relations and could cause tensions between the two countries. The future of the H1-B visa programme could be an important issue. Shalabh Kumar, one of Trump's prominent Indian-American donors and a close confidant, claimed today that there won't be an executive order to limit the visa category and told reporters that "the number of people on H-1B from India is certainly going to increase". Considering Trump's latest actions, this seems somewhat unlikely. Under the visa scheme, US companies can hire foreign workers for limited time periods to perform specialised tasks. It is especially popular with American tech companies but has also been criticised heavily by labour experts. They claim that Indian outsourcing companies are dominating the programme and that American companies wishing to hire legitimate foreign specialists are often squeezed out of the process. In other words, the visa programme is actually pushing jobs abroad in the long-term and hurting American workers. In that sense many share Trump's concern that reform is needed and Democratic Senators might be willing to pass legislation on the matter. However, it seems more likely that Trump would want to abolish the scheme altogether, as it is an easy way to reduce immigration. This would be a huge problem for Prime Minister Modi. Not only are outsourcing companies important tax payers but Indians working under the visa scheme also send considerable remittances back home. Often the jobs move back to India with them, which is obviously also a reason why the scheme is so controversial. In other words, this scheme is a big economic factor for India and Trump might be about to end it.

The Indian government's "Make in India" initiative also stands in stark contrast to Trump's "America first" pledge. Even though the initiative has been extremely ambitious from the start, it hasn't really increased foreign direct investment (FDI) to manufacturing, which is actually lower than in the 2011-2012 period - before Modi was prime minister. The share of manufacturing has also decreased - albeit only very slightly. Red tape, corruption and poor infrastructure still remain big problems that have discouraged a lot of investors. Despite this, India is obviously still highly interesting for many companies due to the huge size of the market and the political stability. While many companies currently move their production to India to sell to the domestic market, the long-term goal of the government is to make India a manufacturing hub akin to China. Needless to say that Trump and Modi will be at odds.

Okay, he might have threatened India's outsourcing industry before. But trade between the two countries is by no means a one-way street. Even though America has a trade deficit with India, it exports mostly high-end, sophisticated commodities, such as machinery, medical equipment and aircrafts to India. Moreover, New Delhi is one of the largest military spenders in the world and is planning on expanding its military even further. In 2015, the country spent $51.3 billion - slightly more than France, making it the 6th largest spender. Between 2012 and 2015, the United States were the second largest provider of military equipment after India's traditional partner, Russia, with American companies securing over $4 billion. Further, since 1991 India has become a key strategic ally to the US to counter Chinese dominance in the region and fight terrorism. Hence the increased military expenditure, especially with US equipment, must be seen as a strategic partnership and not merely commercially motivated.

It seems clear that Trump doesn't necessarily see India as a strategic and economic competitor, at least not openly. Maybe India is part of a greater plan to counter China's growing assertiveness in the region and could prove to be the less controversial partner than Russia to achieve this. In other words, a continuation of Obama's "Pivot to Asia" strategy with a focus on India and without the multilateral trade deal TPP. While Trump might tighten the H-1B visa scheme in the future, he would be ill-advised to scrap it altogether and possibly prompt an angry reaction from New Delhi. But this is completely speculative as Trump's first two weeks in office have only proven how unpredictably predictable he is - if it doesn't fall under his definition of "America first", it isn't in the interest of America. Yet Modi seems to be in a rather comfortable situation, especially compared to Enrique Peña Nieto or Xi Jinping. Moreover, only time will tell what role Trump will play in the strained India-Pakistan relationship or with domestic communal tensions; so far he has only sent very mixed, or rather contradictory, messages.

"I am a big fan of Hindu and a big fan of India; big, big fan, big, big fan. Let me start by saying right upfront that if I'm elected president, the Indian and Hindu community will have a true friend in the White House and I can guarantee you that."

U.S.-AFGHANISTAN STRATEGIC PARTNERSHIP AGREEMENT

On May 2, 2012 Afghan president Hamid Karzai and US president Barack Obama signed in Kabul signed a strategic partnership agreement between the Islamic Republic of Afghanistan and the United States of America, after the US president had arrived in Kabul as part of unannounced trip to Afghanistan on the first anniversary of Osama bin Laden's death. The U.S.-Afghanistan Strategic Partnership Agreement, officially entiteled the "Enduring Strategic Partnership Agreement between the Islamic Republic of Afghanistan and the United States of America", provides the long-term framework for the relationship between Afghanistan and the United States of America after the drawdown of U.S. forces in the Afghanistan war.

NATO Chicago Summit: Troops withdrawal and longterm presence

On May 21, 2012 the leaders of the NATO-member countries endorsed an exit strategy during the 2012 NATO Summit in Chicago. The NATO-led ISAF Forces will hand over command of all combat missions to Afghan forces by the middle of 2013, while shifting to a support role at the same time and then withdraw most of the 130,000 foreign troops by the end of December 2014. A new and different NATO mission will then advise, train and assist the Afghan security forces.

Possibility for early presidential elections

In April 2012, Afghan President Hamid Karzai raised the possibility to hold presidential elections in 2013, instead of 2014 as scheduled. He issued the concern that having the complete security handover and a presidential election take place in one and the same year could be a problem. Karzai said, "This is a question that I've had and I've raised it in my inner circle. I've not had a final decision yet, but it will not be soon."

Cost of war

The cost of the war reportedly was a major factor as U.S. officials considered drawing down troops in 2011. A March 2011 Congressional Research Service report notes the following about Operation Enduring Freedom (OEF) Afghanistan: 1) following the Afghanistan surge announcement in 2009, Defence Department spending on Afghanistan has increased 50%, going from $4.4 billion to $6.7 billion a month. During that time, troop strength has gone from 44,000 to 84,000, and it is expected to be at 102,000 for fiscal year 2011; 2) The total operational cost for Afghanistan from the beginning of the conflict in 2001 through 2006 only slightly exceeds the amount spent in 2010 alone – $93.8 billion. The projected total cost relating to Afghanistan from inception to the fiscal year 2011 is expected to be $468 billion. The estimate for the cost of deploying one U.S. soldier in Afghanistan is over US$1 million dollars a year. In a 2011 news story, the *CSM* reported, "The United States and other Western nations that have borne the brunt of the cost of the Afghan war have been conspicuously absent from the bidding process on Afghanistan's mineral deposits, leaving it to mostly to regional powers."

Risk of a failed state

In a 2008 interview, the then-head U.S. Central Command General David H. Petraeus, insisted that the Taliban were gaining strength. He cited the recent uptick in attacks in Afghanistan and in neighbouring Pakistan. Petraeus also insisted that the challenges faced in Afghanistan are more complicated than the ones that were faced in Iraq during his tour and to turn around the recent events this would require removing militant sanctuaries and strongholds, which are widespread inside Afghanistan.

Observers also have argued that the mission in Afghanistan is hampered by a lack of agreement on objectives, a lack of resources, lack of coordination, too much focus on the central government at the expense of local and provincial governments, and too much focus on Afghanistan instead of the region.

In November 2009, Malalai Joya, a former member of the Afghan Parliament and the author of "Raising My Voice," expressed opposition to an expansion of the U.S. military presence in Afghanistan and concern about the future of her country. "Eight years ago, the U.S. and NATO – under the banner of women's rights, human rights, and democracy – occupied my country and pushed us from the frying pan into the fire.

Eight years is enough to know better about the corrupt, mafia system of President Hamid Karzai. My people are crushed between two powerful enemies. From the sky, occupation forces bomb and kill civilians... and on the ground, the Taliban and warlords continue their crimes. It is better that they leave my country; my people are that fed up. Occupation will never bring liberation, and it is impossible to bring democracy by war."

In November 2009, Afghanistan slipped three places in Transparency International's annual index of corruption perceptions, becoming the world's second most-corrupt country ahead of just Somalia.

Pakistan is playing a central role in Afghanistan. A 2010 report published by the London School of Economics says that Pakistan's ISI has an "official policy" of support to the Taliban. The ISI provides funding and training to the Taliban. "Pakistan appears to be playing a double-game of astonishing magnitude," the report states. Amrullah Saleh, former director of Afghanistan's intelligence service, criticised:

We talk about all these proxies [Taliban, Haqqanis] but not the master of proxies, which is the Pakistan army. The question is what does Pakistan's army want to achieve...? They want to gain influence in the region.

About the presence of foreign troops in Afghanistan he stated: hey fight for the U.S. national interest but... without them we will face massacre and disaster and God knows what type of a future Afghanistan will have.

Capacity of Afghan security forces

The plan to transfer security responsibility to Afghan forces is the centerpiece of U.S. President Barack Obama's revised Afghanistan strategy. Current U.S. policy calls for boosting the Afghan National Armyto 134,000 soldiers by October 2010. By May 2010 the Afghan Army had accomplished this interim goal and was on track to reach its ultimate number of 171,000 by 2011. This increase in Afghan troops would allow the U.S. to begin withdrawing American forces in July 2011, as now planned. The transfer of security responsibilities cannot happen unless the Afghan government and the coalition can recruit, train and retain soldiers.

At present, the Afghan National Army has severely limited fighting capacity. Even the best Afghan units lack training, discipline and adequate reinforcements. In one new unit in Baghlan Province, soldiers have been found cowering in ditches rather than fighting. Some are suspected of collaborating with the Taliban against the Americans. "They don't have the basics, so they lay down," said Capt. Michael Bell, who is one of a team of U.S. and Hungarian mentors tasked with training Afghan soldiers. "I ran around for an hour trying to get them to shoot, getting fired on. I couldn't get them to shoot their weapons." In addition, 9 out of 10 soldiers in the Afghan National Army cannot read.

The Afghan Army is plagued by inefficiency and endemic corruption. U.S. training efforts have been drastically slowed by the corruption, widespread illiteracy, vanishing supplies, and lack of discipline. U.S. trainers report missing vehicles, weapons and other military equipment, and outright theft of fuel provided by the U.S.

Death threats have been leveled against U.S. officers who try to stop Afghan soldiers from stealing. Afghan soldiers often find improvised explosive devices and snip the command wires instead of marking them and waiting for U.S. forces to come to detonate them. The Americans say this just allows the insurgents to return and reconnect them. U.S. trainers frequently must remove the cell phones of Afghan soldiers hours before a mission for fear that the operation will be compromised. American trainers often spend large amounts of time verifying that Afghan rosters are accurate – that they are not padded with "ghosts" being "paid" by Afghan commanders who quietly collect the bogus wages.

Desertion also is a significant problem in the Afghan Army. One in every four combat soldiers quit the Afghan Army during the 12-month period ending in September 2009, according to data from the U.S. Defence Department and the Inspector General for Reconstruction in Afghanistan.

The Afghan National Police provides support to the Afghan army. Police officers in Afghanistan are largely illiterate. Approximately 17 percent of them test positive for illegal drugs. They are widely accused of demanding bribes. Attempts to build a credible Afghan police force are faltering badly, according to NATO officials, even as they acknowledge that the force will be a crucial piece of the effort to have Afghans manage their own security so American forces can begin leaving. Taliban infiltration is a constant worry; incompetence an even bigger one. A quarter of the officers quit every year, making the Afghan government's goals of substantially building up the police force even harder to achieve.

U.S.-INDIA CIVIL NUCLEAR DEAL

For many observers, however, the challenge of managing this Chinese initiative has been complicated by the U.S. decision to renew civilian nuclear cooperation with India, which like Pakistan is also a non–nuclear-weapon state under the NPT and does not accept full-scope safeguards as a matter of national policy. The fact that the United States has treated India differently from the rest of the NPT outliers—creating a unique "carve out" that enables New Delhi to engage in peaceful nuclear cooperation internationally despite its refusal to sign the NPT—is often viewed as weakening Washington's ability to oppose the current Chinese transgression. As one reporter summarized the situation, "China wants to sell two nuclear reactors to

Pakistan. The Obama administration thinks that's a bad idea—but how to oppose that plan while dodging charges of hypocrisy, given [that] the administration only last year sealed a U.S. deal to supply India with civilian nuclear equipment?"

Others, such as Brad Glosserman, executive director of the Pacific Forum Centre for Strategic and International Studies, have gone further, arguing that the U.S.-India deal has in fact opened the floodgates for exactly such transactions as are now proposed by China toward Pakistan: "We all knew at the time that an agreement such as the India-U.S. one would have consequences for the nonproliferation regime and that's what you are seeing now.... The India-U.S. deal was a bad, troubling example to set, for proliferators, however justified the desire in Washington to improve ties with India." In other words, if the U.S.-India agreement had not been consummated, the currently proposed Chinese sale of new nuclear rectors to Pakistan would likely not have occurred. These claims, however, are not persuasive.

Whatever one's views of the U.S.-India civilian nuclear cooperation agreement, the accord reached between President George W. Bush and Prime Minister Manmohan Singh is fundamentally different from the proposed Chinese effort to export additional power reactors to Pakistan. *Pace* the recent claims of Maleeha Lodhi, the U.S.-Indian agreement is not "a fundamental violation of the [Nuclear Non-Proliferation] Treaty" 3 because nothing in the treaty forbids agreements for peaceful nuclear cooperation—to include the export of reactors, other nuclear technologies, and nuclear materials—with states that are not signatories to it. All that the NPT requires is that every nuclear transaction with any non-signatory state be solely for peaceful uses and that all transferred items be fully safeguarded by the International Atomic Energy Agency (IAEA). The U.S.-India civilian nuclear cooperation agreement meets both these conditions and, therefore, cannot be considered a violation of the NPT by any stretch of the imagination.

The bilateral agreement between Washington and New Delhi, however, was clearly in conflict with the full-scope safeguards criterion encoded in the 1978 U.S. Nuclear Nonproliferation Act (NNPA) and adopted by the NSG at its Warsaw meeting in 1992 (which enjoined its members to refrain from any significant nuclear exports to non–nuclear-weapon states that had not adopted comprehensive safeguards). Consequently, the Bush administration expended enormous political capital in the U.S. Congress to amend the relevant components of American law, primarily of the Atomic Energy Act, which previously had permitted nuclear cooperation agreements with non– nuclear-weapon states only after they had accepted full-scope safeguards.

Thereafter, the administration, working in concert with the government of India, committed significant diplomatic resources to convince the NSG to accord India an exceptional waiver from the full-scope safeguards criterion that would have otherwise stymied international nuclear cooperation with New Delhi. From the very beginning, President Bush always had the option of pursuing nuclear cooperation with India in the manner now pursued by China toward Pakistan.

That is, the United States—after amending its own national laws— could have unilaterally begun nuclear trade with India, disregarding the sentiments of its NSG partners and abusing the normative character of the NSG's guidelines. Because maintaining the integrity of the global nonproliferation regime, however, was always important to the United States— and was perhaps even more important because of the exceptional treatment contemplated for India—the Bush administration spent considerable energy from October 2005 until the final extraordinary plenary in September 2008— consulting with its NSG partners *during eight meetings over four years*, not to mention the bilateral discussions that occurred in national capitals—to finally secure the special waiver for India that exempted it from the constraining condition of fullscope safeguards.

The current Sino-Pakistani nuclear transaction could not be more different. For starters, the interstate agreement governing the potential export of the two Chinese reactors to

Pakistan is a secret covenant, secretly concluded. Unlike the U.S.-India nuclear initiative, whose terms were public and vociferously debated in both countries starting with the initial announcement in July 2005, the conditions regulating the proposed Chinese sale (and any potential future transfers) are unknown to the international community.

Furthermore, the Chinese have sought to advance this transaction with Pakistan by subterfuge. By insinuating privately, but without any accompanying formal declaration, that the prospective sale of two nuclear rectors to Pakistan is grandfathered, in Maleeha Lodhi's masterfully equivocal formulation, "under the [Sino-Pakistani] agreement dating back to the 1980s that provided for an understanding in 2003 for further long-term collaboration," Beijing has sought to convey that all Chinese sales to Pakistan are *ipso facto* exempted from its obligation to uphold the NSG's requirement of full-scope safeguards because China joined the NSG only in 2004, well after the latest "understanding" reached with Pakistan.

This minor detail, however, eluded Chinese diplomats when they provided the NSG with a rendition of their outstanding commitments upon joining the organization. As Mark Hibbs has described it, "China then explained to the NSG that a longstanding framework agreement with Pakistan committed China to provide a second reactor, Chashma-2, more research reactors, plus supply of all the fuel in perpetuity for these units."

Notice there is not a word about additional power reactors beyond the already contracted Chashma-2, which began construction in 2005, the year after Beijing joined the NSG. Finally, and most conspicuously, unlike the U.S.-Indian civilian nuclear initiative, China has made no effort thus far—and is unlikely to make any in the future—to seek a specific NSG exemption for its nuclear trade with Pakistan. The Bush administration campaigned for a waiver from the NSG's full-scope condition for India on two defensible grounds: first, India's nonproliferation record justified its progressive integration into the international nuclear regime and, second, its growing technological mastery over different nuclear fuel cycles made the international regime stronger through its inclusion rather than its continued exclusion. After long and arduous diplomatic efforts, these arguments finally carried the day—but not before the NSG wrested from New Delhi a strong reiteration of its disarmament obligations.

What is most pertinent, however, is that the United States made the investment over several years to persuade the NSG and, further, that the NSG's members took their time to consider the American proposal in all its complexity. To be sure, many were torn by the nature of the U.S. initiative; some were frustrated by what was perceived as strong American pressure; others had to balance their long-standing commitment to nonproliferation with their strong ties to India and/or the United States; and all had to struggle to figure out how best to integrate India into the global nuclear regime.

When the consensus finally came, it did only after all the competing interests were weighed and adjudicated in 44 national capitals—which is exactly what the process was meant to do. China, in contrast, has chosen a different route: seeking to short-circuit the NSG rather than appeal to its judgment. Knowing full well that Pakistan's poor nonproliferation record and its continuing reluctance to come clean on the activities of A. Q. Khan and his cohort will prevent the NSG from granting Pakistan any waiver from the full-scope safeguards requirement, Beijing appears committed to persisting with the course of action it has adopted thus far: namely, to attempt consummating various nuclear trades with Pakistan secretly if it believes it can get away with such dealings because of either diffidence or contrivance on the part of the international community.

The glaring differences between the U.S.-Indian agreement and the proposed Chinese-Pakistani transaction thus say more about, in Hibbs' apt phrase, "China's growing nuclear assertiveness" 7 than they do about any purported similarity between these two initiatives. Consequently, the United States can— and should—oppose China's current effort to sell new reactors to Pakistan without fear of "charges of hypocrisy." If duplicity is at issue on this question, it emanates only from Beijing and not Washington.

U.S. LEADERSHIP IS INDISPENSABLE

Whether China chooses to respect the NSG's guidelines and follow the process adopted in the case of the U.S.-Indian nuclear accord, however, will depend greatly on the U.S. response to Beijing's prospective sales to Pakistan. Although it is tempting to believe that the United States has few options and that the Sino-Pakistani deal could go through because China would simply disregard the NSG given its strategic interests in Pakistan, the historical record suggests otherwise. For all of China's supposed nonchalance, Beijing is in fact quite sensitive to both American and international pressure on issues regarding proliferation, given its own past history with Pakistan, Islamabad's nonproliferation record, and the discomfiture associated with visible but awkward and undeniable transactions. Determined U.S. opposition to China's planned sales to Pakistan would engender caution in Beijing and energize resistance from other NSG members, most of whom are already apprehensive about Beijing's efforts to circumvent the existing guidelines.

This is especially relevant because the dramatic expansion of China's civilian nuclear power program has already made Beijing more dependent that ever before on international cooperation for its success; China's reliance on imported fuel, new reactor technology, and alternatives to the uranium cycle, in fact make it all the more important for Beijing to stay in the good graces of key NSG member states. As Hibbs has concluded succinctly, "... countries like Australia, the United States, Canada, countries that are in a position to support China's nuclear energy development, these countries are not powerless and would be in the position to engage China to restrain its behaviour."

In the NSG, as in any other international organization, however, a demonstration of robust U.S. leadership is indispensable. Resolute opposition by Washington will mobilize the pervasive international discomfort that might otherwise lie recessed and, in the case of Sino-Pakistani nuclear cooperation particularly, would be the single most important factor that makes the difference to whether China's plans in current form are realized or frustrated. Unfortunately, the Obama administration's early response on this issue was hesitant and fumbling. T. P. Sreenivasan, formerly India's ambassador to the IAEA, has written about a closed meeting in Washington of nonproliferation experts in early June where a senior White House official despairingly remarked, "India imitates China, Pakistan imitates India. What can we do to stop their nuclear activities?" Further noting that Washington "did not want to displease China or Pakistan at this juncture," the official argued that American priorities today apparently cannot stray from "the economy and the war on terror." Commenting acidly that such observations reflect the attitudes of "a weak state, not a superpower," Sreenivasan chastised both U.S. policy makers and his own government for not standing up to China for its disregard of NSG processes.

It is indeed regrettable that many in Washington today conclude that the American "need" for China and Pakistan at this juncture in history prevents the administration from issuing a more tough-minded riposte toward their transgressions. This conclusion is certainly confounding because the United States arguably does not rely on China and Pakistan any more today than it has since 2001 and, consequently, has no reason to be more forgiving of their challenges today.

In any case, the mark of superior American diplomacy has always been its ability to integrate cooperation and resistance—depending on the issues—vis-à-vis a given state. Accordingly, pressing Beijing and Islamabad is by no means doomed to failure, especially since Washington *has* managed to successfully navigate complex competing pressures involving both countries in disparate issue areas during the last several years and because, at the end of the day, the United States still wields far more power than either or both of these countries combined. Fortunately, the Obama administration is becoming more resolute than it was initially, thanks partly to the fact that the nonproliferation community within the U.S. Department of State has succeeded in slowly forcing change on this issue. As has often been the case in the past, internal divisions within the State Department have been largely responsible for the hesitant position initially adopted by Washington.

Thankfully, it appears as if the United States is gradually recovering both its wits and its fortitude. The State Department's spokesman, P. J. Crowley, for example, recently asserted publicly that the Sino-Pakistani plans regarding the Chashma-3 and -4 reactors "appear to extend beyond cooperation that was grandfathered when China was approved for membership in the Nuclear Suppliers Group," thus amplifying the position taken earlier by another State Department spokesman, Gordon Duguid, who had declared pointedly that the United States "expects Beijing to cooperate with Pakistan in ways consistent with Chinese nonproliferation obligations." The U.S. representative at the NSG meeting, Richard J. K. Stratford, also clearly reiterated this position at Christchurch.

3

India Confident of Strategic Partnership Under Trump

A strategic partnership built between India and the United States in the last two years is expected to deepen under a Trump administration. However, India's famed information technology sector could suffer, along with Prime Minister Narendra Modi's plan to turn the country into a manufacturing hub, if President-elect Donald Trump acts on campaign pledges to restrict immigration and bring jobs back to the United States, some Indian analysts and observers say.

"When the dust settles down, I don't think India will have cause for complaint under a Trump presidency," said Lalit Mansingh, a former Indian ambassador to the United States

He added that Modi, who has vowed to diplomatically isolate Pakistan for its alleged support of cross-border terrorism, will hope to get more support from Trump, who advocated a tougher stance on terrorism during the campaign. India accuses Islamabad of backing Islamic militant groups fomenting terrorism in India, a charge Pakistan strongly denies.

Mansingh predicted Trump would be a stronger ally on terrorism: "I expect that he will go a step further than what his predecessors did in applying pressure on Pakistan, because all the previous administrations have said the right things but have hesitated from putting pressure on Pakistan because it might affect their operations in Afghanistan. I think Trump may be more forthcoming." But there is much more uncertainty about how a Trump administration will affect wider Asian geopolitics. Concerns about China's growing assertiveness in Asia and its expanding influence in India's neighborhood helped prompt Modi to deepen India's military cooperation with the United States, shedding its traditional hesitations about moving too close to Washington.

Modi optimistic

For his part, Modi has sounded an upbeat note on the future of India-U.S. ties under Trump. In a phone call to the president-elect after his victory, Modi said he hoped the two nations would continue to build on the "bedrock of strong Indo-U.S. ties" and tweeted about taking bilateral relations "to a new height."

But Jayadeva Ranade, a foreign policy analyst in New Delhi, warned of major changes in Asia Pacific geostrategic landscape if the U.S. opts for a more insular policy. He pointed to the possibility of the U.S. scaling back its presence in the South China Sea.

"What he [Trump] has said about not wanting to be engaged in military terms in the Asia Pacific in effect would mean ceding space to China," Ranade said. New Delhi, conversely, wants to see Washington deepen its engagement in the region.

Economic concerns

India's bigger uncertainty relates to how a Trump administration will redraw economic and trade policies at a time when New Delhi has been wooing U.S. companies for more investment and business to boost its economy. If election rhetoric targeting both immigration and outsourcing translates into policies, India's $150 billion information technology sector, already battling a slowdown, could face more turbulence. The United States, one of India's largest investors, employs millions there and accounts for 60 percent of the country's software exports. The biggest perceived threat is to H-1B visas, which allow foreign professionals to work in the U.S. and are heavily used by Indian software companies. Indians received more than two-thirds of the H-IB visas in 2014.

Trump's earlier statements that these visas hurt American workers and serve as a "cheap labor program" have raised fears that his administration may move to restrict or raise costs. This would hit Indian IT companies, according to Shivendra Singh, who heads global trade development for the National Association of Software and Services Companies (NASSCOM), which represents India's technology industry.

Singh said he hopes the flow of professionals from India will not be restricted. "It is not that we don't want to hire locally. Definitely that is not the case," he said. But until the United States can address a domestic shortages of STEM skills – in science, technology, engineering and math – "this approach has proven well."

Investment concerns

The possibility of growing U.S. protectionism under Trump also has raised fears of a slowdown in investment flows from the world's biggest economy. Since taking office, Modi has been wooing foreign firms to set up manufacturing bases in India, hoping to usher in a manufacturing revolution of the kind that China has experienced. But many analysts feel that India does not have much to fear. They point out that the U.S. is also looking for export markets, and India's growing economy and huge middle class will lure American companies.

Among those who think that Trump will look favorably on strengthening economic ties with India is Mansingh. "Particularly as Trump himself comes from a business background," the former ambassador observed, "he will be sympathetic to a greater role for business on both sides."

INDIA MUST PITCH FOR MORE STRATEGIC PARTNERSHIP WITH US UNDER DONALD TRUMP'S PRESIDENTSHIP

With Donald Trump set to take charge as the next US president, New Delhi needs to pitch for a more energetic strategic partnership with Washington. We need to especially focus on policy cooperation in the domain of power and energy. It would have very favourable implications for the global environment, and hugely boost infrastructure and investments. The capital markets have been very buoyant since his election, and surveys suggest that consumer confidence in the US is also up. The dollar has also strengthened since the November election.

Trump has confidently stated that he would double the rather lacklustre US economic growth rate. 'Make America Great Again' was his campaign slogan. It remains to be seen how he can, now in office, rise to the occasion and walk the talk.

The world's largest economy, after all, has had a weak and hesitant recovery since the global financial crisis of 2008, which was, of course, home-grown in the US. Yet, it would make eminent sense to boost fiscal policy and step up investment. Which, in turn, should boost the growth momentum there.

The figures show that net of depreciation, US public capital investment has been falling as a share of national income for years. While it was 3% in the 1960s, the figure dropped to as low as 1.3% of GDP in 2007. It rose for a few years after the financial crisis, but has fallen since, pegged at a lowly 0.4% in 2014. It should be possible for Washington to chalk out a medium-term plan to build and construct infrastructure, so as to coagulate funds on the groundand raise the growth momentum.

The US and India need to join hands and rev up thermal efficiency at power plants in both economies. Power producers in the US have indeed been able to demonstrate cutting-edge technology to quite dramatically increase productivity in conventional thermal stations. But the know-how needs to be commercialised and adapted to suit Indian conditions and resource endowments. To diffuse leading-edge technologies for power plants across India would require huge long-term resources at fine rates. For this purpose, we would need to gainfully seek multilateral funding.

Meanwhile, the policy of ultra-low interest rates in the US since the crisis seems, ironically, to have raised the value of all capital assets across the board. And the consequent power of corporates to be in a position to shift production across national boundaries — often simply to seek tax benefits — may have been one of the main reasons why Trump won more than enough electoral college votes in the so-called 'rust belt' states, although he did comprehensively lose the popular vote.

Trump unambiguously opposed such production shifting during his campaign, threatening to slap steep duties on the finished items shipped back to the US. And the threat seems to have worked, at least for now. Major automobile and white goods producers have reportedly decided to stay put in the US. The phenomenon of ultra-low interest rates raising the value of capital assets across the mature markets but especially in the US is real. It may well explain Trump's rather unexpected victory in last year's close race to the White House.

The point is that the bond market is massive and thriving in the US. The lower the rate of interest, the greater the capital value of bonds. This is because in a regime of low interest rates, the prices of bonds are high at maturity, taking into account the low (coupon) rates. But there is no reason why the rise in capital value remains confined only to bonds. It would favourably affect all capital assets and raise value, particularly in those markets where there is much recourse to arm's-length bond finance. It can raise corporate power as well.

The capital value of any asset is the (discounted) value of its future earnings. A lower rate of interest does increase the value of all capital assets. It essentially raises total wealth. The wealth appreciation can have untoward implications, like corporates seeking to move production (and attendant jobs) purely for reasons of tax arbitrage. Hence the rationale for a proactive policy such as penal duties to stem the capital flight at least temporarily, which anyway is due to distorted interest rates in the first place. It seems notable that Trump had his ear to the ground in the rust-belt states.

The US-India energy engagement needs to boost efficiency in conventional thermal stations, shore up capacity-building in the proposed International Solar Alliance here, and speedily actualise India's long proposed membership of the Nuclear Suppliers' Group (NSG).

IS PRESIDENT TRUMP A GEOPOLITICAL OPPORTUNITY FOR INDIA?

In India, public support during the American election campaign have been overwhelmingly in favour of Democratic candidate Hillary Clinton. This also holds true for the majority of the 3.3 million Indian Americans. Altogether five Indian Americans – the highest number ever – have been elected into both houses of Parliament, all Democrats. The Indian government, and Prime Minister Narendra Modi in particular, will be pragmatic in their approach to this new situation.

The USA is India's leading foreign trade partner. Former Foreign Secretary Kanwal Sibal predicts that the current dynamic of bilateral relations will slow down in the immediate future. India will have to learn about the new personnel, who will be largely unknown. Nirupuma Rao, a former Foreign Secretary and ambassador to Washington, noted that "the American President-elect is generally not acquainted with the salient details of the India-U.S. strategic partnership."

Geopolitical implications of the Trump Presidency

Substantial geopolitical changes are expected under Donald Trump, who, in his political style and some of his opinions, is quite similar to Narendra Modi. From an Indian perspective much will depend upon his relationship with China, particularly in view of the sharpening differences between India and China.

Since Trump is against the 'US pivot to Asia', this would permit China to assert itself more in the western Pacific and allow it to expand faster into the Indian Ocean. This would be contrary to the strategic vision built with Obama for the Asia-Pacific and Indian Ocean regions, which was supposed to counter Chinese muscle-flexing.

If this does happen, India must either try to influence the expected American strategy or to fill the expected vacuum.

C. Raja Mohan, director at Carnegie India, has pointed out that Trump's election presents a rare opportunity for Delhi to expand its own influence and agency in the Eurasian region, rather than being the 'lynchpin' of the US pivot to Asia, and indeed become a leader in its own right.

Improved relations with Russia under Trump are seen in India as another good opportunity, in that Russia will lean less towards China and cooperate less with Pakistan, creating changes in the Middle East that could benefit India. Here a coordinated partnership between India, the EU and Britain could be envisaged.

A statement from former Ambassador Rao was telling: "Trump came across during the campaign as having a much more rational and less prejudiced approach to the situation in Syria and Russian involvement in the region, and it is hoped that his advent to office will see more collaborative, well-reasoned policy approaches and dialogue with Moscow to defeat the Islamic State instead of just pursuing the prospects of regime change in Damascus."

Others have suggested that Trump's election could have indirect implications for Pakistan, in that Trump could pull Putin away from Chinese premier Xi Jinping, and thereby ruin Pakistani ideas of a Beijing-Moscow-Islamabad axis.

Economic implications

The prospect of protectionist policies being put in place by Trump are only partly seen as directed against India. It has been noted that India is not necessarily ready for major free-trade agreements, and that the country could benefit geopolitically from the negative economic effects that American protectionism could have on China. That said, if Trump does start to fine outsourcing companies, as he has said he would, this could have a negative effect on the Indian IT industry.

According to Shyam Saran, a former Foreign Secretary and architect of the Indo-US Nuclear Deal, the strategic community in India is confident that in view of the consensus about good bilateral relations and a "strengthening of the strategic relations with India", no negative tendencies are to be expected with the new administration.

There is are similarities between the Hindu-nationalist NDA-government's economic and social policies and what can be expected from Trump. Therefore it is to be expected that in India there will be less criticism of Trump's domestic politics and a greater focus on his future foreign policy.

INDIAN ELITE WELCOME TRUMP'S ELECTION

India's ruling elite has enthusiastically welcomed the election of Donald Trump as US president, calculating that his aggressive anti-China and anti-Pakistan positions will boost New Delhi's geo-political interests against its principal Asian rivals.

While there are apprehensions about the lack of previous interaction between the Indian government and likely key figures in the Trump administration, the Indian media has been full of reports touting the president-elect's praise of India and its Hindu supremacist prime minister, Narendra Modi, in his campaign speeches. Said Trump of the "Hindu strongman" who presided over the 2002 Gujarat anti-Muslim pogrom and whose two year-old Indian government has incited communalism and suppressed dissent, "I look forward to working with Prime Minister Modi who has been very energetic in reforming the economy and bureaucracy. Great man. I applaud him."

Modi, for his part, has voiced confidence that New Delhi's "global strategic partnership" with Washington will continue to expand.

Under Modi's BJP government, India has effectively become a "frontline state" in Washington's military-strategic offensive against China. It has opened its military bases to routine use by US warplanes and battleships; parroted Washington's provocative stance on the South China Sea dispute; and dramatically increased bilateral and trilateral military-security cooperation with Japan and Australia, US imperialism's principal Asia-Pacific allies.

Modi, according to a *Times of India* report, boasted at a private dinner for Indian political leaders this week about his "good relations" with Trump and said that "there was no reason" to fear "any dramatic change in bilateral relations."

Modi dispatched India's highest-ranking diplomat, Foreign Secretary S. Jaishankar, to the US this week to meet with Trump transition team leaders and press them for a Trump-Modi meeting soon after the billionaire demagogue assumes the presidency in mid-January.

A *Firstpost* opinion piece by Sevanand Gaddala, titled "What does Trump's election mean for India?" argues "India could stand to gain more" from a Trump-led administration than a Democratic one, because of Trump's "harsh stance on China and Pakistan." Gaddala points to Trump's labeling of Pakistan as "the most dangerous country in the world" and his calls for India to act "as a check to Pakistan." He adds he expects Trump's administration to "be keen on cutting aid to Pakistan," because it will be dominated by those in Washington's military-security establishment who argue that Islamabad has not borne enough of the burden of the US war in Afghanistan. This faction, notes Gaddala, contends Islamabad "has been collecting US aid" while only "pretending" to fight the Taliban.

Seeking to leverage its enhanced partnership with Washington, India under Modi has mounted a campaign of threats, bullying and military pressure aimed at compelling Islamabad to forego any logistical support for anti-Indian Islamist militants in disputed Kashmir. In late September, this reached a qualitatively new level when the Modi government abandoned New Delhi's purported policy of "strategic restraint" vis-a-vis Pakistan and proclaimed that it had carried out cross-border raids inside Pakistan, inflicting heavy casualties on "terrorists" and their Pakistani "protectors".

The Obama administration at first tacitly and then explicitly endorsed India's patently illegal and highly provocative attack on Pakistan. New Delhi is now hoping that the incoming Trump administration will give India even greater latitude in pursuing confrontation with its nuclear-armed archrival.

Writing in the *Times of India*, Arun Kumar Singh, who was India's US ambassador until last August, emphasized the strong bipartisan support for Washington's policy of using India as a strategic counterweight to China. Singh said his interactions with senior Republicans and Trump campaign officials at the Republican convention in July "reinforced my conviction that a Trump administration would continue the presently articulated US policy of embracing the rise of India, seeing India as a positive net security provider, and looking at the US-India relationship as a defining partnership of the 21st century"

Indian strategist C. Raja Mohan, a strong advocate of India forging ever closer ties with Washington to "balance"—that is, counter—China, is arguing that Trump's call for traditional US allies to assume more of the financial and military costs of upholding the US-led world capitalist order can be used by India to advance its own ambitions to become a major Asian and Indian power. "On the geopolitical front," wrote Mohan in his regular *Indian Express* column, "Trump's reconsideration of US military burdens on the Eurasian landmass provides a rare opportunity for Delhi to expand its own contributions to regional security. Rather than act as a 'lynchpin' of the US pivot to Asia, India can become the leading element in the regional balance of power system. If the U.S. under Trump views itself as a distant power that will help support rather than direct regional systems, India will have greater space and agency to construct a strong Eurasian coalition."

The BJP's Hindu right allies in the shadowy RSS have effusively praised Trump, not least because of his anti-Muslim bigotry. "Trump has a soft corner for Bharat (India) and Hindus," exclaimed the cover story in the RSS's *Organiser*. Reprising the false and reactionary "war on terror" narrative, the article continued, "Bharat will be a major beneficiary of Trump's election since both the countries are prime targets of Islamic terrorism." It concluded by calling for a "Bharat-US-Russian partnership" to prevent "Chinese domination of the world economy."

The Indian elite, as a whole, is pleased by Trump's hostility to China. But there is also considerable concern that India could be sideswiped by his America First protectionist program. At his election rallies, and as part of his chauvinist denunciation of foreign countries for "ripping off" US jobs, Trump repeatedly said he would take steps to limit H1-B visas, which allow US companies to hire foreign professionals. Large numbers of Indians are currently employed in the US under H1-B visas, especially in the IT sector. H1-B workers supply significant remittances to India. However, the biggest concern for India's elite is that a reduction in the H1-B quota, to say nothing of the scrapping of the program, would disrupt the operations of Indian-based IT companies in the US.

There are also concerns that Trump's aggressive stance against Iran—he has threatened to scrap the Iran nuclear deal—could cut across a surge in Indo-Iranian economic and strategic ties. The Iranian port of Chabahar is the pivot of Indian plans to build an economic corridor to Central Asia, where it is competing with China for strategic influence and access to energy resources.

While in India the political and corporate elite have responded to Trump's election with enthusiasm, in Pakistan it has been met with trepidation. As in India, it is widely anticipated in Islamabad that a Trump administration will further downgrade US ties with Pakistan, while strengthening the Indo-US alliance.

Islamabad has repeatedly warned, and in ever shriller tones, that Washington's strategic embrace of New Delhi has upset the balance of power in the region. With Washington ignoring these warnings, Pakistan has moved to enhance its longstanding alliance with Beijing, a development that has only caused US-Pakistani ties to fray further. Formally, however, Pakistan remains a "major non-NATO ally of the US" and the logistical linchpin of the US occupation of Afghanistan.

"America will not abandon Pakistan," wrote Lahore-based foreign policy analyst, Hasan Askari Rizi. "But definitely, Trump will be a tougher President than Hillary Clinton for Pakistan. ... I think India will have a better and smoother interaction compared to Pakistan."

Writing in the *Dawn*, PPP leader and former Pakistani Ambassador to the U.S., Sherry Rehman, warned of a "rough road ahead." "While Trump," she said, "may not openly question" the US-Pakistani alliance "or lock Pakistan out as China's key ally, Pakistan's interests will need vigilance to say the least. Worst-case scenarios like sanctions can be staved off, but not without urgency and agency applied to foreign policy."

Within the Pakistani elite there is widespread resentment of the US, which is viewed as having repeatedly "used" Pakistan as a pawn in its geopolitical power plays only later to "abandon" it. Nonetheless, the Pakistani bourgeoisie is desperate to maintain its alliance with Washington, as US imperialism has been a pivotal bulwark of its rule.

In a gesture that speaks both to the Pakistani government's eagerness to ingratiate itself with Trump and its fears about the heightening war crisis with India, Pakistani Foreign Office spokesman Nafees Zakarai appealed last week for Trump to "mediate" the seven decades-old Kashmir dispute.

INDIA MAY MATTER LESS IN WORLD POLITICS DURING A TRUMP PRESIDENCY

To increase its wiggle room, Delhi needs to find ways to express its strategic autonomy in ways that suits India's interests while ensuring that US, Russia and China do not perceive its moves as being (too) opportunistic.

The reality of a Donald Trump presidency is unnerving many capitals. European leaders are unsure if the US will stick to Nato treaty commitments and hold firm if Russia destabilises the Baltics states, for instance. Japan wonders if Trump's talk of greater financial burden-sharing on security will impact its own preparedness in the wake of threats from China and North Korea.

India too has plenty reason to be uncertain. This has less to do with Trump's rhetoric about outsourcing and the number of H1-B visas granted – although that is politically important for Prime Minister Narendra Modi. The real danger of a Trump presidency for India is in the unsettling of the international order that it promises, and the changed power equations between Russia, China and US which potentially work to Delhi's disadvantage.

To get a sense of the wholly different situation India finds itself in, consider the context India operated in during Barack Obama's presidency. The Asian theatre was marked in recent years by US-China tensions owing to Beijing's belligerence in the South China Sea. The US countered this through a set of revitalised strategic partnerships, including with India. Modi's enthusiasm led him to sign the India-US joint strategic vision for the Asia-Pacific and the Indian Ocean – that explicitly spoke of ensuring freedom of navigation and over flight throughout the region. Modi went one step further and signed a logistics agreement that enables US military's access to Indian bases for repair and supplies.

The diplomatic cover afforded by the Obama administration allowed the Modi government to focus its energies on isolating Pakistan internationally and get away with a heavy-handed policy in Kashmir – both policies that served to bolster the BJP domestically. Russia and China were relatively marginal to India's diplomatic considerations, even though Delhi valued Moscow as a source of weapons and energy while the enhanced trade with China created a measure of interdependence that managed tensions. Delhi could choose not to participate in China's ambitious One Belt One Road (OBOR) infrastructural initiative because the US, Western powers and Japan were envisaged as the primary sources of security, legitimacy and resources for India.

This entire calculus now stands upended. Trump is keen on dismantling the pillars of US foreign policy in a manner that makes the US' political and bureaucratic machinery deeply uncomfortable. He wants to scale back American commitments abroad, he'd like to focus on an 'America first' policy and is expected to be explicitly transactional in his dealings with other countries. He has chosen a pro-Russian figure in Rex Tillerson as his Secretary of State and picked China hawk

Peter Navarro to head the National Trade Council, leading many to anticipate serious tensions with China on trade issues.

Some in Delhi may believe that an aggressive US that counters an assertive China works for India. But policymakers will know that it is one thing to play geopolitical chess in peace time, i.e. strengthen regional partnerships to counter a rising power, and quite another being on the cusp of a US-China conflict in Asia and having to choose sides. It's not clear if such developments will materialise soon, but the scene of global politics will move to great power dynamics between US, Russia and China. India will be peripheral to the concerns of all three for different reasons.

As far as the US is concerned, it is not clear how much attention Trump will devote to India while he is preoccupied with the inevitable domestic turbulence his presidency will generate and the resetting of ties with Russia and China. India's leverage abroad now appears to depend on the Washington security establishment's ability to normalise Trump and make him aware of Delhi's utility to American strategy in Asia. But that establishment itself will take time recovering and coping with the changes he wants and India as a priority could slip in the process. Trump did not mention India in his foreign policy speech on April 27, 2016 and it is not clear if he has any definite ideas as to what to do with the relationship.

Russia and China, meanwhile, understand India's importance as a trade partner but neither are particularly predisposed to do India any favours. The rhetoric of India-Russia joint statements remains solemn and upbeat but Vladimir Putin – known not to forget insults – will be aware of the extent to which India's foreign policy and its cultural elite has gravitated to the United States in recent years. As if to make its point Russia conducted a military exercise in September with Pakistan, the country which armed and trained mujahedin fighters to drive the Soviet Union out of Afghanistan. China, meanwhile, remains critical of Modi's pro-US slant.

Moscow and China will now act in concert to enhance their international influence, take positions that undermine the US, strengthen key partnerships and pursue regional agendas while Washington sorts out its foreign purposes. Beijing will press ahead with the $46 billion China-Pakistan Economic Corridor. Russia, China and Pakistan will coordinate strategies on Afghanistan – they recently announced their readiness for flexible approaches including delisting Taliban figures from UN sanctions list as part of efforts to promote dialogue between Kabul and the insurgents. Russia and Iran are also reported to have improved ties with the Taliban which they see as a counter to growing influence of Islamic State in the country. Iran has close ties with both Russia and China.

India appears adrift amid all this. As noted, its ties with the US are moving into unchartered waters. Russia and China will be key players in the neighbourhood and their interests don't necessarily align with India's. Their reach out to the Taliban is a serious setback to India which has long opposed its return to the political mainstream. India may have got its South Asian neighbours to boycott the SAARC summit but Islamabad is no longer as isolated as it was a couple of months ago (the incoming US Defense Secretary Gen. James Mattis has good links with Pakistan's military leadership).

China will imperiously extend its geographic footprint through OBOR while India stays away and limits itself to scoring rhetorical points on Pakistan and watches its relations with Nepal and Sri Lanka fluctuate with domestic changes. Overall, India looks confined to South Asia while the great powers look to carve up spheres of influence across the world.

Some would contend that this is overwrought. They will argue that India remains a major economy, a mass market the world is still keen on cultivating. Yes, India will be a major weapons importer and still offer attractive trade deals but there too the news isn't great. The country's economic prospects have been dealt a severe self-inflicted blow through demonetisation, which has done great damage to India's reputation abroad. The criticism of economists like Lawrence Summers matters as does the credit rating agency Moody's reported refusal to upgrade India's rating, despite Delhi's lobbying. The characterisation of demonetisation as "sickening and immoral" by Steve Forbes, editor-in-chief of Forbes, will reinforce doubts about the Indian economy. Former PM Manmohan Singh's view that demonetisation can threaten GDP growth by 2% also carries weight and India's poor indicators on higher education, skills and job creation add to the welter of unhelpful perceptions abroad.

So as it braces for a Trump presidency, India finds itself both geopolitically outflanked and economically bereft. The reason for the former is that the Modi government abandoned 'strategic autonomy' and tilted towards the US in ways that aggravated Russia and China – leaving Delhi unprepared for a scenario where Washington's priorities itself change with the election of a maverick figure.

What then can India do in changed circumstances? Some will say nothing – for things may turn out fine; Washington can tame Trump and he may turn out to be a predictable figure who will not hurt India much. American soft power and its public institutions will endure; bureaucratic and people-to-people contact will continue and help weather new political currents. India could also try and strike a set of deals with Trump that appeals to his transactional instincts, vanity or both. There's no guarantee that such methods will work over time with a temperamental politician. As a coping strategy, Delhi will need to accept that a Trump presidency threatens to shrink India's influence by the effects it promises to generate in world politics. To increase its wiggle room, Delhi needs to find ways to express its strategic autonomy in ways that suits India's interests while ensuring that US, Russia and China do not perceive its moves as being (too) opportunistic.

TRUMP ADMINISTRATION WOULD BE GOOD FOR INDIA

"I think US needs India for its presence in the region itself," Mukesh Aghi, president of US India Business Council (USIBC), a representative body of top American businesses having a footprint in India, told PTI. Noting that geopolitically as India sits in a very turmoil arena, New Delhi needs Washington more.

"We feel that from the Indo-US relationship perspective, Trump administration will be good for India," Aghi said, adding that two principles could drive Indo-US relationship. "First, this administration sees that the economic prosperity of India is good for America. Second, it also sees the military growth of India as a stabilising factor in the region itself," he said.

"We believe that India wants to see the US as a strong nation, sending a strong message out there because at this stage while India is trying to grow economically you do not want too much disruption in global order. We feel that the ties between the Trump administration and Modi government will be positive and much more deeper also," Aghi said. Trump and Modi will also look at Indian IT companies to create and hire more Americans, Aghi said.

"The Indian companies will restart hiring Americans in the US. Geopolitically, India will stand by the US and US will support India. "I feel that the partnership is going to reach a higher level as it settles down and the team takes shape in the US itself," Aghi added.

Trump and Prime Minister Narendra Modi are expected to meet sometime later this year. Foreign Secretary S Jaishankar is currently in the US, probably for preparing ground work for Modi's visit and draw a road map of Indo-US ties under the Trump administration.

In addition to the political and strategic partnership, the two leaders in their forthcoming meeting are expected to talk about enhancing the economic and trade ties, Aghi said. "I also believe that Make in India and Buy America, Hire America is not in conflict. They basically support each other.

"Make in India is more for domestic market. India is not a very large export benefaction country. India can support the US very much on pharma side. Indian pharma companies provide cost benefits to American companies and the country.

Trump wants to bring the cost down. So he looks at Indian companies to help from that perspective," Aghi added.

TRUMP CAN IMPROVE TIES WITH INDIA

Beyond the din of post-election protests lies a place where many Americans – as well as like-minded observers in India and elsewhere – who lament the selection of Donald Trump as president of the United States can seek relief from their dismay and anxiety. There, concerned Americans will find a role that is critically important to the capable functioning of a democratic system.

It has various names, including the "loyal opposition." The point is that – without questioning the legitimacy of a government that emerges from a free and fair election – those who find themselves philosophically in disagreement with it have every right to speak out in a clear voice and hold the new leadership accountable.

That way, the political system has a chance to evolve, rather than devolve (as some observers pessimistically predict for the United States). It is also not too early to be thinking about the next election; better results happen when strategizing and follow-up efforts are proactive instead of reactive.

In the meantime, the United States cannot afford disruptions in its work as a nation, either domestically or abroad. More specifically, relations between the United States and India, as well as other countries, must proceed.

So, how might Indo-U.S. ties develop under the incoming Trump administration? For insights, I turned to various specialists, including Ronak Desai, an affiliate of the India and South Asia Program at Harvard University's Belfer Center for Science and International Affairs, and a Fellow at New America, a think tank and civic enterprise in Washington, D.C. Desai says "if a Clinton presidency would have represented continuity in U.S.-India relations, a Trump triumph has injected some uncertainty." On the one hand, Desai continues, Trump expressly declared last month that the United States and India would be "best friends," should he win the White House. Such sentiments are consistent with the bipartisan consensus that has formed around the growing strategic partnership between the United States and India over the past decade and a half.

However, Trump's views on multiple issues could potentially generate friction between the two countries. This is particularly likely in areas such as trade, immigration and climate change. Trump's "isolationist and nativist tendencies also remain cause for concern," according to Desai, especially if the president-elect follows through on his promises to dramatically reduce immigration and diminish U.S. engagement in the Asia-Pacific region. Still, Desai notes, there is reason to remain cautiously optimistic that Trump will align his effusive rhetoric for stronger U.S-India ties with reality.

In that event, the bipartisan consensus supporting the strategic partnership is likely to endure.

What are the key issues that demand attention from the United States and India at present? They remain largely the same, Desai observes: strengthening strategic and economic ties, increasing trade, combatting extremism, and promoting regional and international stability. In his opinion, combatting extremism and enhancing security cooperation will likely garner greater prominence and importance under Trump. The central question, which Desai correctly identifies, is "whether the full range of issues affecting U.S.-India ties, and on which the two countries cooperate, will be afforded the same level of priority moving forward."

I also sought input from Brigadier General (ret.) Stephen Cheney, CEO of the American Security Project (ASP), a non-partisan public policy and research organization in Washington, D.C., and his staff. Cheney and Andrew Holland, ASP's director of studies and a senior fellow for energy and climate, indicate that – like everything in America's international relations – the U.S. relationship with India is suddenly open to reinterpretation under the incoming Trump administration. They do not anticipate significant changes, though. According to Cheney and Holland, "there are no major trade deals that Trump would want to 'renegotiate' (like he wishes to do with NAFTA or the Trans-Pacific Partnership), nor is there a treaty alliance between the nations that he has questioned (like the U.S.-Japan alliance or NATO)."

If anything, Cheney and Holland say, Trump may lean more towards India. Why? Because that posture would provide a counterweight to China in Asia, and strengthen India's role as a partner in anti-terrorism operations across South Asia and the Middle East.

On the issue of climate change, Cheney and Holland suggest the major discontinuity between the Obama and Trump administrations in the context of Indo-U.S. relations will be over international climate policy. While the United States has worked with India and pressed it hard on climate policy in both the Montreal Protocol and the Paris Agreement, Cheney and Holland say, the Trump approach will likely not follow suit and may even seek to abrogate American commitments to those treaties. In response, they advise, India should push the new U.S. administration to ensure that it meets America's climate commitments.

Further, Cheney and Holland are right to remind us that the United States remains concerned about tensions between India and Pakistan, especially in light of their nuclear arms. The two countries need to show restraint, embrace cooperation and resist military confrontation, Cheney and Holland recommend, and they feel confident Trump's administration will share their view.

Lastly, I talked with Akhil Gupta, director of the Center for India and South Asia at the University of California, Los Angeles. He expects the new administration will be very friendly towards India, will likely take tougher stances on China and Pakistan, and could move closer to Russia. That might create a new geopolitics in South Asia, Gupta says, prompting Pakistan to get cozier with China and distance itself from the United States. If that happens, he anticipates seeing greater military and diplomatic cooperation between the United States and India.

The major issue for India, Gupta says, will be free trade in services and other goods. If the incoming Trump administration "clamps down on B-1 visas and IT enabled-services exports, it will impact the Indian economy in a big way," he cautions. As for other issues, the sale of military hardware and nuclear power will be important items for the bilateral agenda. Gupta also warns that if racist attacks against people of Indian origin in the United States go up, it will put a strain on relations between the two countries.

Gupta notes that the top priority for India should be to improve the lives of large numbers of people living in abject poverty, but immediately adds that such an outcome is unlikely to gain the attention of policymakers in either New Delhi or Washington. Aside from that issue, Gupta believes the chief priorities should be the danger of nuclear conflict between India and Pakistan, and the achievement of a peaceful political solution in Kashmir.

To the opinions expressed above, I would add the following, specific suggestions for President-elect Trump to set Indo-U.S. relations on the proper course upon taking office:

1. Immediately extend a firm hand of friendship, respect, consultation and cooperation to India.
2. Designate Indian-Americans for key appointive positions in the Trump administration, especially in areas that affect U.S.-India ties.
3. Invite Prime Minister Narendra Modi to visit the White House as soon as possible.
4. Begin planning for a reciprocal trip by Trump to India early in his term.
5. Publicly recognize India as the linchpin U.S. relationship in South Asia.
6. Re-commit to closer coordination with India in areas such as global and South Asian security, defense and counter-terrorism.
7. Strongly support India's bid to become a permanent member of the U.N. Security Council.

An opportunity exists during the next few months for the Trump transition team to take a careful look at U.S.-India ties, and prepare the new administration to define for Americans and Indians what the nature of that relationship will be. It is time to move past fulsome campaign rhetoric, and embrace substantive policy positions that will shape and reinforce America's much-needed strategic embrace of India.

ECONOMIC AND TRADE RELATIONS OF US AND INDIA

However, the U.S. government is concerned that India's economic reforms are progressing too slowly and unevenly. Bilateral merchandise trade has grown from $6 billion in 1990 to $33 billion in 2006. Although India was only the 21th largest export market for the United States in 2006, the United States has become India's leading trading partner, mostly due to the growth in India's exports to the United States. However, recent increases in trade with China have made it a close second to the United States. In 2006, the U.S. bilateral trade deficit with India totaled $13 billion. In 2006, India's gross domestic product (GDP) grew by 9.2%, a growth rate second only to China among Asian nations. India's economic growth has also brought about the emergence of a sizeable "middle class" and the largest number of billionaires in Asia, but the country's mostly rural population remains comparatively poor and largely isolated from the benefits of growth. In addition, there is growing concern that the economy is "overheated," as evidenced by rising rates of inflation. Moreover, despite several years of strong growth, investment in infrastructure is lagging, creating a potential bottleneck for long-term economic expansion. Finally, attempts at additional economic reforms aimed at resolving these and other economic problems are constrained by India's political dynamics.

Economic and trade relations between the United States and India have experienced a number of ups and downs since India's independence in 1947. During much of the 1950s and early 1960s, the United States was a leading trading partner for India, providing the nation with about a third of its imports. However, those economic ties quickly subsided when India fostered closer ties with the Soviet Union following the Indo-Pakistani War of 1965. For the next 40 years, political and economic relations between India and the United States were rather cool.

Since 2004, Washington and New Delhi have been pursuing a "strategic partnership" based on numerous shared values and improved economic and trade relations. India is in the midst of a rapid economic expansion, and many U.S. companies view India as a lucrative market and a candidate for foreign investment. For its part, the current Indian government sees itself continuing the economic reforms started in 1991, aimed at transforming a quasi-socialist economy into a more open, market-oriented economy. However, the U.S. government is concerned that India's economic reforms are progressing too slowly and unevenly.

According to official U.S. trade statistics, bilateral merchandise trade with India has grown from under $10 billion in 1996 to nearly $31 billion in 2006 — a trebling in a decade. In 1996, India was the 32nd largest market for U.S. exports and the 25th largest source of imports. By 2006, India had risen to be 21st biggest export market for the United States and the 18th biggest supplier of imports. The United States' total trade with India in 2006 exceeded that with Israel, Nigeria, and Thailand.

Both governments appear to be committed to improving trade relations. On March 2, 2006, President George W. Bush and Indian Prime Minister Manmohan Singh endorsed the goal of doubling bilateral trade in three years. On December 18, 2006, President Bush signed into law H.R. 5682, the Henry J. Hyde United States-India Peaceful Atomic Energy Cooperation Act of 2006 (P.L. 109-401), signaling an intent to waive restrictions on civil nuclear cooperation with India.

Despite the growth in bilateral trade and the improvement in trade relations, there are still a number of economic and trade issues between India and the United States. Both nations seek greater market access to the other's domestic markets, as well as the lowering of perceived trade barriers. In addition, both India and the United States would like to see changes in the other nation's legal and regulatory policies to help protect and promote exports and foreign direct investment. Moreover, there are significant differences in the stances of the two countries in various multilateral trade fora, including the current Doha Round of negotiations.

For Congress, resolution of some of the key economic and trade issues may involve alterations in current federal law. In particular, changes in laws pertaining to agricultural goods, pharmaceuticals, nuclear and dual-use technology, and immigration may be considered as part of an effort to foster closer trade relations with India. Plus, Congress may consider heightened oversight of U.S.-India trade relations. This report provides a summary of India's current political climate (with a focus on its effects on the nation's economic and trade policies), its economic condition and policies, the recent trends in bilateral trade and foreign direct investment, and key economic and trade issues between India and the United States. Where suitable, the report also compares India to China to provide a different perspective on U.S. relations with both nations.

POLITICAL AND ECONOMIC CLIMATE OF INDIA

India is the world's most populous democracy and remains firmly committed to representative government and the rule of law. With a robust and working democratic system, India is a federal republic where the bulk of executive power rests with the prime minister and his or her cabinet (the Indian president is a ceremonial chief of state with limited executive powers). As a nation-state, India presents a vast mosaic of hundreds of different ethnic groups, religious sects, and social castes. Most of India's prime ministers have come from the country's Hindi-speaking northern regions and all but two have been upper-caste Hindus.

Larger than Alaska, Texas, and California combined, India is a land of great demographic, geographic, and climatological variety. From stark deserts in the west to thick jungles in the northeast, the towering Himalaya mountains of the north to the vast tableland of the Deccan Plateau of the south, and with the fertile Indo-Gangetic plain between, India dominates the Asian Subcontinent and shares long borders with its six other continental states. About one-third of the population lives in urban areas; an overwhelming majority of the remainder is engaged in the agricultural sector. Most of India's people inhabit either the alluvial soil of the Indo-Gangetic plain across the north, or the eastern and western coasts of the southern Deccan Peninsula. About 290 million Indians live in the densely-populated northern states of Uttar Pradesh and Bihar; another 100 million live in the western state of Maharashtra. These three states account for more than one-third of the country's total population.

The 543-seat Lok Sabha (People's House) is the locus of national political power, with directly elected representatives from each of the country's 28 states and 7 union territories. A smaller upper house, the Rajya Sabha (Council of States), may review, but not veto, most legislation, and has no power over the prime minister or the cabinet. Although India's political stage is crowded with numerous regional and caste-based parties, recent years have seen an increasingly dyadic battle between two major parties that vie for smaller allies in a system that now requires coalitional politics. No party has won a national election outright since 1984.

India has one of the largest and fastest growing economies in the world. India's real gross domestic product (GDP) rose by 9.2% in 2006 — a growth rate second only to China among Asian nations. The strong GDP performance in 2006 capped five years of rapid economic expansion, transforming India into the third largest economy in Asia (after Japan and China). Its recent economic success is generally attributed to a combination of internal and external factors. Internally, a series of economic reforms (begun when the current prime minister was finance minister) have stimulated solid growth of India's manufacturing and service sectors. Externally, a relatively strong global economy, combined with India's trade and investment liberalization policies, have stimulated increased trade and investment flows to and from India.

Despite the recent growth, India's economy confronts several challenges to its future prosperity. First, although the nation's manufacturing and services sectors have grown rapidly, there has been relatively little job creation. Second, its agricultural sector has experienced relatively slow growth for many years. With more than half of Indian households still reliant on agriculture for their income, the standard of living for much of the country's population remains relatively low. There are indications that most of the Indian populace remains untouched by and thus unimpressed with the country's widely touted economic boom.

Third, the standard of living of India's rural and urban poor is being threatened by an emerging economic challenge — inflationary pressures. After seven years of modest inflation at or below 4% per year, inflation in 2006 was nearly 7% and has risen to about 8% in the first part of 2007. India's poor have been especially hard hit by major increases in the cost of food in recent years. In the longer run, India faces three additional barriers to economic growth — lack of infrastructure, bureaucratic obstacles, and environmental degradation. India's economy is already hindered by its inadequate transportation system and electricity shortage. Similarly, India's complex and entrenched bureaucracy frequently creates a barrier to implementing new economic policies and programs. At the same time, its large population and recent rise in industrial output are putting more and more pressure on India's environment, exacerbating existing problems in providing its people with clean, potable water, as well as clean air.

The continued strength of the economy and the Singh government's attempt to balance its economic policies, many analysts see India facing a number of economic challenges and believe there are still several important economic reforms that India should make to increase the benefits generated by its restructured economy. In particular, critics of the current economic policies point to the unequal distribution of the benefits of the economic reforms, noting that the rapid economic growth has not brought a corresponding reduction in poverty in India, particularly in rural areas. For some, the solution is to press forward more aggressively with the economic reforms by greater liberalization of India's domestic economic and international trade policies. For others, the solution is reverse elements of the reform and refocus agriculture and India's rural population.

Prime Minister Singh addressed a roundtable hosted by the *Economist* magazine. In his remarks, Prime Minister Singh provided a fairly comprehensive overview of his administration's view of the current status of the Indian economy, arguing that India's economy will probably continue its rapid growth for another decade or more. However, Singh also pointed out India's need for additional reforms, including changes to its banking and financial system, its labour markets, and its "public service delivery mechanisms." In light of India's past and planned reforms, he stated, "I find it surprising when I continue to hear complaints about our economy still being a relatively inward-looking economy." The Bush Administration seems to hold a different view of India's economic conditions, maintaining that the Singh government ought to push forward more actively with its economic reforms. In September 2006, U.S. Ambassador to India, David Mulford, said to an audience in New Delhi:

Today's business environment in India is more favorable to trade and investment. But there are signs of a pause in the reform process in recent months. Privatizations have stopped, and political reality suggests that reform of other key sectors and policies of central interest to investors will take longer than envisioned. It is important to bear in mind there are serious economic costs to any loss of momentum on the reform front.... The solution to attracting much greater private sector investment in energy and infrastructure development is a blend of policies that includes better governance, market sensitive regulatory regimes, continued liberalization of the financial sector that enables foreign and domestic private capital to finance major projects, and the timely resolution of investor-state disputes.

One U.S. trade official opined that it is only through meaningful reforms in India's vast and poorly performing agricultural sector that the country's true economic potential can be realized. This, he says, will require rural infrastructural improvements, land reform, and changes that will allow foreign direct investment in the farm sector.

INDIAN POLITICAL ECONOMIC HISTORY

A review of India's economic and trade policies over the last 60 years reveals a pattern of conceptual economic theory moderated by pragmatic political and economic considerations. Major shifts in economic policy were typically initiated with significant changes and then followed by a period of gradual adjustments.

The government of Prime Minister Jawaharlal Nehru of the Indian National Congress Party (INC) adopted an economic policy emphasizing rapid industrialization, import substitution, and relatively high levels of government participation in economic production. Monopolies were granted to state enterprises in a number of industries considered of economic or strategic importance. Private companies in other industries were often subject to licensing requirements and legally constrained in their size of operation. The agricultural sector was a key focus of the First Five Year Plan, with the implementation of various subsidy programs, food price controls, and restrictions on the transport of agricultural crops. Labour laws provided workers with protection from managerial misconduct, but also significantly reduced labour mobility. Both exports and imports were controlled by licenses and tariffs. Foreign direct investment was also severely restricted both by industry and size.

Prime Minister Nehru, remained relatively true to these policies for both its First and Second Five Year Plans (1951-56 and 1956-61) with moderately successful results. Real GDP grew at an average annual rate of 3.6% for the First Five Year Plan, and 2.5% for the Second Five Year Plan. Agricultural production rose 44% and manufacturing output increased 144%.

However, the economic policies were also leading to growing merchandise trade and current account deficits that were depleting India's foreign reserves. For the Third Five Year Plan (1961-66), Prime Minister Nehru and the INC made an adjustment in its economic policies, shifting focus away from "rapid industrialization" over to a program of "self sustained growth." At the same time, India's trade policy shifted from "import substitution" to "efficient substitution of imports," which in effect opened up new trade opportunities for goods considered crucial to economic growth and development. This adjusted economic policy remained in effect until the end of the Seventh Five Year Plan in 1990.

In 1990 and 1991, India was struck by a number of political and economic shocks. On the political side, the INC refused to form a coalition government following a poor showing in the elections of 1989. The next largest party, the Janata Dal, was able to form a coalition government, headed by Prime Minister V.P. Singh, but it proved unstable and collapsed in December 1990. During the election campaign of 1991, ex-Prime Minister Rajiv Gandhi was assassinated, and P.V.

Narasimha Rao was selected as the new leader for the INC. Following the INC's success in the 1991 elections, Rao became prime minister. During the political tumult of 1990 and 1991, the combined effects of rise in oil prices (precipitated by *Operation Desert Storm* in the Persian Gulf) and the demise of the Soviet Union, a major trading partner and a key source of foreign aid, led to a rapid devaluation of the rupee, a depletion of India's international reserves, and fears of an impending severe recession. In response, Prime Minister Rao made a major and controversial change in economic policies designed to restore faith in the rupee, replenish the nation's international reserves, and stimulate economic growth. These reforms were overseen by his finance minister, Manmohan Singh. The initial round of reforms included several elements. First, efforts were made to reduce India's perpetual fiscal deficits at both the federal and state levels. Second, the number of sectors reserved solely for the public sector were reduced from 18 industries to just three — military aircraft and warships, nuclear energy generation, and railway transport. Third, India liberalized international trade by reducing import tariffs, eliminating import restrictions, and opening up India to foreign direct investment. Fourth, India liberalized its financial markets, by dismantling its interest rate controls, reducing government regulations and permitting greater competition.

Following the initial round of economic reforms, India's real GDP growth rate accelerated from around 3-4% per year in the 1980s to 5-7% during the early 1990s. However, toward the end of the decade, India's economic growth began to slow. Some analysts attributed the economic slowdown to a failure of the federal government to continue and to complete the economic reforms initiated at the beginning of the decade. Other analysts argued that economic problems generated by the reforms were creating structural barriers to continued growth.

The ensuing debate over the merits of the 1991 reforms contributed to a second period of gradual economic reform in the second half of the 1990s and into the current decade. Since 1991, India has made a number of significant changes in the structure of its economy, including:

- The termination of state monopolies for all but three industries;
- The elimination of the "License Raj" — prior to the reforms, there was a rather elaborate system of licenses and regulations governing the establishment of a business in India, making it a very timely and expensive process to start a new concern;
- The abolition of import licenses for most commodities;
- A major reduction in average and peak tariff rates for imports;
- A reduction in domestic price controls for key consumer goods; and
- A restructuring of many of the nation's various subsidy programs.

However, some analysts argue that many Indians are skeptical about economic reforms in general, thus posing a "marketing" problem for the government in a democratic system. Some suggest that even segments of the private sector oppose reform efforts. Still, representatives of the Indian business community insist that all of New Delhi's progress in economic reform has been voluntary and is not made under external pressure, and that the general path of liberalization will continue to be followed regardless of what party or coalition is in power.

PRESENT POLITICAL CLIMATE AND ECONOMIC IMPROVEMENT

Present ruling United Progressive Alliance (UPA) coalition was seated in May 2004, when the INC, long associated with the Nehru-Gandhi families, won 145 of the Lok Sabha's 543 seats and built a ruling coalition with the support of 14 smaller parties. The election unseated a National Democratic Alliance (NDA) coalition led by the Bharatiya Janata Party (BJP), which had been in power under Prime Minister Atal Vajpayee since 1998. Some analysts saw in the election results a rejection of the BJP's neo-liberal economic reform program. INC President Sonia Gandhi surprised supporters and opponents alike by declining to assume the office of prime minister, instead nominating her lieutenant, Manmohan Singh, a former finance minister. The May 2004 poll results were notable for the best-ever national showing of a leftist alliance — commonly known as the Left Front — led by the Communist Party of India (Marxist) (CPI-M). Although this Left Front is not part of the UPA coalition, it provides crucial parliamentary support from the outside and was described as being "militant" in its opposition to the BJP's privatization efforts. The CPI-M seated the third largest number of parliamentarians in 2004 (43), but its vote bank is almost wholly limited to the states of West Bengal and Kerala.

Immediately following the election, investor fears that a coalition government including communists might curtail or halt India's economic reform and liberalization process apparently led to huge losses in the country's stock markets. Market recovery began when INC leaders quickly offered assurances that the new government would be "pro-growth, pro-savings, and pro-investment." Indian industrial leaders also sought to assure foreign investors that Left Front members are not "Cuba-style communists," but could be expected to support the UPA reform agenda. The Chief Minister of West Bengal, Buddhadeb Bhattacharya, a CPI-M member, has himself actively sought corporate investment in his state. However, since coming to power, the Congress-led coalition has slowed certain aspects of its economic reform program, including suspending major disinvestment and special economic zone initiatives. These moves are widely viewed as gestures to the Left Front.

While there are indications that both Prime Minister Singh and party chief Gandhi remain fairly popular figures in India, February 2007 state elections in Punjab and Uttaranchal saw INC candidates decisively defeated by the main opposition BJP and its allies, causing some pundits to suggest that national economic policies and rising inflation may be damaging the ruling coalition's standing. Some analysts saw the "neoliberal policies" of the UPA as harming its electoral position. In June, eight regional parties formally launched a new "Third Front" that might emerge as a national alternative to the UPA and NDA. Well-known Tamil Nadu leader Jayalalithaa is likely to lead. August 2007 political wrangling between the UPA and its Left Front allies over planned U.S.-India civil nuclear cooperation (the leftists oppose the plan) has added to political instability in New Delhi and led some to foresee early national polls if Singh's coalition loses Left Front support.

Political information and institution

Several governmental figures and trade-related institutions wield influence over India's economic policies. The following is a selected listing of key economic players in the current government:

- Prime Minister Manmohan Singh, INC member and widely-respected Oxford-educated economist who, as finance minister from 1991-1995, was the architect of a comprehensive set of national economic reforms;

- INC President Sonia Gandhi, the Italian-born widow of former Prime Minister Rajiv Gandhi, while not formally a member of the central government, oversaw the UPA's 2004 poll victory and wields considerable influence over the coalition's policy making;
- Finance Minister Palaniappan Chidambaram, a Harvard-educated lawyer from the southern state of Tamil Nadu (and member a regional affiliate of the INC) who served as finance minister in the late1990s, is considered to be a highly-competent, pro-market fiscal manager;
- Commerce and Industry Minister Kamal Nath, an INC stalwart from the east-central Madhya Pradesh state, has launched major trade policy initiatives and is a key interlocutor for the U.S. government;
- Planning Commission Deputy Chairman Montek Singh Ahluwalia, a widely-respected, Oxford-educated economist who works directly under Prime Minister Singh and has close ties to Washington;
- Oil Minister Murli Deora, INC member and former mayor of Mumbai who was appointed in 2006, by some accounts due to pressures for a more pro-business, pro-U.S. oil minister;
- Power Minister Sushilkumar Shinde, an INC stalwart and former Chief Minister of Maharashtra;
- CPI-M General Secretary Prakash Karat, a vocal critic of many economic reforms and of India's warming relations with the United States, is the most notable leader of the UPA-supporting Left Front;
- BJP President Rajnath Singh, a Hindu nationalist from the Uttar Pradesh state who served in the government of former Prime Minister Vajpayee, is seen as a new-generation leader for India's main opposition party and has been critical of the UPA for slowing the process of economic reform;

- The Federation of Indian Chambers of Commerce and Industry (FICCI), a nationwide grouping of corporations, chambers of commerce, and business associations that claims to speak directly or indirectly for more than 250,000 Indian business units; and
- The Confederation of Indian Industry (CII), a nongovernmental industry group with a membership of more than 6,300 private and public sector organizations that employs advisory and consultative processes aimed at improving India's business climate.

POLITICAL PARTIES AND COALITIONS

Political power in India was monopolized by the Indian National Congress. However, starting in the 1970s, INC dominance was challenged by the emergence of other, increasingly influential political parties. In 1977, nearly 30 years after independence, the Janata Dal Party's Morarji Desai became India's first-ever non-INC prime minister. Later, in the 1980s, political party fragmentation in India led to an era of coalition governments, variously led by the INC, the Janata Dal, or the BJP. As noted above, no party has won a national election outright since 1984.

India's political landscape offers no clear division between proponents and opponents of economic reform. Prime Minister Nehru and the INC oversaw decades of centralized economic planning — and today the UPA coalition relies on leftist forces that strongly oppose liberalizing policies — yet it was also later INC governments that launched India's major reform and liberalization programs. At the same time, the main opposition BJP accelerated "second generation" economic reforms during its time in power from 1998 to 2004, even as the BJP is home to some Hindu nationalist and "*swadeshi*" (self-reliance) forces that maintain a deep scepticism of neo-liberal economic systems.

The UPA and the Indian National Congress. Generally perceived as being a centre-left coalition, the UPA is an alliance among the INC and 14 smaller regional parties, including the Bihar-based Rashtriya Janata Dal (RJD) and the Dravida

Munnetra Kazhagam (DMK) of Tamil Nadu. INC members hold about two-thirds of the coalition's 219 Lok Sabha seats, as well as all of the four major cabinet posts (External Affairs, Defence, Home, and Commerce). In forming a government, the UPA coalition created a "Common Minimum Program," a document providing the basic principles of governance that would guide the UPA, along with a policy framework for specific issue-areas. Left Front support for the UPA — which is necessary for the coalition to maintain majority status in the Parliament — has been predicated on government strategies that were seen as compatible with the provisions of the Common Minimum Program.

In addition to taking credit for India's dramatic economic growth during the 1990s and criticizing the BJP for "mismanaging" the economy in general and reform efforts specifically, the INC's economic agenda for the 2004 elections, entitled "An Expanding Economy, A Just Society," called for achieving up to 10% annual GDP growth, while also seeking a shift of emphasis from a rapid rate of growth to "a specific pattern of growth" that would benefit all segments of the population, with ambitious (and far from realized) promises to "abolish" an array of societal ills, including hunger, unemployment, poverty, and illiteracy. A major aspect of this proposed effort would involve creating "a congenial atmosphere" for both domestic and foreign investment. The INC also blamed the BJP-led government for abject failure in the agricultural sector (which employs more than two-thirds of India's workforce), vowing major public investments in rural infrastructure.

The NDA and the Bharatiya Janata Party. The right-leaning NDA, which held power in New Delhi from 1998-2004, is dominated by the BJP, which holds nearly three-quarters of the alliance's 189 Lok Sabha seats (12 smaller regional parties hold the remainder). The surprise emergence of the BJP as a national political force in the early 1990s gave voice to a repudiation not only of the Nehru-INC secular version of Indian nationalism, but also of its concepts of state-directed economic planning. Instead, the BJP called for major liberalization efforts, including abolition of India's complex system of permits and licenses, as well as a selling off of most public sector enterprises. Many early BJP economic policy recommendations were, in fact, adopted by Prime Minister Rao's INC government in the early 1990s.

However, the BJP subsequently moderated some of its liberalization policies, and also had to deal with tensions between Hindu nationalism and the entry into India of major multinational corporations, which some feared would lead to an erosion of "Hindu culture."

This led to measured support for trade protectionism and what the party called "calibrated globalization." While also asserting a goal of "complete eradication of poverty and unemployment," the BJP's 2004 economic agenda was more enthusiastic about unfettered continuation of economic reform efforts and did not place the same degree of emphasis on "social justice" as did the INC.

The NDA's premier statement in 2004 promised an energetic continuation of economic reforms across a multitude of sectors. BJP leaders subsequently have been critical of the INC-led government for significantly slowing the reform process, sometimes accusing the UPA of buckling under pressure from leftist parties.

Moreover, the BJP has been critical of the way in which the Singh government has entered into an agreement on civil nuclear cooperation with the United States, claiming that provisions of such an agreement will constrain India's nuclear weapons program.

Organized resistance to proposed economic reforms has come from Hindu nationalist groups that were influential under the BJP government from 1998 to 2004. As a "sister organization" to the Rashtriya Swayamsevak Sangh — a leading Hindu nationalist organization — the Swadeshi Jagaran Manch (SJM) has taken the lead in efforts to forward the *swadeshi* (self-reliance) cause. According to the SJM, "The Western notion of a global market does not fit into the *swadeshi* approach," nor does the "Western notion of individual freedom, which fragments and compartmentalizes family, economy, culture, and social values...." Such anti-globalization policies continue to enjoy limited, but still substantial backing among Indians. The swadeshi lobby did, however, welcome the UPA's Common Minimum Program document in 2004.

The Left Front and the CPI-M. Long-time and bitter rivals of the INC, India's major communist parties now provide outside support to the INC-led ruling coalition as part of their mutual efforts to keep the BJP from power. The current Left Front alliance is dominated by the CPI-M and, secondarily, the Communist Party of India, which combine to account for about 85% of its 60 Lok Sabha seats. During the 1950s — and in correspondence with growing Soviet support for the new Indian state — India's various communist groups resolved to abjure revolutionary ideology and work within the parliamentary system. These parties, however, remain proponents of government-directed economic and industrial development, moderate land reform programs, and strong labour protection laws.

Initially and still nominally opposed to the essence of New Delhi's reform and liberalization efforts since 1991, communist party leaders in their stronghold of West Bengal have continuously sought both domestic and international investments in their state, thus demonstrating a willingness to compromise in some areas of economic policy. Still, such leaders maintain an intensive focus on caste-based and poverty issues, styling themselves as the champions of minority groups and farmers, along with a deep-seated scepticism about the intentions and goals of U.S. and Western political, military, and economic interests in India.

On economic policy, the Left Front has taken firm stands against raising limits of foreign direct investment, against government efforts to privatize public sector enterprises, and against the government's initial plans to launch hundreds of Special Economic Zones in India. Along with its considerable influence at the national level, the Left Front wields administrative power in the states of Kerala and West Bengal, where important trade unions have caused disruption in the course of major strikes and protests over inflation and unemployment.

Since 2004, the Left Front has accused the UPA government of "serious violations" of the Common Minimum Program, including its planned disinvestment from a major public sector undertaking (PSU) in the summer of 2006. Communist parties characterize such moves as "anti-working class, neoliberal" policies being pushed by the UPA coalition. Moreover, these parties view New Delhi's apparent pro-U.S. foreign policy tilt as accentuating such neoliberal initiatives. It is the Left Front's opposition to "alliance" with the United States that is at the root of its vehement opposition to planned U.S.-India civil nuclear cooperation.

4

Trump and Indian Foreign Policy: An Era of Uncertainty

In 2011, the Obama Administration announced its 'pivot to Asia' strategy, which envisioned a political, economic, and military "rebalancing" toward the Asia-Pacific region by strengthening existing alliances, forging new partnerships and increasing US military presence and its economic engagement in the region. The administration saw India as a "linchpin" in its pivot to Asia and declared that it is "investing in a long-term strategic partnership with India to support its ability to serve as a regional economic anchor and provider of security in the broader Indian Ocean region." Donald Trump's election as president of the United States not only raises questions about the future of the US rebalancing strategy but also poses new challenges for Indian foreign policy.

... uncertainties and potential challenges that the Trump administration might pose for India are likely to reignite the debate about the reliability of the United States as a strategic partner and reinforce India's desire for strategic autonomy in world politics.

Since the end of the cold war, Indo-US relations have gradually developed into a "global strategic partnership" based on common democratic values, a growing convergence of interests and pan-partisan support in both countries. Regular high-level political visits and the establishment of various dialogue mechanisms have provided the bilateral relationship with an institutional framework for sustained and multi-sectoral cooperation in various policy-fields ranging from defence and security to investment, science and technology. A milestone was the 2008 nuclear agreement which de facto recognized India as a nuclear weapons state.

With a powerful appeal to economic nationalism and to put "America First", Donald Trump questioned main pillars of US foreign policy: the US' long-standing commitment to a liberal international order based on expansive internationalism, economic globalization, global rule-based regimes, open borders and strategic alliances with regional powers. For example, Trump called NATO "obsolete" and withdrew the United States from the Trans-Pacific Partnership trade agreement – a key component of Obama's 'pivot to Asia' strategy. For America's allies and partners, a new era of uncertainty has begun, forcing them to reconsider their trust in US commitments. Trump's first months in office did not bring clarity but rather more confusion. The surprising airstrikes against Syria, which led to a further deterioration in US-Russia relations, the dropping of the largest non-nuclear bomb on Afghanistan, or the hawkish approach to North Korea do not only contradict his election pledges, but also appear to lack a coherent strategy, thereby making the US an unpredictable partner for India.

Trump's turn to a more nationalist, isolationist and mercantilist foreign policy undermines some of the foundations of Indo-US engagement in the post-Cold War era. Having pursued an economic policy of import substitution in the decades after independence, India gradually opened its economy and embraced the logic of globalization in the post-cold war era and actively sought to attract investments from US corporations by encouraging them to offshore services and manufacturing to India. While seeking access to the markets of the industrialized countries and criticizing their protectionist policies, India resisted US and European pressures for a further liberalization of its economy in order to protect it from international competition. As the US is now – in line with Trump's motto "buy American, hire American" – turning inward and seeking to strengthen its declining manufacturing sector and reduce the outsourcing of services to India as well as the insourcing of cheap skilled labour from India through the H1B visa system, India's post-Cold War economic model might be over.

Another driving force of the US-India strategic partnership has been the shared concerns about China's rise to power and its growing assertiveness in Asia. Though Indian governments neither seek to balance or contain China – nor do they want India to be perceived as a junior partner to the US in Asia – they believed that the strategic partnership with the US would increase India's room for manoeuvre towards China and serve as a strategic hedge against the uncertainties emanating from China's rise. This hedging strategy, however, presupposes the military presence of the United States in Asia and a willingness to uphold, and if necessary to defend, the regional order.

By renouncing American internationalism and implicitly threating its allies in Europe and Asia with a withdrawal of the United States, Trump raised doubts about US commitments to defend its allies and to provide global public goods. There are fears among US allies and partners in Asia that China might seek to fill this power vacuum created by the potential retreat of the United States and alter the regional order. While uncertainties regarding the US role in the Asia-Pacific region potentially reduce India's strategic leverage towards China, Trump's allegation that US allies took advantage of the US and promoted their own interests at the expense of the United States might also lead to increased pressure on India to share more international responsibility and to show a greater appreciation for US interests.

These uncertainties and potential challenges that the Trump administration might pose for India are likely to reignite the debate about the reliability of the United States as a strategic partner and reinforce India's desire for strategic autonomy in world politics. Though successive Indian governments have signalled their commitment to a close partnership with the US, they also sought to avoid strategic entanglements and one-sided dependencies which could not only undermine India's strategic autonomy but also negatively affect its relations with other countries and state groupings. Rather, India pursued a policy of multi-alignment and tried to develop comprehensive strategic partnerships with all major powers.

While some political observers view this policy as a desperate attempt to preserve the notion of non-alignment and urge India to enter into a strategic alignment with the United States, India's striving for strategic autonomy is rather driven by the conviction that India should hedge its bets and pursue a multi-directional foreign policy in a world order that is characterized by a complex mixture of inter-state competition and cooperation and requires issue- rather than nation-centric partnerships. Against this backdrop, the unexpected election of Trump and his renunciation of established tenets of US foreign policy appears to substantiate the advantages of strategic autonomy than lead ing to a 'bromance' between Trump and Modi – who both came to power as self-styled, anti-establishment populists – not the least because two nationalistic leaders, who promise to put their country first, are not necessarily good negotiating partners.

DONALD TRUMP BRINGS UNCERTAINTIES FOR INDIA

Will a Donald Trump presidency be good or bad for India? The honest answer: It's too soon to tell. It will depend on how that presidency shapes up and what India and other countries do in response. The key word for now is "uncertainty".

Observers will be looking for clarity on (1) the extent to which Trump's campaign rhetoric will be translated into policy; (2) his domestic and foreign policy priorities; (3) policy specifics—including on trade and immigration, which cross the domestic-foreign divide, where his base will want action; (4) Trump's leadership style and personnel appointments, as well as the relationship between Trump and administration officials and advisers, and among them; (5) the dynamics between the Trump White House and the Republican-led Congress; (6) the extent to which he will change the presidency or it will change him;

(7) the level and kind of strategic and economic interest and engagement in the world—will he seek a more limited global engagement based on a narrower definition of American interest and scepticism of allies suggested by campaign rhetoric, moderate the view, or revert to more traditional Republican foreign policies? Which relationships and policies will he care enough about to oversee himself, which will he delegate or even outsource to advisers? (8) The reaction of other countries—will they test Trump or transact with him? (9) The way Trump will react in a crisis.

This comes at a time of global uncertainty, with regional orders in flux and a debate about globalization. It also comes at a critical time for India, which has envisioned the US playing a crucial role in facilitating its rise and ensuring a multipolar Asia. Some potential Trump policies that concern others won't trouble Delhi, for example, outreach towards Russia or lack of emphasis on human rights. But it will also have to see how some questions are resolved.

First, to India's east, what approach will Trump take to the Asia-Pacific, particularly towards China and Japan? Trump has promised to be tough on China on the economic front, but has been less clear on the strategic front. During the campaign, the president-elect suggested a reduced or contingent US role in Asia, but some of his advisers have talked about continuing commitment to Asian allies and greater military—especially naval—spending related to this arena.

Second, to India's west, the Trump administration's policies towards Afghanistan, Pakistan and Iran. On the latter, he's called the Iran nuclear deal a "disaster"—will he seek to overturn or renegotiate it or will Syria-related imperatives prevent that? On Pakistan, he has highlighted the danger of nuclear weapons and the presence there of terrorists targeting the US. But he's also talked about wanting to maintain a relationship with it, declined to take sides on India-Pakistan, and suggested that India could help solve the Pakistan problem (Delhi, on its part, has wanted Washington to help do so). Will his policy be any different? What will be his administration's views on

Afghanistan and nuclear proliferation that will also shape Pakistan policy? Will he see terrorism directed against India in the context of global terrorism or focus on targeting terrorism directed against the US?

Third, economic policies. Delhi might not mind a tougher American approach towards China on trade and market access if it leads to a change in Beijing's policies that negatively affect India as well and doesn't lead to a trade war. However, given US concerns about Indian trade policy, will Trump's promise to be tough on trade extend to India? Trump's rhetoric has indicated that he neither likes the Trans-Pacific Partnership (which India is no fan of) nor the World Trade Organization (which New Delhi prefers), so will he focus on bilateral deals and what will he expect India to offer? On the investment side, the Narendra Modi government wants to attract American investment (particularly of the job-creating variety), but will Trump implement policies like imposing tariffs on American companies setting up facilities abroad?

Fourth, policies affecting immigration and minorities. How will a Trump administration deal with the H-1B visa programme, or the optional practical training programme associated with student visas? What will be the fate of the "Muslim ban"? How will minorities, including millions of non-resident Indians and Indian Americans, be treated in Trump's America?

Fifth, on climate change, will Trump withdraw from or try to renegotiate the Paris agreement? India won't necessarily mind the reduced criticism of its fossil-fuel usage, but given that India's commitment to renewables was partly predicated on climate financing and technology transfer, there's also the question of whether American commitments in this regard will be kept.

Sixth, the priority that India will get in a Trump administration. It will partly depend on whether India is seen as successful, useful (particularly relative to others), and respectful of the new president and responsive to his priorities. It will also depend on personnel appointments—some of the names doing the rounds are not so familiar to India; others have had mixed views on India (for example, they have expressed concern about H-1B visas, Indian trade and investment policies, human rights, the US-India nuclear deal and India-Iran ties). New Delhi will also watch—and hope—that others from the traditional Republican foreign policy establishment join the Trump team.

Finally, Trump is far more transactional than his predecessors and would likely want India to put more on the table. What would that entail for New Delhi? Defence deals? Greater market access?

The Indian government has already reached out to the president-elect. It will continue to engage with his advisers directly, as well as through its contacts in Congress, states, the business community and the diaspora that have links to the next president. It will likely seek a meeting between Modi and Trump as soon as possible, extend an invitation to the new president to visit India, and go on a charm offensive. Policymakers will also seek to shape the new administration's views of India's utility, the relationship's mutual benefits and regional issues, and draw contrasts between India and China. Additionally, New Delhi will have to be ready to be more transactional. Finally, given the uncertainties and unpredictabilities, it will have to prepare for them, accelerate its own strengthening and double down on diversifying its portfolio of partners.

THE AGE OF UNCERTAINTY: US FOREIGN POLICY IN THE TRUMP ERA?

In April 2016, Donald Trump declared 'We must as a nation be more unpredictable.' In a speech on foreign policy during the Republican primary campaign, Trump – who at that point was the front-runner for the GOP nomination – set out what the New York Times in its editorial described as a 'strange worldview,' one that appears to be a throwback to the isolationist movement of the 1930s – 'America First' – but which betrays a total misunderstanding of the complexities of the world in which America is deeply embedded. Dissecting that worldview and extrapolating what the Trump administration's foreign policy will look like over the coming months and years is something of a fool's errand; this is a man who prides himself on being unpredictable, in keeping allies and enemies second-guessing his intentions, and using his personal Twitter feed to make policy pronouncements.

Yet amidst the chaos, some things are all too clear. The first is that the world as we know it has been upended, and is now violently spinning on its axis. Most of us in the West have grown up in a world defined by certain core principles – democracy, liberty, the rule of law, human rights, freedom of speech and expression, freedom of worship, freedom from want and fear – embedded in a liberal order that the US – more than any other nation – has sought to defend, maintain and advance since 1945. It is in part because we live in such a world that Donald Trump now finds himself sitting in the White House, democratically elected (though not by a majority of the American people) with the freedom to express the views he holds. But by doing so, he is undermining many of the values on which liberal order rests: refugees who find themselves being turned away from American airports are living in fear, their yearning to breathe free suffocated by the stroke of a pen; the LGBT community in the US feels more afraid than at any point since the end of the Cold War, while women in America face the prospect that their right to an abortion will be stripped away; Muslims in America are increasingly vilified and demonised, no longer free to worship in peace. Protestors are dismissed and derided; in the world of @readldonaldtrump these are not the legitimate acts of a people with the constitutional right to 'peaceably assemble,' but the product of manufactured outrage created by a liberal elite hell-bent on undermining the will of the people.

Internationally, Trump represents the greatest deviation from the liberal bipartisan consensus that has underpinned US foreign policy since 1990. In Obama's parting speech to the UN he spoke passionately about the threats facing liberal international order. That liberal order has rested not only on a set of core ideas and values, but also an institutional architecture centred on the UN and NATO. Yet in his policy pronouncements thus far, Trump appears to be re-writing the script. He has injected a greater degree of instability into America's relations with Europe and NATO than any presidency since the end of the Cold War, and is far more willing to embrace, rather than reject, the alternative vision of international order promulgated by Russian President, Vladimir Putin. Trump's election has injected a new element of uncertainty into an already perilous state of affairs in Eastern Europe; not only are Putin's intentions unclear, so are Trump's. Lawrence Freedman once wrote that credibility is the 'magic ingredient' of deterrence. It is one thing for NATO to be facing uncertainty over Putin's intentions, it is quite another to be facing its own crisis of credibility caused by uncertainty over the Trump administration's policy towards both Russia and NATO; this at a time when Europe is witnessing the biggest deployment of US military forces to the continent since the Cold War.

Relations with Moscow may well prove to be one of the most pivotal elements of Trump's foreign policy; between them, Trump and Putin have the ability to shape international order in ways that affect us all. A matter of weeks after the election of Trump, Putin signed a new Foreign Policy Concept, outlining Russia's ambitions to play a leading role on the international stage and boost cooperation with the administration of the new US president. It remains to be seen whether these two goals are mutually exclusive – whilst the early atmospherics surrounding both the Russian and US camp have been positive, there are still many obstacles ahead. Moscow has consistently opposed what it views as a US dominance of the international system and has made frequent reference to the destabilising influence of Washington, DC's international actions.

Trump's election success was greeted with elation in Russia, with Trump 'fever' leading to some interesting images being published in the Russian media: boxes of sugar bearing Trump's smiling face, the Army of Russia store offering a 10% discount for US citizens and embassy employees on the day of Trump's inauguration and Vladimir Zhirinovsky, the leader of Russian far-right party, the LDPR, drinking champagne with members of his party in celebration of Trump's election victory. But these images contrast sharply with the realities of the state of the current relationship between Washington, DC and Moscow, which had hit rock-bottom during Obama's presidency. Whilst it remains unclear what the direction of the Trump administration's foreign policy will be, there are already signs that it will take a hard line, particularly with regards to international terrorism and the threat from IS – Trump has indicated that torture is an acceptable tool in the fight against IS, a hard-line stance that will appeal to the Kremlin, which has never shied away from the use of force (legitimate or not) in pursuit of its strategic objectives. This highlights one of the key potential drivers of any future US-Russia relationship: similar personality traits. Both presidents like to portray themselves as 'strong men' who are seeking to make their countries 'great' again. Relations between the two are currently in a honeymoon phase, with each president apparently delighted to have found a similar character in the other, but there could be problems ahead if neither is willing to embrace compromise or concession.

Following UK PM Theresa May's visit to Washington, DC on January 27, Trump and Putin held an hour-long telephone conversation during which both leaders apparently undertook to repair bilateral relations. During a wide-ranging conversation, they discussed the fight against terrorism and ongoing instability across the Middle East, as well as the possibility of expanding their economic ties. This latter issue raises the possibility of US sanctions against Russia being lifted, although the topic was not discussed during their call. Trump has mooted the possibility of lifting the sanctions regime, imposed in the wake of Russia's annexation of Crimea in 2014 and ongoing support for pro-Russian separatists in eastern Ukraine. This position is at odds with that of Europe: European leaders including May, Angela Merkel and Francois Hollande, have all expressed their opposition to any lifting of sanctions until Moscow complies fully with the terms of the Minsk agreement. Any attempt by the Trump administration to ease the sanctions regime risks the emergence of further rifts between the US and Europe, which is precisely what the Kremlin is seeking.

The new Foreign Policy Concept suggests that Russia will continue its pivot towards Asia, partly driven by the lack of access to Western markets, a consequence of the ongoing sanctions regime. However, it also makes clear that Russia will continue to consolidate its position as a 'centre of influence in today's world'. Encouraged by its use of the military lever in Syria, Russia is likely to take an even more assertive line on the global stage over the coming year and will seek to boost its international influence by both hard and soft means.

Since Putin came to power in 2000, the Kremlin has demonstrated an increased willingness, and ability, to use the military lever to achieve broader strategic and foreign policy goals. Despite this, many in the West continue to be surprised by the primacy of hard power in Russian policy-making, particularly the use of force. Russian involvement in Syria has undoubtedly demonstrated that it is now able to project power beyond its own strategic 'backyard' and that it is determined to play a global role. The Kremlin appears to have high hopes for a considerable improvement both in its relations with the US and its position on the global stage. However, whilst relations between Trump and Putin are currently very positive, this could change dramatically if either oversteps and finds themselves in an opposing position.

However, as the relationship unfolds between Trump and Putin, one thing appears clear: we are living in an era of instability and uncertainty, the likes of which many of us have never experienced before.

TRUMP'S FOREIGN POLICY OF CONFUSION

When Donald Trump was elected as the US President in November 2016, foreign policy observers predicted an era of uncertainty. If the first few weeks of President Trump are anything to go by, we will have to expect the unexpected. What do the first few weeks of the Trump Administration have the say about his foreign policy over the next four years? What impact would these have on the US' allies? These are questions many around the world have been asking since November 2016.

Trump's election campaign had given glimpses into his potential foreign policy stance. He was clearly up in arms against trade deals like the NAFTA and TPP. He openly welcomed the UK's vote to leave the EU. He wanted Mexico to pay for the wall across the US-Mexico border. He also termed the NATO as an obsolete agency and threatened to relook at the US' engagement in the NATO. Most significantly, he openly praised Vladmir Putin, sparking debates of how a Trump-led USA would seek closer ties with Russia. As the President-elect, he broke from tradition, openly criticising President Obama's stance on the UN Resolution against Israel.

Post-January 20, 2017, many expected to see a radical shift in the way US foreign policy is conducted. These predictions have come out to be true so far. Over the past three weeks, we have seen it all. There has been a heated exchange with the Australian Prime Minister over the phone. Trump's tweet, calling for Mexico to pay for the border wall, resulted in the Mexican President cancelling a state visit to the US. His executive order barring citizens from seven Muslim majority countries has sparked angry responses from leaders across the world. A verbal and twitter battle with Iran has led to new sanctions being imposed.

Going by what we have seen so far, is it possible to come up with a rough picture of how US foreign policy under Trump would shape up? Will there be a sift in the way foreign policy is conducted? The answer to the latter question would be more straightforward. As far as the way foreign policy is conducted, Trump has made it clear he does not care much for diplomatic language or protocol. When questioned on the renewed sanctions on Iran, he responded by stating: "They aren't behaving themselves." One would not expect such language to be used when engaging in foreign policy. Trump's use of twitter to express his views on foreign policy is a clear break from tradition. As a presidential candidate, the use of twitter and the undiplomatic language could have been acceptable. However, Trump has shown his inclination to use twitter to express his opinions even after taking over as the President. A harshly worded tweet resulted in the Mexican President cancelling a planned state visit. Trump has also engaged in a twitter war with the Foreign Minister of Iran. The use of twitter and the harsh language Trump has often used is a clear break from diplomatic tradition and protocol. While this is a very hazardous precedent, we should expect more of it during Trump's presidency.

The more challenging question is: what can we say about Trump's overall foreign policy direction? His handling of the NAFTA and TPP has gone on expected lines. Considering his position on the border wall, one expected differences to crop up with Mexico. The cancelled state visit is a sign of growing differences between the US and Mexico. Over the next few years, one can expect more differences to crop up as Trump goes ahead with his plan to build the wall.

Trump's opposition to the TPP during his election campaign raised quite a few eyebrows in Australia. While some friction was expected between Trump and the Australian Prime Minister, no one would have predicted the showdown Trump and Turnbull had over the phone. If news reports are to be believed, then this would mean significant tensions would emerge between the US and one of its closest allies, Australia.

There is a great degree of uncertainty regarding Trump's approach towards Russia. Though his election campaign hinted at a possible US-Russia détente, the US ambassador's speech in the UN criticising Russia's actions in Ukraine has put question-marks over Trump's Russia policy. After taking over as the President, Trump has not given any hints on how he would approach the Russian question. While his election campaign hinted at close ties with Putin, the UN speech sends a different signal. With regard to Israel, Trump's election campaign promised to recognise Jerusalem as the capital of Israel. As the President-elect, he broke all protocol by pushing the Obama Administration to veto the resolution against Israel. When the outcome was not in Israel's favour, in another first, Trump took to twitter openly criticising the US' stance. After taking over as the President, there has been a growing call from lawmakers, including Republicans, asking Trump to mellow down his stance. Considering the fact that his own partymen are calling for a more watered stance, Trump's hands may be tied with regard to Israel.

More than two weeks after taking oath, there is still no clear picture regarding Trump's foreign policy. We can say with some amount of certainty that tensions are bound to arise with Mexico as Trump pushes ahead with his programme to build the wall. With regard to Russia and Israel, there have been mixed signals. The phone conversation between Trump and Turnbull poses serious questions regarding Trump's strategic thinking. Australia is a vital part of the US' security calculations in the Asia-Pacific region. His hardline approach towards Australia throws into question Trump's security calculations.

While the overall picture of Trump's foreign policy position is still not very clear, what is clear is the shift in the way foreign relations is conducted. Protocol and diplomatic language do not feature anywhere in Trump's foreign policy manual. One can expect more twitter outbursts, undiplomatic language and verbal battles over the next four years.

US FOREIGN DIRECT INVESTMENT

Although current levels of U.S. foreign direct investment (FDI) are relatively low when compared to China, there is strong private interest in the Indian market for U.S. companies in certain industries. Annual FDI to India from all countries rose from about $100 million in 1990 to nearly $6 billion for 2005, then nearly doubled in one year to more than $11 billion in 2006. About one-third of these investments was made by U.S. firms; in recent years, the major U.S.-based companies

Microsoft, Dell, Oracle, and IBM announced plans for multi-billion-dollar investments in India. However, current Indian law restricts foreign ownership in many industries to varying degrees, making FDI less attractive to many U.S. companies.

At present, India strictly prohibits FDI in four industries: retail trade (except single-brand outlets); atomic energy; lottery business; and gambling and betting. For other sectors of interest to U.S. companies — including broadcasting, pharmaceuticals, banking, financial services, insurance, defence production, mining, oil and natural gas, and telecommunications — FDI limits range from 26% to 100% of total equity, both across and within sectors. In addition, depending on the sector and the size of the FDI, the investment may be subject to administrative approval. In late 2006, India announced it is considering new legislation on FDI. The so-called FDI Promotion Act would cover all aspects of FDI, including entry conditions, dispute settlement, incentive programs, approval procedures. The Indian government is also considering a proposal to create uniform FDI limits within each sector, as well as raise some of the current FDI limits. Prospects for these two proposals are uncertain. However, New Delhi did increase the FDI limit for the telecommunications industry from 49% to 74% in March 2007.

Especially closely watched are opportunities for investment in India's potentially vast retail sector. Foreign involvement in his sector is a sensitive issue for Indians; in March 2005, Commerce Minister Nath said, "We are very clear that if at all FDI is permitted into retail trade it should lead to incremental economic benefits and not substitute ongoing activities. There is no question of replacing or displacing what we have: it must add to economic activity."

New Delhi subsequently commissioned a report on FDI in the retail sector and, in January 2006, Nath announced new regulations that allow foreign investors to own up to 51% of retail outlets selling only single-brand goods. India has a particularly large number of small merchant shops — perhaps the highest per capita number worldwide — meaning that tens of millions of citizens could be adversely impacted by the appearance in India of "big-box" retailers.

Intellectual Property Rights

The U.S. Trade Representative listed India on the U.S. Special 301 Priority Watch List in 2007, despite recognition of improvements in India's IPR laws, regulations and enforcement. On the administrative side, the United States urged India to "improve its IPR regime by providing stronger protection for copyrights, trademarks, and patents, as well as protection against unfair commercial use for data generated to obtain marketing approval."

The U.S. Trade Representative has also indicated that the United States would like to see India join the World Intellectual Property Organization's (WIPO) Internet Treaties. On the enforcement side, the United States claimed that piracy of copyright materials was "rampant."Opponents of inserting "data exclusivity" clauses into Indian law assert that they constrict India's generic drug industry's ability to compete both domestically and internationally, and place a large financial burden on firms that must repeat expensive clinical trials. By removing the availability of inexpensive and oftentimes life-saving medications, the argument goes, would have a seriously detrimental resulting impact on public health.

India appears to have been active in its IPR enforcement during 2007. On February 6, 2007, India joined 11 other Asia-Pacific entities in a combined sting operation that arrested 870 people and seized nearly 5 million pirate DVDs and VCDs. The operation was called "Operation Trident," and involved operations in Australia, China, Hong Kong, India, Indonesia, Japan, Malaysia, New Zealand, the Philippines, Singapore, South Korea, Taiwan, and Thailand. In India, there were 110 raids, with 118 arrests. Operation Trident occurred while India was hosting the first-ever International Meeting on Intellectual Property and Development. Organized by India's Department of Industrial Policy & Promotion (DIPP), the meeting included representatives from 22 countries, including the United States.

The focus of the February 5-7 meeting was on the relationship between intellectual property rights (IPR) and economic development.

In addition, in May 2007, the U.S.-India Business Council (USIBC) in conjunction with the Federation of Indian Chambers of Commerce and Industry (FICCI), implemented a "Bollywood-Hollywood" anti-piracy initiative aimed at stopping the illegal copying and distribution of U.S. and Indian entertainment videos. The initiative seeks to reduce video piracy both in India and the United States, where the growing popularity of Bollywood movies has given rise to a growing problem of video piracy.

The relationship between IPR and economic development has been of interest to India for several years. In 2003, a group of developing countries, including India, circulated a paper at the WTO making recommendations on actions that could be taken to foster greater technological transfer to developing countries. The United States and other WTO members objected to the paper's analysis, which suggested that the TRIPS agreement and its IPR protection provisions were hindering technological transfers.

In October 2005, India, Pakistan, and the Philippines submitted another paper on the subject of technological transfer and the TRIPS agreement that focused on ways to encourage technical assistance, promote the performance of technological development work by multinational corporations in developing countries, and facilitate the mobility of scientists and technicians under the GATS agreement. The U.S. response to the second paper was more favorable.

The second paper became the focus of discussion in 2006 of the WTO's Working Group on Trade and Transfer of Technology (WGTTT), a body established in 2001 at the Doha Ministerial Conference. According to the USTR's 2007 Trade Policy Agenda, the United States expects that the paper will also dominate WGTTT discussions in 2007.

Beyond the usual concerns expressed by the software, movie, and publishing industries about IPR protection, the U.S.

pharmaceutical industry has of late been very actively seeking improved IPR protection in India. In particular, it would like to improve patent protections, secure test data exclusivity, and limit pre-grant opposition to patent applications. India's pharmaceutical industry, for its part, believes that the level of IPR protection sought by the U.S. companies exceeds those provided for in the TRIPS agreement, and will effectively prevent the introduction of generic drugs in India in the future.

Jewellery

India is a leading exporter of jewellery, especially diamonds and diamond jewellery, to the world and to the United States. In 2006, the United States imported $5.9 billion worth of jewellery (HTS71) from India, or 25.5% of all imports from India. Of this, $3.3 billion (55.5%) were diamonds and diamond jewellery and another $2.4 billion (41.0%) was precious metal jewellery.

The depletion of many of India's diamond mines has pushed its industry to source its diamonds from overseas. In 2005, India imported nearly $10.6 billion worth of diamonds. This has raised concerns about the possible import of so-called "conflict diamonds." In January 2003, India, the United States, and 53 other countries endorsed a UN initiative called the Kimberley Certification Process that certifies that the diamonds do not come from Angola, Liberia, Sierra Leone, and Congo. In 2005, India considered lowering the FDI limit for diamond mines from 100% to 74% in an effort to close a possible back door for the import of "conflict diamonds." However, there are claims that uncut "conflict diamonds" are still finding their way into India, especially into the markets in Surat. If true, then there is high likelihood that "conflict diamonds" could also be making their way into the U.S. consumer market.

Oil

The rapid growth in India's economy has also meant a rapid increase in its demand for oil. Although India has proven oil reserves, production is nearly at capacity, while demand continues to rise. According to the U.S. Department of Energy's Energy Information Agency (EIA), India produced an average of 846,000 barrels per day (bbl/day) of "total oil liquids" in 2006, and used an average of 2.63 million bbl/d of oil, resulting in a shortage of nearly 1.8 million bbl/d. In addition, according to the EIA's estimates, India's oil demand increased by 100,000 bbl/d in 2006, and will increase by similar amounts in 2007 and 2008, leading to the nation's growing "energy deficit."

In order to fill its oil gap, India national oil companies have been actively seeking overseas sources of crude oil, involving the acquisition of equity in some cases. According to EIA, the most active Indian oil company overseas is ONGC Videsh Ltd., which holds interests in 25 oil and natural gas projects in 15 different countries in Africa, Asia, the Americas, and the Middle East. Indian companies have also been actively involved in Sudan's oil industry, as well as the operation of the major oil pipeline and terminus in Port Sudan.India's growing oil demand, along with China's growing demand, are contributing factors in the a tightening global petroleum market and higher crude oil prices. Competition for crude oil and energy in general is becoming an important issue in Asia, pressing nations to develop trade relations outside of the region. For example, India is pursuing closer relations with the repressive regime in neighboring Burma (Myanmar), with an interest in energy cooperation and to counterbalance China's influence there. In response, the United States is exploring ways to foster cooperation with friendly nations with respect to global petroleum market. Legislation specifically on energy cooperation with India has been introduced in both the House of Representatives and the Senate.

Energy Cooperation

There currently is legislation before 110 Congress on the subject of U.S.-India energy cooperation. The United States-India Energy Security Cooperation Act of 2007 (H.R. 1186) would "promote global energy security through increased cooperation between the United States and India in diversifying sources of energy, stimulating development of alternative fuels, developing and deploying technologies that promote the clean and efficient use of coal, and improving energy efficiency." Both the Energy Diplomacy and Security Act of 2007 (S. 193) and the Renewable Fuels, Consumer Protection, and Energy Efficiency Act of 2007 (S. 1419) would, *inter alia*, establish a U.S. petroleum crisis response mechanism in conjunction with China and India. The International Climate Cooperation Re-Engagement Act of 2007 (H.R. 2420) would create Foreign Commercial Service attaches and deploy these to India (and China) for the purpose of promoting U.S. exports in clean and energy efficient energy technologies. The New Direction for Energy Independence, National Security, and Consumer Protection Act (H.R. 3221), introduced in July 2007, contains similar provisions. Moreover, and as noted above, an initiative to launch civil nuclear cooperation with India was provisionally endorsed by the 109th Congress in the Hyde Act (P.L. 109-401) and any future "123 Agreement" guiding such cooperation must be approved by Congress.

Immigration

Immigration reform is a major issue for the 110th Congress. The Comprehensive Immigration Reform Act of 2007 (S. 1348), currently being considered by the Senate, would alter the eligibility requirements for H-1B visas under the Securing Knowledge, Innovation, and Leadership Act of 2007 (SKIL Act of 2007), and limit the number of "market-based visas" to 115,000 per fiscal year. While this is an increase from the current limit, it is below the level sought by both Indian and U.S. information technology companies. Nor does the bill address the industry's desire to see the creation of a new visa category for short-term training of foreign nationals in the United States.

Trade in Information Technology

At present, most of the focus of Indo-U.S. service trade is in the information technology (IT) sector. Over the last few years, U.S. companies have been outsourcing many aspects of their IT work to India and other nations. According to one recent study, U.S. banks will increase the share of their IT work overseas from 6% to 30% by 2010, representing a transfer of over $10 billion of IT services. The study also predicted that the nature of the overseas IT work will shift from "low-level applications" to more sophisticated IT activities. Another study projected that U.S. IT outsourcing would increase at a compound annual growth rate of 5.9% over the next five years, reaching a total value of $17.7 billion in 2011. This later study indicated that an impending shortage of IT skills among government employees will be one of the key stimuli of the outsourcing.

U.S. companies are not limiting their activities in India to IT; they are also utilizing India to provide a growing array of services related to the financial sector. On April 11, 2007, Citigroup announced the elimination of 17,000 jobs — or nearly 5% of its global workforce — and the relocation of 9,500 jobs to "low-cost" locations. However, in the same news story, sources close to Citigroup said that between 5,000 and 8,000 jobs would be moved to India in the near future. Most of these relocated jobs would involve equity research, investment banking, and backoffice transaction-related services.

Meanwhile, India's domestic IT industry is attempting to branch out of the lower value-added activities (such as call centers and payroll processing) into higher value-added services (such as product design, software development, and chip engineering). Many U.S. companies are establishing tech centers in India to take advantage of the greater availability and lower cost of Indian engineers. Plus, leading Indian IT companies — such as Tata, Infosys, Wipro, Satyam, and HCL Technologies — are developing their international IT service capacity.

H-1B Visas. The growth of trade in IT services has placed pressure on the U.S. H-1B visa program. The H-1B visa permits U.S. companies and universities to temporarily employ foreign workers who have the equivalent to a U.S. bachelor's degree.

While there is an annual quota of 78,200 visas, exemptions have allowed the U.S. Citizenship & Immigration Services to issue over 100,000 H1-B visas in 2004 and 2005. Recipients of an H1-B visa may remain in the United States for up to six years (ten years for Defence Department related work) so long as they remain employed by the same company. H1-B visas are not transferable.

Both U.S. and Indian companies have complained that the current quota is too restrictive, making it difficult for U.S. companies to hire enough engineers and technicians to remain competitive in the global market. Also, some companies would like to see the creation of a new visa category that would allow foreign nationals to work and/or train in the United States for a short period of time. However, there is opposition to the expansion of the current H1-B program.

In May 2007, two senior U.S. Senators wrote letters to nine Indian companies that account for nearly one-third of all H1B visas issued in 2006 and requested further details about their use of the special visa program. The Senators expressed concern that fraud and abuse in such programs may have negative impact on U.S. workers.

The Farm Bill

Many provisions of the current omnibus farm bill, the Farm Security and Rural Investment Act of 2002 (P.L. 107-171), expire in 2007. India, along with Brazil and other nations, have argued that certain aspects of the current U.S. farm program are "trade distorting,' and are pushing the United States to change various agricultural programs, including its farm subsidies.

It was previously hoped that the Doha Round would be completed in time for Congress to consider the enabling legislation under Trade Promotion Authority (TPA), and that any changes in U.S. agricultural policy could be including the enabling legislation. However, since the Doha Round discussions are not completed, Congress is considering the expiring programs without the benefit of knowing the terms of any new WTO obligations. The recently introduced H.R. 2419 provides for the continuation of the expiring farm programs, but may not prove to be in compliance with the results of any agreement coming out of the current Doha Round discussions.

Outsourcing and Displaced Workers

The growth of outsourcing various services to India, as well as other nations, is a serious concern for many U.S. workers. Current U.S. law provides some assistance to "displaced workers" via the Trade Adjustment Assistance (TAA) program authorized by the Trade Act of 1974 (P.L. 93-618), the Worker Adjustment and Retraining Notification (WARN) Act of 1988 (P.L. 100-379) of 1988, and the Workforce Investment Act of 1998 (P.L. 105-220).

However, various groups and individuals have called upon Congress to revisit these programs, and strengthen the provisions protecting U.S. workers from job losses caused by outsourcing.

There are currently two bills before Congress that offer additional assistance and/or protection to displaced U.S. workers. The Trade Adjustment Assistance Reform Act (H.R. 1729) expands eligibility for displaced textile and apparel workers for trade adjustment assistance, arguably in response to the growth in clothing and textiles imports from India. The second bill, the Worker Empowerment Act (S. 1330), would amend the Social Security Act to provide for wage insurance for dislocated workers.

Foreign Direct Investment

The 110 Congress is considering legislation pertaining to the operation of the Committee on Foreign Investment in the United States, or CFIUS, an interagency committee that overseas the security implications of foreign investments in the United States.

While U.S. laws governing FDI are generally viewed as being very liberal, there has been recent concern about the security implications of some proposed overseas investments, especially their implications for national defence and port security. Proposed legislation would require CFIUS to investigate all foreign investment transactions in which the entity is owned or controlled by a foreign government, regardless of the nature of the business. Given the recent increase in Indian FDI in the United States, this could cause some tension with India, as well as weaken U.S. efforts to persuade India to lower its current barriers to FDI.

A PERMANENT U.N. SECURITY COUNCIL SEAT FOR INDIA?

During his address to Indian parliamentarians, President Obama received thunderous applause for his endorsement of a permanent Indian seat on the U.N. Security Council as part of elevating that country to "its rightful place in the world." This was the most explicit such endorsement to date; previously, the U.S. government had endorsed only Japan as a new permanent member of that body. There is evidence of U.S. congressional support for a permanent Indian role on the Council. Although this unprecedented expression of support was widely hailed as a positive shift in U.S. policy, some Indian observers noted that the President's statement was not nearly as explicit an endorsement as was received by Japan and that, in the absence of a timeline for Security Council reform, it could be taken as little more than a "vague promise." In neighboring Pakistan, the endorsement met with expected resistance; Islamabad claimed India is undeserving of such status given New Delhi's "conduct in relations with its neighbors and its continued flagrant violations of Security Council resolutions on Jammu and Kashmir."

Reactions to the President's Visit

President Obama's India trip was widely considered successful as a diplomatic exercise, although reviews of the substantive outcome were somewhat mixed. As External Affairs Minister Krishna later reported to his Parliament: "The visit was successful in strengthening mutual understanding on regional and global issues, accelerating the momentum of bilateral cooperation, and creating a long-term framework to elevate the India-U.S. strategic partnership to a new level." Assistant Secretary of State Robert Blake later said the trip "will be remembered as a watershed, when the U.S. and India embarked at a new level on concrete initiatives to build a global partnership." The President's visit was itself seen by many in India and abroad as reflective of the country's rising visibility on the global stage. Even in the absence of major new initiatives, there was a sense among some observers that the visit had exceeded expectations, with the U.S. President's "calm demeanor and soaring rhetoric" winning over a previously skeptical Indian audience.

Other commentators, however, saw President Obama turning a blind eye toward or underestimating the seriousness of India's ongoing struggles with poverty, government bureaucracy, and health and education issues while remaining overly focused on the country's high-technology innovation successes.

In these accounts, the New Delhi government's failure to push forward with economic reforms has made foreign investors wary, a problem only exacerbated by recent corruption scandals. There also continued to be contentions from some quarters that India's polity is skeptical about being subsumed into a U.S. "imperialist agenda," with fears that Indian commercial markets will be opened in ways that do not benefit the country's people and that India will be drawn into a military alliance with the United States.

July 2011 Strategic Dialogue

Another Strategic Dialogue was held in New Delhi in July 2011. Given the persistence of doubts about the robustness of the U.S.-India relationship, there were hopes that Secretary Clinton's attendance could reinvigorate a relationship that many analysts still see as incomplete and in need of more specific focus. Clinton traveled with a group of nine other senior U.S. officials, including the Director of National Intelligence. Yet even before the final Joint Statement was issued, commentators were lowering expectations with the assumption that neither government's circumstances was ripe for new large-scale initiatives.

Upon her arrival, Secretary Clinton highlighted three issue areas: (1) *trade and investment* ("This is a good news story, but... Each of our countries can do more to reduce barriers, open our markets, and find new opportunities for economic partnership"); (2) *security cooperation* (especially on counterterrorism and maritime security); and (3)*the civil nuclear agreement* ("[T]o reap the benefits of that investment and to see returns on the political capital that has been spent on both sides, we need to resolve remaining issues....").

The resulting Joint Statement highlighted a bilateral commitment to "broaden and deepen the U.S.-India global strategic partnership" in the cause of global stability and prosperity, and to enhance the partnership in numerous issue-areas. Among the notable clauses of the Statement were:

- a reaffirmation of the two countries' "commitment for consultation, coordination, and cooperation on Afghanistan," to include a reconciliation process there that is "Afghan-led, Afghan-owned, and inclusive";
- a call for Pakistan "to move expeditiously in prosecuting those involved in the November 2008 Mumbai terrorist attack";
- a continued commitment to "full implementation of the U.S.-India civil nuclear energy cooperation agreement"; and
- plans to resume technical-level negotiations on a bilateral investment treaty.

In a major policy speech in the southern Indian city of Chennai (formerly Madras) the next day, Secretary Clinton laid out the Administration's vision for future relations, emphasizing India's growing leadership role in the world, especially in the Asia-Pacific and in South and Central Asia.

On the former, and in what could be seen as a thinly veiled expression of concern about China's rise, she sought India's close cooperation in seeing formation of a regional architecture that adopts "international norms on security, trade, rule of law, human rights, and accountable governance." In this respect she welcomed New Delhi's "Look East" policy of closer engagement with the ASEAN countries. She also took the opportunity to issue an unusually open criticism of India's Burma policy, contending that, "As India takes on a larger role throughout the Asia-Pacific, it does have increasing responsibilities, including the duty to speak out against violations of universal human rights."This last reflects a pervasive view in Washington that New Delhi is too hesitant to exercise India's growing power and influence.

On South and Central Asia, Secretary Clinton focused on three key issues. First, a reiteration of a strong and lasting U.S. commitment to Afghanistan well beyond the planned 2014 withdrawal of American combat troops, and a reiteration of "unambiguous redlines" for reconciliation with Afghan insurgents (their renunciation of violence, divorce from Al Qaeda, and acceptance of the laws and constitution of Afghanistan). She acknowledged New Delhi's "rightly expressed concerns about outside interference in the reconciliation process" and vowed to consult closely with India on this shared concern. Second, and related, Clinton stated that lasting peace and security in the region will "require a stable, democratic, prosperous Pakistan free from violent extremism," and assured listeners that the United States continues to press the Pakistani government to seek those ends. Finally, the new "Silk Road" initiative was raised: "an international web and network of economic and transit connections" that would facilitate regional commerce and prosperity. According to senior U.S. officials speaking later, this regional economic integration would be "anchored in the Indian economy."

As with President Obama's earlier travel to India, the Administration's second Strategic Dialogue session and Secretary Clinton's public appearances in New Delhi and Chennai were widely hailed as successful in moving the bilateral relationship forward. Yet, in another indication that current U.S.-India relations have no obvious, specific focus, the read-outs from two major wire services highlighted very different issue-areas.

INDIA'S FOREIGN POLICY AND FOREIGN RELATIONS

The end of Cold War political constraints and the rapid growth of India's economy has allowed New Delhi to more energetically engage global diplomacy. Expanded engagement is evident through the huge increase in the number of bilateral defence arrangements the Indian government has made in the past decade, more than tripling from 7 in 2000 to at least 26 today. During the latter half of 2010, every major world leader paid a visit to India, including those from all five permanent U.N. Security Council members. Much of the international attention on India is due to the country's vast market potential—the retail sector alone is worth an estimated $450 billion.

Some observers argue that the New Delhi government acts too timidly on the global stage, and that the country's regional and domestic difficulties continue to hinder its ability to exert influence in geopolitics. As a rising power, India has appeared unwilling to take the kinds of policy stances expected of major global players, in particular those who sit on the U.N. Security Council, as India has been in 2011. From vague positions on Middle East uprisings to the appearance of fence-sitting on issues such as U.S.-led efforts to isolate Iran and Burma, New Delhi's leaders may be finding it increasingly difficult to avoid taking on the responsibilities many in Washington and elsewhere are looking for.

One example is New Delhi's largely hands-off response to uprisings in the Arab world, with External Affairs Minister Krishna saying India would not "jump into the fray" unless invited and would maintain a "very cautious" approach to the Libyan conflict. In March 2011, India officially opposed NATO's military action in Libya and notably abstained—along with Brazil, China, Russia, and Germany—from voting on U.N. Resolution 1973, which approved of such action. More recently, Secretary of State Clinton has sought greater Indian assistance in pressuring the faltering Syrian regime. Human rights activists have joined foreign governments in prodding India to be more proactive on key foreign policy issues, even those in India's own neighborhood such as in Burma and Sri Lanka. One such observer has criticized New Delhi for issuing "bland propositions" that "can convey indifference to the plight of subjugated people." She challenges India's leaders to "stand with people or with dictators."

Many analysts view India's foreign policy establishment—its foreign service, think-tanks, public universities, and relevant media—as being too small and/or too poorly developed for India to achieve true great power status in the foreseeable future. By one substantive account, without a major modernizing and revamping of this establishment, "India's worldview will be parochial, reactive, and increasingly dominated by business rather than by strategic or political concerns." Thus, even as India's rising stature commands greater attention in many world capitals, the country's diplomatic influence remains limited—especially in comparison to that of China—and the central government continues to concentrate mainly on domestic development and poverty alleviation. Indeed, India's domestic and social indices continue to rank it as a developing country, or what one former senior Indian diplomat called a "premature power." Moreover, Indian bureaucrats' prickly and sometimes distrustful attitude toward their American counterparts survives long after the Cold War's end, and is sometimes evident in New Delhi's vehement reactions to what many Americans would consider minor and essentially meaningless slights.

MAJOR STREAMS OF THOUGHT IN INDIAN FOREIGN POLICY

In the assessment of one former U.S. diplomat and longtime South Asia expert, there are two major schools of thought in India's current foreign policy approach: "21st century Nehruvian" and "great power advocates." The former is notable for its essential continuation of Jawaharlal Nehru's emphasis on developing world unity and an attendant skepticism regarding U.S. power, which, from this view, may require taking action to balance against. The latter, energized by India's rapid economic growth and higher visibility on the world stage, concentrates on New Delhi's triangular relations with Washington and Beijing with an eye toward increasing India's relative power, mainly through economic growth and innovation. Yet both schools share several important basic characteristics, including a view of India as a more-or-less natural regional hegemon; limited attention to global governance issues; a commitment to maintaining India's "strategic autonomy"; and a preference for hedging strategies, be they balancing against a more aggressive China by welcoming a continued major U.S. presence in the region, or by working with China and Russia to preclude an excessively dominant American presence.

In an informal but extensive survey of Indian elite opinion about the United States, this same expert found broad areas of consensus and concluded that Washington has now supplanted Moscow as New Delhi's most important external partner. As is reflected in opinion surveys of the Indian public more broadly, views of the United States, its varied power capabilities, and its continued substantive presence as a player in Asia are widely welcomed by Indian decision makers.

The United States is seen to possess a unique ability to turn innovation into wealth and military power, both coveted by aspiring global powers such as India. America's national will and soft power tend to be admired by Indians, and the leading U.S. role in international institutions may serve as a model for New Delhi. Moreover—40 years after the Nixon Administration was seen to "tilt" toward Pakistan by sending the *USS Enterprise* carrier task force into the Bay of Bengal—American military capabilities and ability to project significant power into the Indian Ocean Region are no longer viewed as threatening to most in New Delhi, where there is a widely held view of the United States as the only viable hedge against the rise of a potentially adversarial or revisionist China.

The above-noted schools of thought correspond closely to what two other senior observers identify as India's "traditional nationalist" and "pragmatist" strains of foreign policy visions. These analysts see policy makers tending to "split the difference" by mouthing traditional nationalist rhetoric while pursuing a largely pragmatic course. While nationalists are inherently opposed to any international alliance that would constrict India's autonomy and tend toward legal-moral rather than political arguments, pragmatists are accepting of a balance of power approach emphasizing a flexible pursuit of Indian national interests over ideological positioning.

One result is that pragmatists are less averse to alliance-making and international treaties. Their rising influence thus opens greater possibilities for closer and more meaningful U.S.-India ties, perhaps especially in the area of nonproliferation (New Delhi's Iran policy has become a bellwether issue of contention between nationalists and pragmatists).

Rivalry and Conflict With Pakistan

Three full-scale wars—in 1947-1948, 1965, and 1971—and a constant state of military preparedness on both sides of their mutual border have marked more than six decades of bitter rivalry between India and its western neighbor, Pakistan. The acrimonious partition of British India into two successor states in 1947 and the unresolved issue of Kashmiri sovereignty have been major sources of tension. Both countries have built large defence establishments at significant cost to economic and social development, and the bilateral conflict has precluded the development of meaningful regional organizations.

A major factor in U.S. interest in South Asia is ongoing tension between India and Pakistan rooted largely in competing territorial claims and in "cross-border terrorism" in both Kashmir and major Indian cities. In the interests of regional stability, the United States strongly endorses a recently revived India-Pakistan peace initiative, and it remains concerned about the potential for India-Pakistan to cause open hostilities between these two nuclear-armed countries. Senior Indian officials continue to press the U.S. government to convince Islamabad to take stronger action against anti-India terrorist groups operating inside Pakistan. The effects of this bilateral conflict are seen to negatively affect U.S.-led efforts to stabilize Afghanistan.

Most observers assert that U.S. success in Afghanistan is to a significant degree dependent on improved India-Pakistan relations, the logic being that Pakistan will need to feel more secure vis-à-vis a perceived existential threat on its eastern front in order to shift its attention and military resources more toward the west. Some in Pakistan believe that, by feeding their country's insecurities, the increasingly warm U.S.-India relationship actually foments regional instability. In 2010, Indian decision makers became discomfited by signs that the United States and its allies are preparing to leave Afghanistan in such a way that would provide a central role for Pakistan in mediating between Kabul and Taliban elements, perhaps even to include a role for the latter in Afghanistan's governance. Such an outcome would be anathema to Indian leaders, who wish to limit Islamabad's influence in a post-war Afghanistan. During his 2010 confirmation hearing, the U.S. military commander in Afghanistan (and current Director of Central Intelligence), Gen. David Petraeus, said India "without question" has a legitimate interests in Afghanistan.

Also in 2010, conflict over water resources emerged as another major exacerbating factor in the bilateral relationship. Some in Pakistan accuse India of violating international law, bilateral agreements, and ethical principles of peaceful coexistence through the allegedly illicit manipulation of water flows into Pakistan. Of particular concern for Indian and Western observers has been the fact that some of these complaints are emanating from the leaders of militant Pakistani Islamist groups such as Lashkar-e-Taiba. Pakistan's then-foreign minister said water was "emerging as a very serious source of [bilateral] tension," but a senior Indian official denied that India is in violation of the Indus Waters Treaty and called Pakistani rhetoric a "political gimmick" meant to distract from Islamabad's own poor water management.

The Indian government suspended the bilateral peace process following the late 2008 terrorist attack on Mumbai that was traced to a Pakistan-based terrorist group. In early 2011, New Delhi chose to reengage dialogue with Islamabad despite the fact that many of the alleged planners of that attack have not been brought to justice. A panel of experts of security and terrorism brought together by *India Today* magazine in 2010 outlined ten strategies for India-Pakistan dialogue. Each of the top three involved actions to be taken by Pakistan: (1) firmer and more rapid action the perpetrators of the 11/08 Mumbai attack; (2) extradition of the fugitives most wanted in India; and (3) action against the "terrorist infrastructure" on Pakistani soil. The experts also called for establishment of a regular dialogue between the two countries' intelligence chiefs. These remain among New Delhi's key concerns.

The immense pressures now faced by Islamabad—ongoing and widespread Islamist militancy and extremism, the unprecedented embarrassments of bin Laden's discovery and an attack on a naval base in May, and deteriorating relations with the United States foremost among them—may have the effect of shifting the focus of Pakistan's military decision makers away from conflict with New Delhi. This may in turn open a window of opportunity for India to pursue improved relations with Pakistan.

5

'Defence, Counter-terror to Indo-US ties under Trump'

India would be "absolutely critical" in Trump's foreign policy, said Alexander Gray, a senior military advisor and author of several of the ambitious defence policies of Trump. Defence and counter-terrorism would be two key pillars of Indo-US strategic ties under Donald Trump, his top military advisor has said while asserting that India will be "absolutely critical" to the Republican candidate's foreign policy as president.

"This is a country that shares our values, this is a country that shares a lot of geo-political interest and I think, his (Trump's) work is going to be continuing the tradition of Bush Administration which made a lot of progress in that regard," said Alexander Gray, a senior military advisor and author of several of the ambitious defence policies of Trump.

"We (Trump Administration) would be looking to strengthen not just the cultural and economic aspect, but also on the defence side there is so much common ground with India. At a time when India's foreign policy is changing because of China and Pakistan, because of Islamic terrorism, we need to be there to greet them with open arms. I think, the Trump Administration is ready to do that," Gray said giving an insight into the India policy of a possible Trump administration.

Trump is the only presidential candidate to have addressed a meeting of Indian Americans and directly spoken about a strong India-US relationship. Gray, who has emerged as a key player in evolving the defence and military policies of the Trump Campaign, said India would be "absolutely critical" in Trump's foreign policy.

Co-author of a major policy paper on 'Donald Trump's Peace Through Strength Vision for the Asia Pacific' which was published in the prestigious Foreign Policy magazine, Gray said India is "on top of the list" of Trump's Indo-Asia Pacific policy to which the defence aspect would be an important pillar.

"Strengthening defence relationship with India would be at top. This is what the Congress has been looking at for a long time," he said, indicating that a Trump Administration would be looking at legislative changes towards strengthening India-US defense ties.

"The Trump Administration would not give a passage to what China is doing in South China Sea, what it is doing in East China Sea, what it is doing along the border in India," Gray said in response to a question.

A strong partnership with US would deter China from making any aggressive posture against India, said Puneet Ahluwalia, a member of the Trump's Advisory Committee on Asian Americans.

"A strong US defence with India would give India much dependable ally to fight of threats from its neighbours and from terrorism by creating strong navy and latest technology in cyber and other areas," he said.

Ahluwalia, a Washington DC-based lobbyist, said he will work aggressively with the Trump Administration and the Pentagon to remove the obstacles in regards to transfer of technology and enhance defence trade and develop the blue economy.

U.S. - INDIA DEFENCE RELATIONSHIP

The U.S. and India are working to build the architecture of a durable defence partnership that will support our common interests in maintaining security and stability, defeating terrorism and violent religious extremism, preventing the spread of weapons of mass destruction and associated materials, data and technologies, and protecting the free flow of commerce via land, air and sea lanes. Since the signing of the New Framework for the U.S.-India Defence Relationship by Secretary Rumsfeld and Minister Mukherjee on 28 June 2005, the U.S. and India have made considerable progress in enhancing the relationship, through signing foundation agreements, conducting exercises and engaging in ongoing dialogue on a variety of security issues. President Bush and Prime Minister Singh announced their intent to increase U.S.-Indian cooperation to improve security in the maritime domain. The two countries will soon sign an agreement for mutual logistics support that will enable our militaries to cooperate more easily during combined training, exercises and disaster relief operations. In January 2006, Secretary Rumsfeld and Minister Mukherjee signed the Research, Development, Test and Evaluation Agreement which will facilitate new avenues of cooperation in the area of scientific exchanges and joint development.

The U.S. and India's Military Services are improving their interoperability through increasingly sophisticated and complex exercises. The MALABAR Naval exercise conducted in September and October 2005 was the largest naval exercise to date between the U.S. and Indian Navies, and was the first to involve both U.S. and Indian aircraft carriers. The U.S. and Indian Air Forces conducted the third Cope India air exercise in November 2005 at Kalaikunda Air Station, West Bengal, India, the first U.S.-India exercise to involve Airborne Warning and Control System aircraft. U.S. and Indian Armies held a company-size exercise – their largest ever – in the foothills of the Himalayas in January 2006. Most recently in February 2006, the U.S. and Indian Navies were able to quickly organize a passing exercise with aircraft carriers from both countries, demonstrating capabilities that can be used to respond collaboratively to future emergencies at sea.

The U.S. and India seek to expand defence trade, co-production, joint development, and technology transfer, all of which will improve interoperability and cooperation. We are working through several forums to achieve this goal. The U.S. intends to transfer the USS TRENTON amphibious transport ship to India in early 2007. U.S. firms will compete with contemporary technology in the Indian Air Force's upcoming tender for Multi-Role Combat Aircraft and a U.S. firm is competing in the Indian Army's commercial tender for a new light helicopter.

The U.S. Department of Defence and the Indian Ministry of Defence conduct ongoing dialogue on several topics of mutual interest under the auspices of the annual Defence Policy Group meetings, including counter-terrorism, missile defence cooperation, and strategic planning. A U.S. Defence Department delegation will travel to India soon to discuss the Quadrennial Defence Review with senior Indian officials and influential strategic thinkers. U.S.-Indian defence cooperation is a force for good. The U.S. and India cooperated closely in providing aid to tsunami victims in December 2004-January 2005. In January 2006, the U.S. Navy rescued Indian mariners off the Horn of Africa whose ship had been hijacked by Somali pirates. Under the auspices of the U.S.-India disaster relief initiative, approved in July 2005, India airlifted supplies and made a contribution to the American Red Cross following Hurricane Katrina, and the U.S. and Indian militaries are working together to expand disaster relief cooperation.

U.S-India Secur®ity Relations

Remarkable changes have taken place in the framework of US-India security relations in recent years. During the Cold War, estrangement characterized the two democracies because of India's non-aligned policy, close relations with the erstwhile Soviet Union and tensions with Pakistan, coupled with the US containment policy towards the Soviet Union, and the US alliance with Pakistan. Based on common strategic, economic and political interests after the end of the Cold War, the US and India have moved from being "estranged democracies" to "engaged democracies". Such a change is primarily due to America's adjustment of its strategy and policy toward India as well as South Asia and the Asia-Pacific. The changing US-Indian security relations will have a great impact on China's security environment. This paper focuses on the implications of these changes for China from three perspectives: the emergence of a Sino-US-India strategic triangle; the complicated security situation in South Asia; and the America factor in Sino-India relations.

The increasing attention being paid to the relationship between the Indian and the US security apparatus – particularly over the last couple of years – is no longer a matter that can be dismissed as mere speculation. Indeed, after India's five under-ground nuclear tests at Pokhran in May 1998, the US initiated a series of strict sanctions under the aegis of the US Nuclear Proliferation Prevention Act of 1994.

The security relationship between Washington and New Delhi had ebbed and suspicion seemed to characterize the bilateral agenda.

President Clinton's visit to India in March 2000, which was the fourth presidential visit in the history of the two countries and the first in the last 22 years, was a turning point in the ambivalent US-India relations of yesteryears. On May 1, 2001, not long after he took office, President George W. Bush made a speech to announce his security policy and plans for developing a missile defence system India had expressed its approval of this programme earlier, and was, indeed, seen to be even more supportive than the US' traditional allies.

Later, in order to win India's support in the fight against terrorism, the US lifted its sanctions on India and the two nations agreed to comprehensively co-operate in the field of the global war against terrorism. Indeed, in May 2002, US Special Forces were flown into India and took part in a two-week military manoeuvre in north India, in the historical city of Agra. This manoeuvre was the first between the two countries in 39 years and demonstrated that their military cooperation had reached a high level. What are the changes in US-India relationship? Why are these changes occurring? What are the implications of these changes for China's security, and how will these affect Sino-India relationships and Sino-US relationships? This paper attempts to examine these questions.

US-India Relations: From Estrangement to Rapprochement

With the beginning of the Cold War, the primary US goal with regard to countries in South Asia was "to orient those nations toward the United States and the other Western democracies and away from the Soviet Union." However, India's geo-strategic interests and considerations were different from those of the US. As opposed to Pakistan, who joined the US led BTO (Baghdad Treaty Organization, later the Central Treaty Organization, CENTO) and SEATO (the South East Asia Treaty Organization), India initially supported the principles of self-government and non-alignment – resulting in its refusal to participate in the US-led strategic alliance against the Soviet Union. India was also opposed to the setting up of a defensive alliance in order to contain China. It recognized the new Communist-led government of China in December 1949, regarded Taiwan as a part of China, and criticized the US for its official stance against the People's Republic. In January 1951, India was the only non-Communist state that voted against a resolution sponsored by the United States in the United Nations (UN) General Assembly labelling China as an aggressor.

As a third corollary, India began to receive military, political, and economic assistance from the erstwhile Soviet Union from the 1960's – an alliance which brought about further estrangement in Indo-US relations. Indeed, India still depended on Moscow for military and political support, and when the Soviet Union invaded Afghanistan in 1979 – which made the US and China stand by Pakistan's side – India complained that the US did not try to find a political method to resolve the Afghanistan crisis. On the other hand, US did not punish India for its close relationship with Soviet Union in the 1980's.

The other important factor was the India-Pakistan War of 1971. The US sent its Seventh Fleet into the Bay of Bengal and this act was regarded as a threat by India and it pushed the already ebbing Indo-US relationship to an all-time low. By supporting Pakistan, New Delhi argued that America had forced India into an unnecessary and costly arms race, that American assistance gave Pakistan the means and the inspiration to challenge New Delhi, and that the Pakistan-US relationship came to be seen as not directed against communism, but against India.

During the Cold War, America's policy toward India was different from its policy toward the two other big Asian nations – China and Japan. America did not include India as its strategic alliance partner nor did it include India as a possible containment target. And just as the United States did not approve of India attempting to balance power between United States and the Soviet Union, India did not endorse the United States' attempt to balance power between India and Pakistan. In sum, with India implementing the policy of non-alignment, maintaining friendly relations with the Soviet Union, and engaging Pakistan; and, the contrasting United States' policy of forming alliances in order to deter the Soviet Union, made it difficult for the US and India to work together. With the end of the Cold War, myriad factors began to push the United States and India to change their relationship from estrangement to one of convergence. The United States and India are two of the largest democracies in the world and, furthermore, they have similar egalitarian values. The US also hopes that India will play an active role in the process of democratisation in Russia. Starting from the 1990s, with India beginning to implement policies to create an open market economy, the United States has been treating India as a newly developed market; United States has progressively emerged as India's greatest source for foreign investment supplies and trading partner. Up to 1998, it seemed that the two countries attempted to form a new relationship that would bring them closer and engender a more robust co-operative relationship. Even though this relationship was damaged in 1998, when India exploded its nuclear bombs and the Americans responding with an embargo, the relationship that had taken off after the Cold War had not ended. Indeed, with eight rounds of security dialogue between US Deputy Secretary of State, Strobe Talbot, and the then Indian Foreign Minister, Jaswant Singh, the security relationship between the two countries normalised.

During the Kargil crisis of 1999, India successfully won sympathy and support from the US. In stark contrast, the US initially cold-shouldered Pakistan's new regime when General Pervez Musharraf rode to power through a military coup. The two situations in 1999 led United States' South Asian policy shift to 'focusing on India and reducing on Pakistan.'

President Clinton's India visit was the first turning point in the Indo-US security relationship. During his visit, President Clinton admitted that the US had ignored India over the preceding 20 years and indicated that it would end the passive impact caused by nuclear issues in future. In a joint communiqué which was termed 'India-US relations: A Vision for the 21st Century', the Indo-US relationship was termed a 'continuous, constructive in political area, and beneficial in economic arena' style of new partnership. This new style of partnership, according to certain independent analyses, was formed on the basis of both the sides deriving mutual strategic benefits, economic benefits, and socio-political benefits.

President George W. Bush continued the policy after he took office. When the then Indian Foreign Minister, Jaswant Singh, visited Washington in April 2001, Bush told him that the new administration would continue and strengthen its predecessor's policy to promote bilateral relations. After Bush declared his new Missile Defence plan on May 1, 2001, Condoleeza Rice, then Special Assistant to the President on National Security Affairs, broke protocol and took an initiative to call Singh and introduce the U.S. missile defence policy to him; US Deputy Secretary of State, Richard Armitage, also visited India in order to muster support. This is the first time that the US has valued India as an important partner in its strategic agenda.

The September 11, 2001, attack and the war on terrorism that followed provided a chance for the US and India to forge an even closer strategic cooperation. It has become a turning point in the Indo-US security relationship. The two countries together implemented a co-operative framework of relationships based on three dimensions: democracy, economy, and security. In the security field, the United States felt that India, as a de-facto nuclear state, had co-operative potential with the US on the proliferation issue.

India actively supported the US missile defence plan as well as that on counter-terrorism. With the end of the US sanctions on India, the two countries improved and increased high level leadership communications, military contact, and economic co-operation. On November 9, 2001, President Bush told the visiting Indian Prime Minister, Atal Behari Vajpayee, that his administration was committed towards developing a fundamentally different relationship with India, based upon both trust and mutual values. After the meeting of the two top leaders, in a joint statement signed by both the countries, expressed their desire to enhance bilateral co-operation in the war against terrorism, and agreed to renew the activities of the Joint Working Group on Counter-terrorism.

The Joint Working Group on Counter Terrorism was established in January 2000 as a first step towards increasing exchange and technology co-operation in the field of defence and security. Thereafter, the two countries maintained a high-level contact frequently and formulated a comprehensive co-operative agenda. Mohammed Ayoob believes that the United States and India can begin close co-operation in the following security arenas: (1) improve the region's security and stability; (2) counter terrorism; (3) promote democracy; (4) prevent nuclear proliferation, and (5) contain China during the first 10 years of the new century. As Stephen Cohen, the celebrated US specialist on South Asia security issues has commented, the United States and India's relationship was 'structurally changing'. However, the partnership between the United States and India has not developed into a possibility of creating an alliance similar to that of the US-Japan or US-UK Alliance. The reasons are as follows:

First, India's five nuclear tests in 1998 greatly damaged the US-led international non-proliferation regime. Though the United States has adjusted its non-proliferation policy to some measure after Bush's taking office, India's nuclear tests and the United State's embargo afterward continue to have some negative effects on the Indo-US relationship. After 9/11, the US pressure on India to join the Nuclear Non-Proliferation Treaty (NPT) and Comprehensive Test Ban Treaty (CTBT) has lessened, although it is still to disappear. This has been perceived as a bargaining chip for the co-operation the United States seeks from India in its fight against terrorism.

Secondly, America realized that India and South Asia is the "most dangerous region in the world". In considering facts such as territorial disputes, the ethnic and religious divergence, and the nuclear confrontation between India and Pakistan; the need for Pakistan to support the United States in its counter-terrorism campaign; and South Asian and American relationships with other major countries in the region, the United States will not create an alliance in the region with any third country. Creating such an alliance to counter a third party does not benefit US interests.

Thirdly, Americans and Indians have very different views of a just international order. These differences have led to specific Indian-American disagreements in three important areas: the limits of humanitarian peacekeeping; the make-up of the UN Security Council; and the emergence of China. Most Indians have trouble accepting the principle of humanitarian interventions and fear that the US would extend the principle to South Asia – which means the United States would support the principle of 'self-determination' and press for a plebiscite in Kashmir. Similarly, the United States is unwilling to accept the Indian demand for a UN Security Council seat. Some Americans would regard it as a 'reward' for India's nuclear programme, and fear that this would further accelerate the trend towards nuclear weapons.

Finally, India and the United States are each groping for a strategy to cope with the emergence of China as a major world power. The United States is especially concerned about China's challenge to its world leadership, while India is especially concerned about China's future relationship with Pakistan. For India, creating or joining an alliance against China does not suit its national interests. One Chinese scholar pointed out that if India does not participate in the containment of China, China's development would lighten US strategic pressure on India. If India joins forces with the United States to contain China, the future of the 21st century will not belong to India. An Indian scholar argued that, as a developing country, India's priority is economic development. India has always attached the highest value to maintaining independence in making her foreign policy and sovereignty and avoided becoming part of an US or western agenda towards China. The United States is also unlikely to be willing to underwrite the costs of guaranteeing Indian security, and it would be foolish for India to entrust her security to a superpower with global interests. Furthermore, The United States and India both have substantive interests in China. Both within the United States and India, there are significant numbers of people that believe that China is a 'threat' to the interests of the two countries. Both countries also have people that advocate close engagement.

United States' South Asia Policy

United States and India's relationship has changed in these various ways because the US has adjusted its strategy and policy in South Asia. The adjustment is demonstrated in the following areas:

United States Security Policy Towards India

In terms of non-proliferation, the US urges India not to carry out nuclear tests, not to produce fissile materials, not to deploy missiles with nuclear warheads, to stop a dangerous nuclear and missile arms race and to control the export of sensitive materials. As anti-terrorism become the United States' greatest concern, it has reduced the pressure on India in the area of halting the spread of nuclear arms. In terms of Kashmir, there is a change from supporting Pakistan's policy which is implementing United Nations policy of giving the residents of Kashmir the right of plebiscite for its future to supporting India's policy of solving the problem through negotiation while respecting Kashmir residents' view. In terms of its relations with India and with Pakistan, the United States, in accordance with its own advantage, and comparing the power of different nations in South Asia, has slowly changed its focus to India.

An article published in *Washington Times*, quoting the Executive Director of US–India Commercial Committee, Michael Clark, stated that, for an American company, the most important thing was not the rising of the Indian middle class, but undoubtedly the information technology corporations in India, which have extraordinary potential. Some scholars in China concluded that the US policy toward India had changed from 'paying equal attention to India and Pakistan' in the early period of the post-Cold War era to 'focusing on India and reducing Pakistan' during the Clinton administration. The focus was once again changed to 'raising India and curbing Pakistan' when Bush took over and 'regarding Pakistan while respecting India' after the 9/11 attacks and the Enduring Freedom campaign in Afghanistan.

Balance of Power to Power Advantage

The advantage is demonstrated in the following manner: (1) US obtains more influence in South Asia, compared to Russia and China; and (2) India wins the dominant position in the Indian sub-continent, compared to the other South Asian countries. Zbigniew Brzezinski, the eminent American strategist, recognized India as "the strongest state in South Asia and to some extent the regional hegemon." But at the same time, he thought that, "as a geo-strategic player, India is not – at least, not to the same degree as either Russia or China – a source of geopolitical concern." However, this kind of judgment undervalues India's position and capability. The US recognizes India as the largest democracy in the world. India's economy increased by six per cent annually in the 1990's and it also has a growing information technology industry. The United States is India's largest trading partner, its biggest investor and its biggest provider of advanced technology. Besides, Indian Americans are playing an important role in shaping the United States' South Asia policy. During his trip to South Asia in March 2000, President Clinton visited India for seven days while halting symbolically in Pakistan only for some hours. It is obvious that U.S. places its relationship with India on the top of its South Asia policy framework. Compared with Pakistan, which experiences economical trouble and political turbulence and has only one-seventh of India's territory, Washington regards New Delhi as the largest democracy and a potentially important economic partner. Nevertheless, the United States is unlikely to discard its Cold War ally – Pakistan. Contrarily, the United States needs Pakistani support and co-operation as an Islamic 'frontline state' in the war against terrorism.

In sum, against the backdrop of the its preferential values in favour of democracy and its long-term benefits, and the comparison of power between different countries in South Asia, the United States changed its strategic policy of focusing on the balance of power during the Cold War to define and implement a new policy in South Asia: 'Focusing on India and Reducing on Pakistan.' This new policy attempted to go beyond the balance of power. However, judgments based on past traditions, concerns regarding the anti-terrorism efforts and the dangerous situation in South Asia, have diluted this perspective to one within which there is a 'focus on India while respecting Pakistan.' Thus, despite the initial intent, the US policy has not entirely gone beyond the balance of power.

Security Policy for the Asia-Pacific Region

This is primarily demonstrated in the United States' increasing focus on the Asia-Pacific region or, more accurately, in the emergence of an integrated military strategy for the Europe-Atlantic region and the Asia-Pacific region. India and the Indian Ocean are expected to play an important role in such a geo-strategy. In the closing days of the Clinton administration, the containment of China gradually increased in importance as a factor influencing America's Asia-Pacific strategy. In addition to causing trouble on the Taiwan issue, the strategy of containment included reliance on Japanese and Indian Forces, and especially on the trend of enhancing India's capabilities to contain China. Giving the fact that counter-terrorism has became the primary issue in American strategy, the United States intends to use the war on terrorism to implement its military strategy in the Asia-Pacific region in addition to strengthening homeland security. The US military strategy in the Asia-Pacific region, consequently, includes securing influence and location in Central Asia; the limiting of Western Asia's development; and a return to South East Asia. Within this context, India and the Indian Ocean constitute the bridge for the United States in its regional military strategy.

The Change in United States and India's Relationship

While Pakistan has attempted to balance Indian superiority by seeking external ties, India has perceived this as a way of upsetting the natural balance of power in South Asia. For America, Pakistan's role in the United States' military strategy is especially important when America's personal interests are in jeopardy (anti-communism, containment of the erstwhile Soviet Union, and counter terrorism). As Pakistan is a traditional ally of the United States and a frontline state in fighting terrorism, without a more normal India-Pakistan relationship, the India-US relationship will remain highly sensitive to Indian perceptions of Washington's relationship with Islamabad.

It is widely accepted both in the United States and India that China is likely to pose a long-term strategic challenge to them. How will China deal with the outer world after it consolidates its economic and technological ascent? There are different assumptions in the United States and India. Some believe that the future role of China in the Asia-Pacific region will be stable and defensive, rather than destructive and offensive. Others assume that – based on aspects of its strategic culture – China may undertake an offensive foreign policy at the point of time when Chinese leaders think the international balance of power is in their favour. The United States and India have mutual interests, but different policies, in terms the nature of their future dealings with a rising China. There are also essential divergences on issues such as Taiwan and human rights between China and the United States. There are also basic differences on issues including border problems and non-proliferation between China and India.

With the end of the Cold War, the balance of power in South Asia has been upset, and the influence of Russia in South Asia has weakened. Russia still maintains a stable co-operative relationship with India, especially in the field of defence. In the joint statement of Russia-India strategic partnership issued on October 3, 2000, the two parties claimed "democratization of international relations" which is obliviously aimed at hegemonies.

During President Putin's three-day visit to India in early December 2002, both sides signed the Delhi Declaration on Further Consolidation of Strategic Partnership, which heightened the bilateral relations to a new level. In conclusion, based on the rise of the Indian power, the importance of South Asia and the emergence of an Asia-Pacific perspective, the United States has gradually changed its balance of power policy. America is using the balance of power (method) to secure a power advantage (goal).

US PRESIDENCY UNDER DONALD TRUMP TO BOOST STRATEGIC TIES WITH INDIA

US presidency under Donald Trump, a confessed big fan of India and Prime Minister Narendra Modi, is most likely to boost Indo-US strategic relationship with a special emphasis on defence ties and counter-terrorism cooperation.

Trump, 70, had recently described India as "a key, and key strategic ally" and looks forward to deepening the diplomatic and military cooperation that is the shared interest of both countries.

The billionaire businessman who has lauded economic policies of Modi had said he wants to work with him.

At an event in New Jersey less than a month from now, Trump had promised to the Indian-American community in him India would find a true friend at the White House.

"I am a big fan of Hindu and I am a big fan of India. If I am elected president, the Indian and Hindu community would have a true friend at the White House," he had said at an event organised by the Hindu Republican Coalition.

Trump said he appreciated "great friend India in the fight against radical Islamic terrorism." India has experienced firsthand "brutality of terror" in the past "including the mayhem in Mumbai," he said and described the 2008 Mumbai terror attack and that on Indian Parliament in 2001 as "absolutely outrageous" and terrible.

"We will defeat radical Islamic terrorism. We will stand soldier-to-soldier in this fight. This is so important in the age of ISIS," he said. "India's is the world's largest democracy and is a natural ally of the US. Under a Trump Administration, we are going to become even better friends. In fact, I will take the word even out because we are going to be best friends. I look forward to working with Prime Minister Modi, who has been very energetic in reforming the economy and bureaucracy. Great man. I applaud him," he said.

"I look forward to doing some serious bureaucratic trimming right here in the US, believe me we need it most," Trump said. "Your great Prime Minister has been a pro-growth leader for India. He has simplified the tax code, cut the taxes and the economy is strong growing at 7 per cent year. Excellent," he said.

On the eve of the November 8 general elections, a key military advisor to the Trump said that India will have an important role to play in the Trump Administration's Asia Pacific policy of "peace through strength." "This is a country that shares our values, this is a country that shares a lot of geo-political interest and I think, his (Trump's) work is going to be continuing the tradition of Bush Administration which made a lot of progress in that regard," Alexander Gray, a military advisor and author of several of the ambitious defence policies of Trump, said.

"We (a Trump Administration) would be looking to strengthen not just the cultural and economic aspect, but also on the defence side there is so much common ground with India. At a time when India's foreign policy is changing because of China and Pakistan, because of Islamic terrorism, we need to be there to greet them with open arms. I think, the Trump Administration is ready to do that," Gray said.

PRESIDENCY UNDER TRUMP BOOST FOR INDIA-US TIES

The US presidency under Donald Trump, a confessed big fan of India and Prime Minister Narendra Modi, is most likely to boost Indo-US strategic relationship with a special emphasis on defence ties and counter-terrorism cooperation.

Trump, 70, had recently described India as "a key, and key strategic ally" and looks forward to deepening the diplomatic and military cooperation that is the shared interest of both countries.

The billionaire businessman who has lauded economic policies of Modi had said he wants to work with him. At an event in New Jersey less than a month from now, Trump had promised to the Indian-American community in him India would find a true friend at the White House.

"I am a big fan of Hindus and I am a big fan of India. If I am elected president, the Indian and Hindu community would have a true friend at the White House," he had said at an event organised by the Hindu Republican Coalition. Trump said he appreciated "great friend India in the fight against" terrorism.

India has experienced firsthand "brutality of terror" in the past "including the mayhem in Mumbai," he said and described the 2008 Mumbai terror attack and that on Indian Parliament in 2001 as "absolutely outrageous" and terrible. "We will defeat... terrorism. We will stand soldier-to-soldier in this fight. This is so important in the age of Daesh," he said.

"India's is the world's largest democracy and is a natural ally of the US. Under a Trump Administration, we are going to become even better friends. In fact, I will take the word even out because we are going to be best friends. I look forward to working with Prime Minister Modi, who has been very energetic in reforming the economy and bureaucracy. Great man. I applaud him," he said. "I look forward to doing some serious bureaucratic trimming right here in the US, believe me we need it most," Trump said.

"Your great prime minister has been a pro-growth leader for India. He has simplified the tax code, cut the taxes and the economy is strong growing at 7 per cent year. Excellent," he said. On the eve of the November 8 general elections, a key military advisor to the Trump said that India will have an important role to play in the Trump Administration's Asia Pacific policy of "peace through strength."

"This is a country that shares our values, this is a country that shares a lot of geo-political interest and I think, his (Trump's) work is going to be continuing the tradition of Bush Administration which made a lot of progress in that regard," Alexander Gray, a military adviser and author of several of the ambitious defence policies of Trump, said. "We (at Trump Administration) would be looking to strengthen not just the cultural and economic aspect, but also on the defence side there is so much common ground with India. At a time when India's foreign policy is changing because of China and Pakistan, because of terrorism, we need to be there to greet them with open arms. I think, the Trump Administration is ready to do that," Gray said.

Indian fan club celebrates victory

A far-right Hindu group which has been one of Donald Trump's most avid overseas cheerleaders began celebrating in New Delhi Wednesday as the Republican pulled off a shock US presidential election victory. Vishnu Gupta, chief of the ultra-nationalist 'Hindu Sena' outfit, said supporters had taken to the streets to bang traditional drums even before Trump claimed victory and would also distribute celebratory sweets. Trump's hardline rhetoric towards Muslims has found favour in some quarters in India, the world's largest democracy which has had its fair share of tensions between the majority Hindu population and its Muslim minority. Indian Prime Minister Narendra Modi was before his 2014 election regarded as an international pariah after deadly communal riots broke out in the state of Gujarat more than a decade ago when he was chief minister. Most of the victims were Muslims.

Trump has called for a ban on all Muslims entering the United States and Gupta said his message had wide resonance. "We predicted that he would win five days ago - there is a huge support for him, his ideas, and we could see that," Gupta said."

Now terrorists will be hunted everywhere in the world, even if they go and hide in a cave. Now only God can help Pakistan. India will now have the support of the US in our efforts against terrorists. We will be together in this.

"Donald Trump will do what no other US president has been able to do before. We are happy. All terrorists should now run and hide. "Gupta's group held a special prayer session for Trump in New Delhi back in May when he was seen as a long shot for the presidency, hailing him as a "fighter and a saviour of humanity". They also celebrated his birth-day in June with a cake, balloons and posters.

Australia wants US to stay focused on Asia

Australia said on Wednesday it was crucial for Washington to stay focused on Asia as Donald Trump won the presidential election, with Canberra keen to see more US involvement in the region, not less. Under President Barack Obama, the United States has pursued a foreign policy "pivot" towards the Asia-Pacific, including stationing marines in Australia, against the background of Beijing's increasing assertiveness.

With tensions high over China's claims in the South China Sea and fears Trump could be a negative for the region's trade prospects, Foreign Minister Julie Bishop said it was critical that the US remain fully engaged. "Countries in our region are looking for more US leadership and not less in the Asia-Pacific," she told Sky News in the first Australian reaction to Trump's win over former secretary of state Hillary Clinton.

As parliament sat on Wednesday, Bishop and Prime Minister Malcolm Turnbull closely watched results flow through on their mobile phones. Bishop said Canberra wanted to continue working closely with any new administration and meet soon "to ensure it focuses on our region and the importance of US leader-ship and a US presence in the Asia-Pacific".

Warm congratulations' sent from Philippines

Philippines President Rodrigo Duterte, who has publicly abused US President Ba-rack Obama and threatened to downgrade ties with the US, on Wednesday sent his "warm congratulations" to US President-elect Donald Trump. "President Duterte wishes President-elect Trump success in the next four years as Chief Executive and commander-in-chief of the US military, and looks forward to working with the incoming administration for enhanced Philippines-US relations anchored on mutual respect, mutual benefit and shared commitment to democratic ideals and the rule of law," Duterte's Communications Office Secretary Martin Andanar said, GMA news agency said.

Duterte, who has expressed outrage almost daily with the Obama administration and threatened repeatedly to end one of Washington's most important Asian alliances, "hailed the success of US democratic system and the American way of life," the statement said.

INDO-US TIES HEADED FOR BEST DAYS UNDER DONALD TRUMP

India-US relationship is headed for the best days ahead under new President Donald Trump, his Indian-American supporters believe. "This is the beginning of a new era, new dawn of new (India-US) relationship," Indian-American Digvijay Singh 'Danny' Gaekwad from Florida told Press Trust of India. Having closely worked with Mr Trump and his campaign during the grilling election campaign last year, Mr Gaekwad, who is a hotelier and a first general successful entrepreneur, said.

"With Trump becoming the president, a new India-US relationship will begin. This is one President in my life time, who has come on a national television and said I love India, I love Indians, I want to help India, I want to fight terrorism. If that is not enough then what is enough," said Mr Gaekwad.

"No President has ever said this on a national television at the election time. He is not afraid. He is the new breath in the time," he said adding that during the election campaign he had a chance to interact with Mr Trump. "He understands India very well. I have not met a presidential candidate in my life time who knows about India, who has been to India and who understands India and who ever dared to say in the middle of a heated political debate that I love India and I love Hindus," said Mr Gaekwad, who hails from the illustrious Mr Gaekwad family of Baroda. He has been living in Florida for 29 years.

Concurred Harry Walia, a member of the Trump's Asian American and Pacific Islanders Advisory Committee. "The relationship is going to be fantastic, because we are natural allies. Trump has already made a statement that we are going to be best friends," he told PTI referring to the October Edison speech of the 45th president of the United States.

With Donald Trump inside the White House, Mr Walia said he expects "a very open dialogue" between India and the US.

"And it would be fruitful on defense side and economic side. Trump recognizes US relationship with India is very different than the rest of the countries that he has been mentioning. Because we bring talent, we are economic engines in America. We are peaceful community. We are activist in mainstream and we do not talk trash to anyone. We contribute a lot to the American society," he said. "Under Trump, the US India relationship would be far better than it has been under any other American president," said California-based KV Kumar.

"He is a businessman. He is going to establish a good business relationship with India. And India will greatly benefit from his administration," Mr Kumar said. A large number of Indian Americans from across the country have gathered in Washington to participate in Trump's inauguration.

ECONOMIC-BASED COUNTERTERRORISM

Under Executive Order 13224, the U.S. Treasury Dept. periodically identifies certain entities as terrorism financing organizations (financiers), and under U.N. Security Council Resolution 1390, all member states must block the assets of such organizations. Terrorist financiers often look like humanitarian aid organizations, an example being Benevolence International Foundation (BIF), an al-Qa'ida front operating out of Illinois since 1992. Attacking terrorism on economic fronts, whether via blocking or freezing of assets, requires extensive knowledge of organizational structure. Certain organizational principles are endemic to all terrorist groups. Organizations employ varieties of command and control structures, but they are frequently organized along the same pattern no matter what causes they endorse.

The typical organization is arranged in a pyramid. It takes many more people to support terrorist operations than to carry them out; therefore, the majority of people who work in terrorist organizations serve to keep terrorists in the field. The most common job in terrorist groups is support, not combat.

According to Fraser & Fulton (1984), the hierarchical structure of terrorist groups is divided into four levels. The smallest group is at the top and is responsible for command. As in military circles, leadership makes policy and plans while providing general direction. Other researchers have often pointed out that the command structure is not as effective as in legitimate organizations because of the demand for secrecy. The command structure in a terrorist organization is not free to communicate openly with its membership; therefore, it cannot exercise day-to-day operational control.

The second level in Fraser's hierarchy contains the active cadre. The active cadre is responsible for carrying out the mission of the terrorist organization. Depending on the organization's size, each terrorist in the cadre may have one or more specialties. Other terrorists support each specialty, but the active cadre is the striking arm of the terrorist group. After the command structure, the cadre of active terrorists is the smallest organization in most terrorist structures.

Under the active cadre is the second largest and the most important level of a terrorist organization. Active supporters are critical to terrorist campaigns. Any group can carry out a bombing or kidnapping, but to maintain a campaign of bombings and kidnappings takes support. Active supporters keep the terrorists in the field. They maintain communication channels, provide safe houses, gather intelligence, and ensure all other logistical needs are met. This is the largest internal group in the organization.

The last and largest category is the organization's passive supporters. This group is extremely difficult to identify and characterize because supporters do not readily join terrorist groups. Many times they are used without their knowledge; they simply represent a favorable element of the political climate. When a terrorist group can muster political support, it will have a relatively large number of passive supporters. When its cause alienates the mainstream, passive support dwindles. Passive support complements active support.

Most terrorist groups number fewer than 50 people and are incapable of mounting a long-term campaign. Under the command of only a few people, the group is divided according to specific tasks. Intelligence sections are responsible for assessing targets and planning operations. Support sections provide the means necessary to carry out the assault, and the tactical units are responsible for the actual terrorist action. Terrorist organizations have two primary types of subunits: the cell and the column.

The cell is the most basic type. Composed of four to six people, the cell usually has a specialty; it may be a tactical unit or an intelligence section. In some organizations, the duties of tactical cells vary with the assignment. Other cells are designed to support the operations.

Groups of cells form to create columns. Columns are semiautonomous conglomerations of cells with a variety of specialties and a single command structure. As combat units, columns have questionable effectiveness. They are too cumbersome to be used in major operations, and the secrecy demanded by terrorism prevents effective intercolumn cooperation. Their primary function is combat support because elements in a column can be arranged to support the tactical operations of cells.

MILITARY-BASED COUNTERTERRORISM

Military special operations are generally used when little is known about the precise details of a terrorist organization. It must be remembered that intelligence gathering and counterterrorism is normally a police responsibility. The reason for this is that even though police agencies share information with spy agencies, it is the police who must testify at trial, not spies. Collaboration between police and spy agencies is essential in military-based counterterrorism.

While the most effective counterterrorist activities involve preemptive strikes at their bases of support, the most commonly used methods involve retaliation and/or hostage rescue. Many nations maintain specialized counterterrorism units, and these units have a long history, going back as far as the Roman Empire with Jewish extremists. Israel has, in fact, been at the forefront of counterterrorism policy. Israel's Golda Meier formed the first modern counterterrorist agency (the Sayeret Mat'Kal) to hunt down and kill terrorists, abiding by what became the world's rules on retaliation:

- No bystanders must be killed, only terrorists
- Terrorists should be killed in the same way as their victims died
- Terrorists should know who is killing them before they die
- Someone must stay behind to clean up the evidence and mislead police investigation

Probably the most effective counterterrorist agency in the world is the British SAS (Special Air Service). They developed the stun grenade and various other noise-flash devices commonly found today. They also developed night vision goggles and special ladders for assaults. Members of this elite unit are anonymous.

They have been used against the IRA and throughout Europe. Many countries around the world receive SAS support or training in forming their own counterterrorist agencies. Spain also operates a little-known anti-terrorist group, the GEO (Grupo Especial de Operaciones), which specializes in "shoot to kill" and hostage rescue operations like the SAS. The Sultan of Oman maintains a special force (SSF-Sultan of Oman Special Forces) that is constantly on fifteen-minute standby in case of terrorist activity against Omani interests in the Persian Gulf. France operates a special police unit (GIGN-Groupment d'intervention de la Gendarmerie Nationale) trained in counterpropaganda and psychological warfare. The Netherlands and Norway have special marine corps units which protect those nations' economic interests at home and overseas. Germany's GSG9 (Grenzschutzgruppe 9) is an elite force of well-equipped volunteers capable of infinite stealth and overwhelming firepower.

The United States has a system of FBI special units who work with local police SWAT teams and the CIA providing intelligence. Delta Force is perhaps the most well known U.S. counterterrorist unit. However, Seal Team Six is the Navy's equivalent. ATF also maintains a special unit. First responder units throughout the U.S. are trained in terrorist scenarios. Local police departments are trained in close quarter combat situations. America's newest agency is the FAST (First Fleet Antiterrorist Special Team).

DIPLOMACY AS COUNTERTERRORISM

Diplomacy is the most frequently used and most successfully used form of counterterrorism. Numerous misconceptions exist about it. What diplomacy is NOT may be easier to describe, and things such as foreign policy and international law are definitely things involving other continuums. These areas might be called the "legislative" branch of diplomacy (Nicolson 1964), but policy and law are things best left to a President, his or her Cabinet, a Legislature, and a Judicial Branch. Instead, diplomacy is mostly "executive" in the sense that a seasoned team of professionals (called the Foreign Service or Diplomatic Service) are used who are dedicated to the practice of diplomacy and nothing else. Diplomacy is also NOT about negotiation, guile, or trickery, which might be expressed in such commonplace definitions as "the art of persuading others to do things that serve mutual interests." This is a bad definition of diplomacy, and in fact, the practice of diplomacy is often all about fixing the problems that nations get into by trying to deceive one another. A true and correct definition of diplomacy requires an understanding of its history, a topic to which we now turn.

Historically, diplomacy began in prehistoric times. When the first tribe of cavemen realized that it might be better to listen to what the messenger from another tribe had to say before killing and eating them, diplomacy was born. The concepts of messenger, emissary, ambassador, envoy, herald, and to some extent, angel, are all concepts similar in meaning to diplomat. The idea that there is a time and place for persons who are "off-limits" or under a "white flag" from harm is the idea of diplomacy. You might begin to see the potential of diplomacy for counterterrorism at this point.

The social taboo against killing well-meaning foreigners on state business is one of the world's oldest taboos. The ancient Greeks called such visitors "heralds" and throughout the centuries, the profession of herald (like one's heraldry or coat of arms) ran in families. The Romans are generally credited with creating "archivists" (specialists in diplomatic precedents and procedures) and so-called "secret" diplomacy, but the Italian states during the fifteenth century created public positions known as "ambassadors". The word diplomat comes from the Greek word "diploun" meaning "to fold" which refers to the stamped metal plates early diplomats used to carry. These metal plates consisted of passes to come and go across international borders, and were called "diplomas" which eventually became associated with documents of academic achievement. As the years went on, the Vatican and England helped spread the practice of housing permanent missions (embassies or consulates) overseas. By 1815 at the Congress of Vienna, every nation officially approved and sanctioned a global diplomacy system, with diplomats recognized as a true profession, distinct from the job of statesman or politician. Diplomacy is today thought of as a *regularized system of establishing channels of communication and avenues of cooperation between inter-state actors*. The standard definition is "the application of intelligence and tact to the conduct of official relations between governments and independent actors" (Satow 1905).

To become a diplomat requires earning a title, inheriting a title, or having one bestowed upon you by the sovereigns of your country. In the United States, the standard procedure is to work for awhile as a career foreign service officer in an agency like USAID (Agency for International Development), and your supervisors will process you for such a title as your career rises. Since the Congress of Vienna, the following standard titles are what one is likely to encounter among diplomatic teams and consulate missions, while it should be noted that representatives to the United Nations are usually required to be at the level of plenipotentiary, and that in most missions, almost all envoys regard themselves as extraordinary. Diplomatic theory and practice are derived from notions of social justice and a relatively little known field of social science called peace studies (Barash 1991). You'd be surprised at how many colleges and schools that offer a degree in peace studies. Programs solely devoted to diplomacy are fewer in number, and usually affiliated with history departments (as Norwich is), political science departments (as George Washington is), or in the case of the Fletcher School of Law and Diplomacy at Tufts, has been around since 1933 and has emerged into a separate college division unto itself.

- Ambassador-the highest ranking officer of a diplomatic mission who is sometimes addressed as Excellency
- Envoy extraordinary or Minister plenipotentiary — someone in charge of a special project or has special responsibilities
- Envoy ordinary or Minister resident — someone working on a regular project, or a regular employee at a mission
- Charge d'affaires — an acting head of a mission when others leave, and who is left behind to express displeasure
- Attaché — military officers, lower-level foreign service personnel, or commercial businessmen performing special services
- Counselor — secretaries or assistants who are regular employees that work at the mission
- Honorary attaché — a volunteer or person of private means who is not a permanent member of a mission

Diplomatic language contains certain phrases, which over the course of centuries, have become part of a common international vocabulary. For example, if a diplomat says his or her country "cannot remain indifferent," that almost certainly means that his or her country will be intervening soon in the affairs of another country. When a diplomat says that matters are of "grave concern," that almost always means a hard line is being taken.

When a diplomat says that something will be interpreted as an "unfriendly act," that almost certainly implies a threat of war. When diplomats are dispatched to settle a conflict or controversy, it is not the same as sending negotiators. The role of a negotiator is to distract the enemy while you are doing other things, like preparing to attack them. With negotiation, there is usually compromise; someone wins, someone loses, or at least both parties never get all they want. The role of a diplomat is to resolve a situation to the ultimate triumph for all; everyone usually wins, and the region is ideally transformed by peace. Diplomats carry letters of credentials and full powers signed by a President or Secretary of State to act on behalf of a sovereignty. Let's take a look at some of the tools of diplomacy:

- Accession — this is a clause in existing treaties by which parties who did not sign off on it can do so later
- Accord — this is a document signed by both parties which is not of sufficient importance to justify calling it a treaty.
- Ad referendum — this is when a diplomat agrees to something but requires his or her government to approve it later
- Agreement — this is a document signed by both parties to formalize what they have sounded out with one another prior to a meeting
- Compact — this is a short-term agreement to continue talking and outlines the course of procedure to follow
- Conference — this is the name for a meeting of diplomats between all interested parties and is called a congress or convention when heads of state are present
- Declaration — this is doctrinal statement of rights or policies to be shared between nations before the diplomats arrive
- Memoire — a memorandum or note passed by diplomats to one another which are expected to get back to their sovereigns secretly
- Note — the ordinary means of communication by diplomats expressing their thoughts on matters
- Protocol — a record of the less formal means of procedure by which agreement may be reached
- Treaty — a bilateral or multilateral document that concludes diplomatic action between parties
- Voeux — these are wishes or recommendations for future good conduct that have no binding force on signatories

The most common uses of diplomacy in counterterrorism include: developing bilateral or multilateral anti-terrorist policies; arranging for the sharing of intelligence; arranging permission for law enforcement authorities from one country to come in and arrest (or interrogate) a suspected terrorist in another country; and establishment of appropriate sanctions on sponsors of terrorism. In some cases, diplomatic overtures are made to the terrorists and their groups themselves, even though they are sub-national actors. Some famous cases where diplomacy worked in the terrorist context include: ending the OPEC hostage crisis at Vienna in 1975; arranging a prisoner exchange with Lebanese hijackers in 1985; catching Carlos the Jackal in 1994; getting the IRA to agree to a laying down of arms in 1998; and numerous cease-fire agreements between Israelis and Palestinians from 2001-2003. Diplomacy also played a part in social reform movements when Spain changed how it was dealing with the Basque rebellion during the 1980s, and when Peru changed how it was dealing with the Shining Path in the 1990s. Diplomacy has positive results, indeed, when it can do things like get terrorists to apologize and change their ways, and also get governments which have fought terrorism repressively become better democracies that respect civil liberties.

NEGOTIATION AS COUNTERTERRORISM

Diplomacy can also have horribly negative results. Conventional wisdom holds that it is never good to negotiate with terrorists or to concede to their demands, at least while they are still engaging in violence. In fact, the U.S. and many of its allies are formally committed to a policy of "no negotiation" with terrorists. However, it is often the case that this policy is not followed. It exists as hard-line rhetoric more than reality. The truth is that history shows democracies are more willing to negotiate and compromise with terrorism than not. When such efforts go wrong, they encourage the terrorists to repeat their acts and become more violent later on. They also embarrass a nation and result in lost credibility for many years. When such efforts go partially right, and that is all they can be- partially effective, the best that can happen is the incident goes away, and there is some closure, for awhile, on the world stage regarding the attention given.

Efforts to negotiate and compromise with terrorists are called concessionary options, and they have been used quite often by a number of parties over the years. Negotiators rather than diplomats are usually involved in these options. A countless number of ransom payments have been made by governments, corporations, and families to terrorists. Numerous prisoner exchanges, prisoner releases, and even mass releases of prisoners have been made throughout history, and the U.S. has been party to it. For all its tough talk, Israel has engaged in almost as many concessions as crackdowns. Perhaps the most famous act of concession involving the U.S. was the Iran-Contra scandal. During 1985-1986, high-ranking officials of the U.S. government sold $30 million worth of guns to Iran in hopes of getting Iranian help for releasing American hostages held by Shi'ite terrorists in Lebanon.

The money from the gun sale was used to support anti-Sandinista forces in Latin America. Iran, for its part, came through and successfully pressured the terrorists to release the hostages in Lebanon. Shortly after, however, more American hostages were seized by the same terrorist group, among others, and the U.S. suffered a major credibility problem in Latin America from which it has not since recovered.

Iran-Contra is just one example of things gone horribly wrong, but in all fairness, it is up to history to decide if short-term expediency options are worth the long-term costs. The best that can be said is that the following concessions are only marginally effective (and for the most part, bad ideas), but they might be conceivably useful under some very specific historical circumstances where they don't reward terrorism or create credibility problems:

- Payment of ransom money to terrorists
- Payment of bribe or protection money to terrorists
- Giving weapons, food, material, technology, or information to terrorists
- Release of imprisoned terrorists upon demand by other terrorists

- Release of imprisoned supporters or sympathizers of terrorism
- Release of political prisoners, dissidents, extremists, and spiritual fanatics
- Provision of transport to another location intra-or internationally
- Provision of political asylum or amnesty within a host country
- Provision of top-notch legal services and a public court forum to air their cause
- Provision of access to the news media to broadcast their propaganda

INTELLIGENCE AS COUNTERTERRORISM

Good intelligence is the best weapon against terrorism, but it should be all-source intelligence, and the kind, which is good for almost all kinds of intelligence — the value-added kind which separates out the signals from the noise, such as what is sometimes called Indications & Warnings (I&W) in the intelligence community. Indicators will be discussed in a moment, but "all source" requires some clarification at this point. This means that all the different platforms (technical and human) of intelligence collection should be used, along with open source platforms like the Internet.

It is best when all the collection assets converge or cover at least one of the indicators an analyst is trying to assess (another meaning of "all source"). From the human asset (espionage) aspect, this involves sometimes dealing with "bad apples," and from the open-source perspective, this involves mining the Internet for what it's worth. For analysis, while reactive (after the fact) investigation may prove useful for some purposes, it's generally considered that with crimes like terrorism, a proactive (before the fact) strategy is best, and a proactive one which accounts for all sorts of strange and unusual contingencies. For example, sometimes sensitivity training may be needed along with proactive efforts, especially when the intelligence resource being used is a community within the U.S. where a significant number of immigrants live. Such communities can be an invaluable resource, but there should be friendly and open relationships between law enforcement and such areas. For example, an organization called PfP (the Partnering for Prevention and Community Safety Initiative) has piloted some techniques for getting the Arab, Muslim, and Sikh communities in Southeastern Michigan, Southern California, and Greater Boston to work cooperatively with local law enforcement. Such "networking" as it would be called in the language of community policing should be fine-tuned to an effective level.

A proactive mode of inquiry will also take advantage of the fact that many terrorists have quite predictable social and psychological motivations. Their "profiling" is somewhat easy to do. In many ways, terrorists behave like common criminals, but they just take politics or religion very seriously. Also, because nonstate or modern terrorists usually have no legitimate sovereignty structure, like a nation-state or official organization, the role of group support and reference groups in the system become extremely important. Strategic thinking toward elimination of terrorism as a "tactic" not an enemy is still evolving (Pena 2006), but traditional techniques have some value too. Indicator collection and efforts toward "profiling" should strive toward including all the following in intelligence gathering and interpretation:

"Indicators" refer to those collectable things which would have to happen and those that would likely happen as a scenario unfolds (Khalsa 2004). Indicators are usually thought of as factors of risk. The three (3) primary factors of risk regarding terrorism are: *adversary capability, adversary intentions, and target vulnerability*.

There is some debate within intelligence circles as to whether the third one is necessary, and some people define "terrorism threat assessment" (as opposed to terrorism risk assessment) as only involving the first two. The third is controversial precisely because it sometimes involves collecting vulnerability information on an ally or friendly force. The following table lists some of these indicators, but it must be borne in mind that the analyst must strive toward including others that are also important in intelligence interpretation:

Additional "profiling" indicators:

1. Group Information — Name(s), ideology (political or social philosophy), history of the group, dates significant to the group, and dates on which former leaders have been killed or imprisoned. *(Terrorist groups often strike on important anniversary dates)* Some groups also have a Bible or manifesto which is important to obtain (*doomsday dates*).
2. Financial Information — Source of funds, proceeds from criminal activities, bank account information. *(Sudden influxes of funding or bank withdrawals indicate preparation for activity)* It's also important to determine the group's legal and financial supporters. Generally, anyone who would write an official letter of protest or gather names on a petition for a terrorist is a legal-financial supporter. Sometimes, an analysis of support will reveal linkages and/or mergers with other terrorist groups.
3. Personnel Data — List of leaders (and changes in leadership), list of members (and former members), any personnel connections between its members and other groups of similar ideology, and the skills of all group members (weapons expertise, electronics expertise, etc.) *(Knowing the skills of the group is an important part of threat assessment)* If the philosophy revolves around one leader, it's important to know what will occur if something happens to that leader. Often, the analysis of family background is useful to determine how radically a leader or member was raised. Group structure, particularly if the organization pattern is cellular, determines who knows whom.
4. Locational Data — Location of group's headquarters, location of group's "safe" houses (where hide from

authorities), and location of group's "stash" houses (where hide weapons and supplies). *(Regular attacks on "stash" houses is the most frequently used counterterrorism technique)* It's important to specify the underground that exists where terrorists can flee. This is harder than determining safe havens. Terrorists like to live in communal homes instead of living alone.

While ordinary street crime is often deterred by crackdowns, target hardening, denying opportunity, and aggressive security (with known displacement patterns), *terrorism frequently defies deterrence* and predictable displacement patterns because they don't seek targets of opportunity, but symbolic targets. As a group, terrorists are very team-oriented, and always prepared for suicide missions. On the other hand, ordinary criminals are undisciplined, untrained, and oriented toward escape. Terrorists are just the opposite. They have prepared for their mission, are willing to take risks, and are attack-oriented. If captured, they will usually not confess or snitch on others as ordinary criminals do. Traditional law enforcement methods are not all that effective when it comes to the investigation or intelligence of terrorism.

6

India's Relationship with the US Enters an Era of Uncertainty

Over the past two decades, relations between India and the United States have improved quite dramatically. There have been some vicissitudes, such as those over India's stance on global trade negotiations and legal issues surrounding the US-India civilian nuclear agreement. But the progress is clear by most measures, such as the volume of trade—while the two countries traded goods worth $9.5 billion in 1996, last year that figure stood at $62.1 billion. Various intergovernmental dialogues, in areas such as education, energy and counterterrorism, also point to the fact that the relationship is now on reasonably secure footing. Donald Trump's assumption of the US presidency, however, has generated several questions, if not actual misgivings, about the future of these ties.

Even before formally assuming office, Trump upended a series of long-established precedents that have served as guiding principles in US foreign policy. For example, he openly questioned the US commitment to the North Atlantic Treaty Organization, raised doubts about the country's adherence to the "One China" policy, suggested that he may oversee a drastic expansion of the US nuclear arsenal and even cast doubts on the utility of the United Nations Security Council in the wake of a controversial vote on Israeli settlements. These statements and the stances they embody have rattled much of the US foreign policy establishment, not to mention key allies and some adversaries.

Given Trump's apparent willingness to move away from a number of key current facets of US foreign policy, a pressing question is how he intends to deal with India. But since he has yet to spell out an overarching framework for his foreign policy, in seeking answers, one is forced to search his public pronouncements for clues.

It is already evident that if Trump is sincere about his stated preferences, tensions with India are bound to arise. Take, for example, his railing against the issuance of H1-B visas, which allow US companies to hire foreign workers for limited periods of time, to perform specialised tasks. On occasion, past US administrations also made noises about restricting these visas. But owing to the needs of US corporations, they rarely, if ever, imposed any meaningful constraints. At most, the visa fees associated with the programme were raised.

Trump fought the election on a blatantly populist platform. In a campaign promise on his website he vowed to "end forever the use of the H1-B as a cheap labor program, and institute an absolute requirement to hire American workers first for every visa and immigration program." Trump reiterated his commitment to restricting H1-Bs after his victory, claiming that the visa was subject to "widespread, rampant abuse." More recently, in January, two members of the House of Representatives—Darell Issa, a Republican and a Trump supporter, and Scott Peters, a Democrat—reintroduced an earlier bill that would significantly tighten restrictions on the H1-B programme.

Among its other provisions, the bill proposes to make it more difficult for companies that rely heavily on H1-B visas to bypass some of the legal requirements of applying for the visas—by making it more expensive for such companies to hire workers under it, and revoking a rule that granted an exemption from those requirements when hiring individuals with Master's degrees.

The proposed legislation, if passed, could have adverse consequences for Indian outsourcing companies such as Infosys and Wipro, which earn significant revenue by sending staffers to work for clients in the United States. Azim Premji, the chairman of Wipro, and Vishal Sikka, the CEO of Infosys, both raised concerns of difficult times ahead in letters they sent to their staff members early in the new year. Sikka specifically cited the US presidential election as an aspect of the "strange year gone by." Policymakers in New Delhi are bound to be concerned about the economic impact of a drastic cut in the earnings of prominent outsourcing firms. These earnings are not only an important source of profits for the companies, but also benefit communities within India in the form of remittances that workers send home.

Trump's rants about undocumented immigrants, though mostly directed against Mexicans and people from Muslim-majority nations, are another cause for worry. The majority of people of Indian origin in the United States are there through legal means; however, according to the Pew Research Center, undocumented Indians form the fastest growing undocumented community among all ethnicities. Pew's data put the number of undocumented Indians in the United States at 500,000, as of 2014; these individuals are among those who stand to face the most persecution under the upcoming administration. Trump's periodic tirades about illegal immigration could also affect those Indians who are documented, by stoking existing hostility towards non-white immigrants, especially among poor, white communities, many of whom have not benefitted from globalisation. The rise of such ill will could easily impact the hitherto very influential Indian diaspora community. Faced with such animosity, they may seek to withdraw from the public arena, and thereby lose their growing voice in the foreign policy realm in general, and Indo-US relations in particular.

Another thing that could spell trouble for India-US relations is Trump's insistence on bringing back industrial jobs to the United States, and his relentless threats to companies that outsource manufacturing abroad. Even though India is hardly comparable to Mexico or China as a destination for US manufacturing jobs, as a *Harvard Business Review* article notes, some American corporations, such as General Electric, Cummins (which makes engines, among other products) and the healthcare company Abbott, do have plants in the country. With Prime Minister Narendra Modi promoting his own initiative to fuel industrial growth under the "Make in India" campaign, the two sides may well find themselves at odds if Trump does carry through his promises.

Defence purchases form another key aspect of the trade relationship between the two countries. India's military expenditure has grown swiftly over the past decade, and it is now the fourth largest military spender in the world. Between 2012 and 2015, India signed deals worth around $4 billion with the United States—second in worth only to those it signed with Russia—making it a significant customer for the US military-industrial complex, and a potential creator of thousands of jobs.

Trump's statements may have raised concerns, but it is also possible to infer that his presidency may not be inimical to India's interests after all. It is already evident, for example, that Trump has little love for China. He has charged the country with currency manipulation, and has also railed against the vast trade surplus that it has enjoyed vis-à-vis the United States. More to the point, he has openly questioned the US's "One China" policy, which officially recognises only the People's Republic of China, and not the Republic of China, also known as Taiwan. Trump spoke to the president of Taiwan over the phone immediately after his victory, and also remained noncommittal in interviews about his plans for the policy, triggering alarm in Beijing.

Trump's intransigence towards China suggests that he might continue the same policies that the Obama administration embraced towards India in its second term. During these years, the two sides carefully built upon limited past efforts to forge the beginnings of a viable strategic partnership. If Trump does view China as a strategic and economic competitor, he will have every reason to continue firming up the security and defence partnership with India. After all, barring Japan and a distant Australia, few countries in the Asia-Pacific region with significant economic and political power have demonstrated much willingness to stand up to the growing assertiveness of China. India, for its part, has been home to the Tibetan government-in-exile, and allowed the Dalai Lama to visit the state of Arunachal Pradesh, to which China claims a territorial right. India has also offered to sell missiles to Vietnam, another antagonist of China. If Indian statespersons evince a willingness to continue the policies that they pursued with the Obama administration, there is little reason to believe that the emerging US-India security partnership will run into troubled waters. Indeed, the recent visits to the United States of two key Indian foreign and security policy officials—the national security adviser, Ajit Doval, and the foreign secretary, Subrahmanyam Jaishankar—both suggest that policy continuity is indeed in the offing.

With regard to the fraught India-Pakistan relationship, one that has huge significance for Indian foreign and security policy, there is little indication of Trump's position apart from his phone call at the end of November to the Pakistani premier Nawaz Sharif. But the sheer vacuity of the conversation, in which, according to a Pakistan government press release, he heaped lavish praise on the country, suggests that his remarks can hardly be seen as serious indicators of policy intentions.

There are other reasons to doubt that Trump intends to cosy up to Pakistan. Chief among them is his choice of Michael Flynn as his national security advisor. Flynn is a retired army officer with considerable experience in dealing with Pakistan while serving in Afghanistan. Though news reports have alleged that he shared classified information with Pakistan, his broader stand towards the country might be more clearly discerned from his statements describing Islam as a "cancer" and the Islamic world as an "epic failure." In light of such sentiments, it is difficult to imagine that he would be especially well-disposed towards Pakistan—an avowedly Muslim state, and one that has long acted against the strategic interests of the

US in Afghanistan, all the while professing to be a staunch US ally.

It remains to be seen how Trump handles the fraught issue of his very substantial business interests in India. According to the *Washington Post*, he is "involved in at least 16 partnerships or corporations" in the country, accounting for "more business ventures than in any other foreign nation or territory." Just prior to his inauguration, he categorically refused to divest himself of his vast real-estate ventures both at home and abroad.

Thus, from what indications Trump has given so far, it is fair to assume that in some areas, unless they are very deftly handled in New Delhi, India and the United States could find themselves in opposition. However, in those realms related to key Indian strategic concerns, fears about the future course of India-US relations under a Trump presidency, though understandable, may well prove to be misplaced.

AMID UNCERTAINTY, INDIA BRACES FOR A CHALLENGING TRUMP ERA

"There will be change in terms of US engagement with the world," Jaishankar said in a seminar at the Institute of Defence Studies and Analysis in New Delhi on his return from Washington DC. "What can be safely predicted is that the Trump administration will have different priorities."

Trump challenged many bipartisan consensuses on US foreign policy during his campaign. And, on November 8, when he finally won the race to the White House, the possibility of major changes in US enga-gements with Europe and Asia indeed see-med real. His "America First" foreign policy, his admiration for Russian President Vla-dimir Putin even after European Union accused Moscow of occupation of Crimea in Ukraine and his dismissive comments about the Nato put US allies in Europe at unease.

He also called into question the value of America's alliances in Asia and suggested that if countries like Japan and South Korea could not "reimburse" the US for ensuring their security, they should be defending themselves, be it from a rising China, or from the rogue North Korea. Trump also vowed to withdraw the US from the Trans-Pacific Partnership, which was signed on February 4 by 12 Pacific Rim countries, notably excluding China.

India is not an ally of the US, but the bilateral strategic partnership grew steadily since the signing of the landmark nuclear agreement in 2008. And, with Narendra Modi at the helm of affairs in Delhi since 2014, India appeared to be entering into a closer emb-race with the US over the past two-and-a-half years. So much so that some critics questioned if the Modi government was compro-mising India's strategic autonomy to build closer security and defence ties with the US.

Modi and US President Barack Obama issued an India-US "Joint Strategic Vision for the Asia-Pacific and Indian Ocean Region" from New Delhi on January 26, 2015. An India-US-Japan trilateral dialogue among senior diplomats was elevated to the level of foreign ministers. The annual India-US Malabar naval exercise was turned into a trilateral drill with Japan's Maritime Self Defence Force joining it. Beijing, of course, was not amused and perceived all these as efforts to contain China. What also raised hackles in Beijing was India's position on China's territorial disputes with its maritime neighbours, as it was almost akin to the stand taken by the US and Japan.

The year 2016 also saw India dropping its decade-long hesitance and finally inking with the US the Logistics Exchange Memorandum of Agreement or LEMOA, which would provide the militaries of both countries' access to each other's facilities for supplies and repairs. The year ended with Obama signing into law a legislation designating India as a "major defence partner" of the US.

As India moved into closer relations with the US, its ties with China soured. Beijing blocked New Delhi's bids to enter the Nuclear Suppliers Group as well as to get United Nations' sanctions imposed on Pakistan-based Masood Azhar. New Delhi – wary of China's "string of pearls" strategic assets encircling India – remained opposed to One-Belt-One-Road initiative of the communist country. India opposed the OBOR, not only because it perceived the move as an attempt to spread China's influence in the region, but also because the initiative included the China-Pakistan Economic Corridor, which is proposed to pass through areas it accuses Pakistan of illegally occupying in Kashmir.

There has not been any progress in India-China negotiations to resolve the long-pending boundary dispute, too.

So New Delhi, undoubtedly, has reasons to worry, as Trump's election to succeed Obama cast a shadow of uncertainty over the fate of "US pivot to Asia" – a major foreign policy initiative of the outgoing administration in Washington DC for strategic rebalance of America's diplomatic and military resources to the continent.

Underwater drone issue

Trump's talks with Taiwan President Tsai Ing-wen over phone and his strong criticism of China after the communist country seized a US underwater drone in international waters signalled that Uncle Sam's hostility with the Middle Kingdom may intensify after he succeeds Obama in the Oval Office. But will America with Trump at its helm come to the aid of its allies (and "major defence partners") in Asia-Pacific, if China reacts to US hostility more aggressively and turns into a security nightmare in the region?

New Delhi had some engagements with Team Trump over the past two months. The interlocutors got a rather clear signal that President Trump will seek to pursue the "transactional approach" that Candidate Trump advocated in managing its relations with allies and partners in Asia.

So, India must be prepared to respond to what the new reality of President Trump's America would mean to Asia after January 20. It, in fact, has already started doing so. Just weeks after the US elections results were out, India launched trilateral talks with China and Russia on Asia-Pacific affairs – a move apparently aimed at creating space for policy manoeuvring to respond to changes in the US approach to the region.

The Asia-Pacific talks saw senior diplom-ats of the three countries noting that China, Russia and India had "extensive common interests and close views" on many regional issues. They also agreed that the trilateral consultations would continue as they would "contribute to strengthening practical coordination on regional and global issues".

"In an evolving global order, India needs to engage with a multiplicity of actors in a multi-polar world," Jaishankar, who served as New Delhi's envoy to both Beijing and Washington, said after his first visit to the US after Trump's election as the 45th president of the US. However, he was quick to acknowledge that it would be a challenge for New Delhi to position itself optimally in its engagements with US, China and Russia.

INDIA AND THE TRUMP ADMINISTRATION'S AGENDA

February 7, 2017: Indians are optimistic about how their bilateral relationship with the United States will fare under the Trump administration. They expect important changes in the U.S. geopolitical outlook. The resulting disruption may bring dangers but also opportunities for India. In assessing its policies for a world of much greater uncertainty, the basic foreign policy goals we wrote about in *India at the High Table* will largely survive, though India, as we anticipated, may need to tweak how it thinks about strategic autonomy. Some aspects of the new administration's approach to the U.S. domestic economy may wind up having an impact on international trade as well – and hence on India.

US-India relations look promising: A recent visit to Delhi found Indians – both official and unofficial – decisively upbeat about the effect of a Trump presidency on bilateral relations with the United States. Most expect that President Trump and Indian prime minister Narendra Modi will quickly develop a strong personal relationship. Both are politicians who beat the odds to become national leaders; both had promised to shake up the political systems in their countries; both like direct and sometimes provocative communications. Especially after a buoyant phone conversation praised in both countries, observers expected the security and economic ties that have built up over the past two decades to carry on.

Trump's strong anti-immigration stance, and word of his dislike for the H-1B visa program that brings many Indian tech workers to the United States, is recognized as a potential problem. It has generated a great deal of excitement, especially as legislation changing the program has been considered once again in the U.S. Congress. A delegation from the Indian tech industry is expected to visit Washington in February to advocate for retaining the program. However, this issue was generally not expected to disrupt the upward trajectory of U.S.-India relations.

The Global Order at an Inflection Point: Trump's campaign said relatively little about foreign policy, but what it did say felt revolutionary. This tone has continued since the election, with Trump publicly calling NATO "obsolete," questioning the viability of the European Union, and threatening trade wars. Observers outside the Indian government expressed uneasiness about unpredictable U.S. behavior which could lead to global uncertainty.

Indian government officials seem to be watching three issues in particular. The first and most important is what will happen to U.S.-China relations. Ideally, India would like the U.S. and China to keep their relations reasonably stable, but not so close as to cut India out of the role it seeks in Asia and on the world stage. China has a big economic relationship with India as well as a profound influence on the security outlook in the Indian Ocean and Southeast Asia – areas critical to Indian security. India's ability to expand its trade and its influence to its East has benefited from the U.S. economic and security profile in Southeast Asia. Now, the watchword is uncertainty.

The second important issue for India is U.S.-Russian relations. Trump's warm words about Putin suggested that U.S.-Russian relations might improve. This would be widely welcomed in India. Finally, Indian officials are closely watching the perennial question of U.S. relations with Pakistan. The effusive reports of a December phone conversation between Trump and Pakistan Prime Minister Nawaz Sharif inevitably left many Indians wondering whether the old U.S.-Pakistan attraction would resume. Those who follow events in the U.S. recognized that Trump and senior figures in his administration are also deeply suspicious of Muslims, and Modi is expected to try to build on this common view. There was remarkably little speculation on whether the U.S. administration was likely to try to broker a Kashmir settlement – an effort we regard as most unlikely, which would be welcomed in Pakistan and rejected in India.

We were particularly impressed with one experienced observer's comments on the strategic implications for India of Trump's global outlook and the nationalist rise in Europe. He noted that the liberal international order that prevailed for the past seventy years might be morphing, perhaps into a Hobbesian "war of all against all." This might not take military form. It could mean that countries that had relied on a predictable set of international relationships might find themselves without support that they could count on. If China's economy went through serious difficulties, this would add a strong element of economic disruption to the geopolitical shifts.

If the basic underpinnings of the world order are shifting for the United States and China, this observer argued, the resulting uncertainty might offer opportunities as well as risks for India. He offered little explanation of what these newly open "doors" might be. Three seemed to us implicit in the rest of his discussion. India might have new opportunities for multilateral leadership. Fluid relations among the United States, China and Russia might offer India opportunities to use its ties with those three major powers to shape the global balance of power.

More broadly, this observer noted, if the United States is fundamentally reevaluating its approach to the world, perhaps India might need to do the same. Looking back over the seventy years since modern India became independent, three foreign policy drivers have been extraordinarily durable. India has consistently sought to maintain regional preeminence. This is likely to become, if anything, even more important in an era marked by uncertainty, fluid international relationships, and a Chinese powerhouse competing with the United States.

A second driver, the commitment to nonalignment and more recently to its intellectual descendant, "strategic autonomy," could come in for some redefinition in a world of more changeable international relationships. India's greater power is unlikely to relieve it of the need to work with other countries to achieve its goals. What is unclear is how complicated it may be to develop sustained friendships in a more Hobbesian international order, should that materialize.

The Economic Dimension: The third major Indian foreign policy driver, nurturing India's expanding economy as an instrument of national power, only achieved its present prominence in the last quarter century. This objective will, if anything, become even more important in Indian foreign policy if early projections of the emerging international order are correct.

India's economic surge and greater openness to the global economy developed as global trade was expanding. The Indian government remains highly cautious, however, in considering further market opening. Trump's decision to withdraw the United States from the Trans Pacific Partnership (TPP) was greeted with relief in Delhi. India had not joined the TPP talks, which it felt would open the doors faster than its economy and its democratic politics could manage. It feared U.S. pressure to join the TPP, but was uneasy about the impact on its export markets of an agreement that gave competitors like Vietnam preferential access to the US market.

The background of President Trump's appointees to senior U.S. government positions, their public statements, and what Trump himself said on the campaign trail, point to a sharp departure from seven decades of U.S. trade policy. India now faces a more inward-looking global economic environment –

and a more inward-looking United States, one of its key economic partners. Consider the priorities that top Trump administration officials have articulated so far:

- Export access was the key U.S. objective during most of the world's trade negotiations since 1947; the accent has now shifted to penalizing imports.
- The U.S. objective is job creation – but not just any jobs: Trump and his appointees are focused chiefly on manufacturing, and specifically on heavy industry: steel, aluminum, automobiles. Services and tech jobs are mentioned much less frequently. One doesn't hear much about encouraging innovation, or about small business.
- Local supply is in. Global supply chains are out. The border tax that has been floated would take direct aim at them.
- Multilateral negotiations are out – too diffuse, too complicated. Even "plurilateral" negotiations with a handful of countries are suspect. Bilateral negotiations are in, with a specific transactional focus. Powerful countries often prefer bilateral encounters, which magnify their power differential (this has generally been true of India as well). But a world of bilateral agreements makes trade rules more diverse, and hence makes trade more complicated.
- The administration, and Trump in particular, want to short-circuit the way businesses made decisions during the globalizing years. They want CEOs to decide on the future of their production facilities based on citizenship, not global efficiency.
- Short term action is in. Trump seems to favor coercive negotiations with business leaders, leading to company-specific deals. Long term planning is out: remedies involving education and training are not immediate enough. Trade adjustment for displaced U.S. workers is seen as too far off to be a solution.

The Trump Administration is nothing if not impatient, but it may take some months – or more – to get a clear fix on the effect of its changed emphasis. Its top trade priorities are likely to be NAFTA and China. India is large enough to be noticeable in U.S. trade, but not weighty enough to have a decisive influence. It may find some of its export markets under pressure. India's successful auto parts exports could be a case in point, especially if they come from U.S.-owned corporations operating in India. India is unlikely to get much support in the U.S. government for retaining short term work visas (the H-1B category, for example); finding an alternative business model may be a more viable strategy. Finding an argument that connects trade growth between India and the United States with job growth in both countries will be key to avoiding nasty surprises.

What kind of partnership? India and the United States have been working toward a partnership since 2000, but both have historical baggage which has made it hard to define what that should mean. As the Trump administration settles in, two basic concepts are in play. One is strategic collaboration resting on some core common interests, including anti-terrorism and similar goals for Asian security. With India, this would not involve agreement on the full range of either country's interests. The other model is a succession of transactional deals, involving trade and investment, but potentially also more specific security issues. These would be agreements in which both parties know with great specificity what they are offering and receiving. These are not incompatible; ideally, a solid and enduring partnership would draw on both models.

The challenge for President Trump and Prime Minister Modi is to keep their eyes on the strategic ball. This should not rule out more specific deals – far from it. But India is not yet a big enough player for a trade agreement here and an anti-terrorism cooperation understanding there to carry the rest of their relationship. President Trump has thus far showed much more enthusiasm for specific deals than for broad strategic partnerships. Prime Minister Modi has built his foreign policy success on larger understandings between leaders. A lot is riding on their ability to find a common "sweet spot."

INDIA'S GREAT TRUMP HOPE

President Trump may be in a hurry to overturn many measures of the previous Obama administration, but he appears to seek continuity of the increasingly close partnership America has developed with India's Prime Minister Narendra Modi. In fact, within five days of taking office, the new president called the prime minister to emphasize that desire.

It was by all accounts a courtesy call, but important in its symbolism, with the president hailing India as a true friend and partner in addressing challenges around the world. According to a White House readout of the call, the two leaders discussed opportunities to strengthen the bilateral partnership in broad areas such as the economy and defense. They also resolved that their two countries would stand "shoulder-to-shoulder" in the global push against terrorism. Mr. Trump signed off with an invitation to Mr. Modi to visit the United States, and it is likely the prime minister will take him up on that invitation this spring.

President Obama made a similar call to Mr. Modi, on Jan. 19, a day before his term ended, when both the leaders discussed the progress they made on shared economic and security priorities, including recognition of India as a major partner of the U.S. in defense and in addressing the global challenge of climate change during his administration.

An early Modi-Trump meeting will sustain the momentum of closer bilateral relations. In a tweet following his phone call with Mr. Trump, the prime minister said he too had extended an invitation to the U.S. president to visit India. "Had a warm conversation with President Trump last evening," Mr. Modi added. "President and I agreed to work closely in the coming days to further strengthen our bilateral ties."

It has not been lost on Indian observers that the new president has appointed as many as six Indian-Americans to his administration. This includes his one-time fierce critic and first woman Indian-American governor of a U.S. state (South Carolina), Nikki Haley. Her appointment as the U.S. ambassador to the United Nations makes her the first-ever Indian-American to serve at the Cabinet level in any U.S. administration and the first non-white female member of the Trump Cabinet.

The other five appointees are Uttam Dhillon, appointed special assistant to the president, where he will be part of the legal team led by White House Counsel Donald McGahn; Seema Verma (head of Medicaid and Medicare Services); Ajit Pai (head of the Federal Communications Commission); Preet Bharara (U.S. attorney for the Southern District of New York, with jurisdiction over Wall Street); and Raj Shah, who is part of the White House Communications team. During his campaign and afterward, Mr. Trump has lauded the 3.8 million-strong Indian diaspora in the United States for its talents and hard work.

At a charity reception hosted by the Republican Hindu Coalition, during his campaign Mr. Trump exulted: "I am a big fan of Hindu and a big fan of India; big, big fan, big, big fan. Let me start by saying right upfront that if I'm elected president, the Indian and Hindu community will have a true friend in the White House and I can guarantee you that." It appears to us that the new president is as good as his word. India is keen on moving swiftly to elevate its strategic partnership with the new U.S. administration, being one of the largest purchasers of American arms, and both countries also have agreed to expand their $100 billion worth of two-way trade five-fold in the near term.

There are challenges, however, given the nationalist and protectionist rhetoric driving his "America first" vision. While the president is restricting visas for citizens of seven Islamic countries in an understandable, if controversial, effort to keep terrorists from gaining access to the American homeland, what is more troubling is his apparent intent to tighten H-1B visas that he believes is facilitating the entry of foreign workers at the cost of deserving Americans. India is the world's largest provider of information technology (IT) services, and 67 percent of its $130 billion IT business is accounted for by the U.S., where some 350,000 Indian engineers work, on H-1B visas, with both Indian and American tech companies. Indian professionals whose visas are due for renewal are understandably concerned about the implications of all this. India's National Association of Software and Services Companies estimates that any rewriting of work visa rules to force cutbacks on outsourcing could cost Indian IT companies $400 million a year, along with large-scale job losses.

With no clearly defined foreign policy as yet from the Trump administration, India is waiting for firmer indications. It is evident that despite their mutual exuberance, both Mr. Modi and Mr. Trump will have a weighty agenda before them when they meet in Washington.

COULD DONALD BE INDIA'S TRUMP CARD? THE FUTURE OF INDIA-US RELATIONS

India-US bilateral relations have reached new heights in the past few years, and developed into a 'strategic partnership'. The regular dialogues between the two countries have enabled them to broaden their bilateral cooperation, and today it covers trade and investment, defence and security, education, science and technology, civil nuclear energy, clean energy, environment, agriculture and health. Further, an ambitious target of $500 billion worth of trade of goods and services has been set. This is a manifold increase from the current figure of around $100 billion.

Investment

The US is also the sixth largest source of FDI into India and increasing Indian investments in the US has been an interesting feature of bilateral ties, which reached a new height due to the close proximity between PM Narendra Modi and President Barack Obama. However, Donald Trump's win in the US presidential elections has raised many concerns about the ongoing bilateral advancement and its impact on the Indian economy. While Trump has been rated as the biggest source of global risk by The Economist, he has shown his admiration for India and its policies towards terrorism and nuclear energy.

Also, there is a clear bipartisan support in the US for a deeper Indo-American strategic as well as economic partnership. During the campaign, Trump has complained about bad trade deals, illegal immigration and terrorism without giving any concrete solutions for them. His manifesto of 'Making America Great Again' is based on the idea of de-globalisation which involves the US policies against free trade and easy immigration policy.

He also blames emerging-market counterparts as one of the beneficiaries from the bad trade deals and high unemployment rates in the US. Trump, in response to high unemployment, hopes to bring back lost manufacturing jobs by slashing tax rates and implementing strict trade policies that involves tariffs and non-tariff barriers.

While this has mostly been targeted against countries like China and Mexico, Trump has addressed India as 'a key strategic ally' and praised PM Modi for his stance to combat and fight terrorism. Trump has insisted on further strengthening the strategic and economic ties that is in the interest of both the countries.

However, the reality is that the two mega trade deals TTIP and TPP are almost irrelevant now given Trump's attitude towards trade. But from an Indian perspective, given the strong relations between the two countries, trade and investment flows should not be affected unless the US raises barriers to trade in goods and services and becomes protectionist with the objective of promoting jobs in its economy.

Trump's win will have significant impact on the India-US trade because of the protectionist policies he seems to favour. The sectors that will be mostly affected include IT services and pharmaceuticals. The IT services exports will undertake a hit where the outsourcing giants like TCS, Infosys, Wipro and other users of H-1B visas will be the most affected, although he has also acknowledged the significance of highly skilled Indian professionals for IT sector in the US.

Trump's strong views on immigration have managed to capture the imagination of American public. Specifically, the issue of H-1B visas is of extreme importance to the Indian IT services sector and any drastic move could affect Indian IT companies and employees. On the contrary, Trump has also said that he wants to attract Indian entrepreneurs and students.

Issue

While Trump has been inconsistent with his views over this issue, it would be interesting to see since Indians are the largest proportion acquiring H-1B visas. In case of stricter H-1 visa regime but lower tax regime under Trump, Indian companies have to open their subsidiaries in the US instead of sending professionals.

On the other hand, pharma sector could actually gain as Trump's proposal to relax import duties and entry restrictions for drug makers that provide cheaper, safe and reliable products, might work in favour of Indian drug makers provided there is no IPR issues. Also, Trump's criticism of China as 'currency manipulators' and bad trade agreements could see India emerge as a major player on the Asia front as far as the US trade policies are concerned.

Alternatively, with the US being a major and founding member of the WTO, Trump cannot be selective in his trade policy. The US would have to have a similar tariff rate for similar goods irrespective of its origins. Thus, a tariff on auto imports from Mexico or China would similarly harm Modi's 'Make in India' move.

Terrorism

Trump's strong stance on terrorism and comments on Pakistan could also turn into deeper understanding between India-US defence and strategic ties. Trump has sought the help of India and other nations to address the problem of a 'semi-unstable' nuclear Pakistan. Also, the Modi government may find one of its biggest allies in Trump who once called India's neighbour 'probably the most dangerous country in the world'.

This could improve the defence ties and strategic cooperation between the two countries while simultaneously boosting economic ties as well. With Trump rising to power, there is a huge scope for revitalising India-US relations and also in curbing cross-border terrorism.

India now conducts more military exercises with the US than any other country. However, there is still some scope for improvement in the bilateral relationship. Another outstanding issue is India's complicated custom tariffs, IPR regime and the uncertainty with regards to the FDI in the retail sector.

THREE CHALLENGES FOR U.S.-INDIA RELATIONS UNDER PRESIDENT TRUMP

President-elect Donald Trump has offered few concrete policy proposals about how he would approach South Asia. With an improbable victory sealed and inauguration less than two months away, his team of advisors will need to put together a vision for the region. Until then, Indian leaders, much like the rest of the world, will be held in suspense. Will Trump stay the course on the Obama administration's policies in the region? Or will he chart a new path?

A few of Trump's campaign statements about India and the region could offer a window into his approach. His foreign policy vision can also help us guess what a Trump administration might mean for India. Here are three critical questions going forward:

Can Trump Replicate the Obama-Modi Partnership?

President Barack Obama and Indian Prime Minister Narendra Modi shared a connection and invested tremendous amounts of time and political capital to improve the bilateral relationship. There is no reason that Trump and Modi can't find similar success. Trump has called Modi a "great man" and has repeatedly expressed an interest in working closely with India. He said that "there won't be any relationship more important to us" than the one with India. This could suggest that Trump might make an overture to Modi early in his time in office. To date, however, this has not happened, in spite of the president-elect's initial outreach to other world leaders.

Related

Modi will be glad that a Trump administration will likely pressure him less on India's domestic policies. Having praised Russian President Vladimir Putin for his "strong leadership" during the campaign, it would be unexpected for Trump to needle world leaders about human rights violations, religious intolerance, and media suppression to the extent that President Obama did, or as much as Hillary Clinton might have. Donald Trump may well prefer maintaining friendship over principle, which could work to Modi's liking. There could be bumps along the road, however.

If Trump pursues the kind of isolationist "America First" foreign policy he sometimes hinted at during the campaign, it would raise doubts in the minds of Indian leaders about whether the United States can be a reliable partner, especially in Asia. Some of Trump's views will directly undermine India's interests and the cooperation Modi secured with Obama. For instance, climate and energy cooperation were top priorities for Obama and Modi. What happens to that legacy if Trump backs away from those commitments and rejects the Paris agreement, as is expected? That would not be looked upon lightly by Modi, who, for the sake of his relationship with Obama, invested considerable political capital in a more forward-thinking stance on climate change and clean energy.

Will U.S.-India Economic Relations Suffer?

Trump criticized Asian economies like China, Japan, and Korea for cheating the U.S. through currency manipulation or bad trade practices. India was one of the few countries that escaped his wrath. However, India will not escape the negative impacts of the trade policies Trump proposed during the campaign. In 2015, India had a positive goods trade balance of $23 billion with the United States. That number will diminish if the U.S. erects trade walls. Just as India is set to benefit from greater integration with the global economy, Trump's actions could depress already sluggish global trade and growth. After growing at a steady pace from 2000 to 2013, bilateral trade has been stagnant in recent years. That might continue under President Trump.

India could also face a confrontation with the U.S. if Trump seeks to reduce temporary work visas. Trump criticized the U.S. H-1B non-immigrant specialty worker visa program during the campaign, saying it "decimate[s]" American jobs. The Indian government has long sought more H-1B visas for its citizens, who are already the greatest recipients of them. If President Trump keeps his promise to reduce H1-Bs, India would likely see fewer of its citizens coming to work in the United States, putting its IT companies under greater pressure.

Such a dispute would certainly also complicate economic cooperation in other areas. And it could generate animosity toward the administration among Indian-Americans — an increasingly important domestic constituency.

Could South Asia Destabilize Further?

Trump has made some controversial statements about India-Pakistan relations, which if translated into policy could be very damaging to U.S.-India ties.

Last month, stating that he would be open to being a "mediator or arbitrator" between India and Pakistan on Kashmir, Trump contradicted U.S. policy and suggested something that is anathema to India, which rejects international interference on the Kashmir issue. On the other hand, earlier in the campaign, Trump's comments criticizing Pakistan over its support of terrorism delighted many Indians.

Trump also described India as a means of keeping Pakistan in check. When asked about how he would handle a crisis in Pakistan, he said, "You have to get India involved. ... They seem to be the real check. ... I think we have to deal very closely with India to deal with [Pakistan]." Such comments earned Trump praise from Indians who have long soured on U.S. support of their neighbor. If Trump does present Pakistan with an ultimatum, it would either have to change its tack or the U.S. would have to pull aid from the country, which would leave the United States with very little leverage.

Related

Asia Society's India Center in Mumbai cultivates nuanced understanding of Asia Pacific affairs through its diverse and multidisciplinary programming initiatives including public lectures, business discussions, policy roundtables, guided art tours, performances, lecture demonstrations, and leadership programs. Learn more

Giving India a freer hand could create its own problems. Historically, the United States has intervened diplomatically during crises between India and Pakistan. For instance, asking India to exercise restraint after a terrorist attack emanating from Pakistan has become a tired U.S. talking point. If the U.S. does not pressure India and lets it "deal with Pakistan," as Trump suggested, tensions could escalate beyond any point we've seen since the two countries attained nuclear weapons — a very dangerous development for U.S. interests in the region. This is especially true after Modi's decision to counter the most recent terrorist attack on Indian soil with surgical strikes in Pakistan that India publicly acknowledged. India's action deviated from a long standing pattern of choosing not to retaliate militarily across the "line-of-control" or keeping mum if it does so. An escalation between the two nuclear rivals could become far more likely given Mr. Modi's more muscular stance toward Pakistan. This would pose serious challenges to the ability of the U.S. to manage a crisis in South Asia.

Finally, Trump's policies on Afghanistan could have a major impact on regional stability. He has repeatedly said that the United States is involved in wars it has no business in and that he is against "nation building." Though he has not presented a clear vision on Afghanistan, his election creates uncertainty about whether the U.S. will continue its support of the Afghan unity government, which is struggling politically and economically, and is increasingly under attack from the Taliban.

If Trump scales back American military and economic support for Afghanistan's government, the country is likely to descend further into chaos. India, which has consistently urged the United States to maintain its presence in Afghanistan, would be loath to see this happen. Ultimately, even if Trump and Modi are able to craft a friendly working relationship, Trump's policies as president will determine whether he will be good for India and U.S.-India relations. The U.S.-India bilateral relationship had been on a solid trajectory since the turn of the century. The Trump administration will certainly attempt to build on that progress. Whether it will succeed remains an open question.

IT COMPANIES HOPE FOR BEST FROM DONALD TRUMP REGIME

The Indian IT industry on Wednesday leaned on US President-elect Donald Trump's business credentials to hope he would not push through with his pre-election anti-outsourcing rhetoric, given the key role the sector plays in keeping American economy competitive. The captains of the industry felt that Trump's victory is unlikely to affect the fortunes of the USD 110 billion Indian technology sector as the US faces crunch of highly-skilled workers and for the fact that the Republican himself is a businessman and will be "pro-business". "We are optimistic that President-elect Trump's administration will focus on making the strategic relationship with India a high priority, including providing a boost to US- India bilateral trade and investment," Nasscom said. Trump, who during his high-decibel campaign had advocated tightening of visa norms for skilled workers and bringing jobs back to America, today beat rival Hillary Clinton in the race to be the US President.

Many had feared that Trump's coming to power could lead to job losses for Indians and a protectionist approach by the US, a market that accounts for about 70 per cent of Indian IT industry's revenue. However, Nasscom claimed that many of Trump's observations during the campaign concerning high-skilled immigration and outsourcing were based on "fabrications put out by critics" of the sector.

BPO industry stalwart Raman Roy said the sector is integral part of the economic growth story of the US. "I have no hesitation in saying there will be no issues. He (Trump) cannot produce a million people overnight to do the job. He cannot say we will shut off the switch... there is commerce that is going to happen... card queries, insurance and mortgage queries that have to be answered that are being done from here (India)," Roy added.

Industry veteran and former HR head of Infosys TV Mohandas Pai feels that it is still early days. He added that India's prowess is well-established in technology and the country plays a crucial role for US enterprises.

Genpact founder Pramod Bhasin said that while he was "stunned" by the election outcome, he did not expect any negative ramification for the Indian technology players as Trump being a businessman "will always be pro-business".

Given the softer conciliatory tone adopted by Trump towards the end of his election campaign, the industry said it is keen to work with the new administration to highlight the sector's contributions to the US economy and ensure the US leaders understand the depth of investments made by Indian firms. "Our sector plays a key role in helping US businesses innovate and grow and make corporate America more competitive," Nasscom said.

INDIA-US RELATIONS

The foreign policy of the United States is the way in which it interacts with foreign nations and sets standards of interaction for its organizations, corporations and individual citizens. The U.S. is highly influential in the world. The global reach of the United States is backed by a $15 trillion economy, approximately a quarter of global GDP, and a defence budget of $711 billion, which accounts for approximately 43% of global military spending. The U.S. Secretary of State is analogous to the foreign minister of other nations and is the official charged with state-to-state diplomacy, although the president has ultimate authority over foreign policy; that policy includes defining the national interest, as well as the strategies chosen both to safeguard that and to achieve its policy goals. The current Secretary of State is Hillary Clinton.

The officially stated goals of the foreign policy of the United States, as mentioned in the Foreign Policy Agenda of the U.S. Department of State, are "to create a more secure, democratic, and prosperous world for the benefit of the American people and the international community." In addition, the United States House Committee on Foreign Affairs states as some of its jurisdictional goals: "export controls, including nonproliferation of nuclear technology and nuclear hardware; measures to foster commercial intercourse with foreign nations and to safeguard American business abroad; international commodity agreements; international education; and protection of American citizens abroad and expatriation." U.S. foreign policy and foreign aid have been the subject of much debate, praise and criticism both domestically and abroad.

When asked if the WikiLeaks of 2010 would damage American relations with other countries, Secretary of Defence Robert Gates noted that "governments deal with the United States because it's in their interest, not because they like us, not because they trust us, and not because they believe we can keep secrets."

Long considered a "strategic backwater" from Washington's perspective, South Asia has emerged in the 21st century as increasingly vital to core U.S. foreign policy interests. India, the region's dominant actor with more than one billion citizens, is often characterized as a nascent major power and "natural partner" of the United States, one that many analysts view as a potential counterweight to China's growing clout.

Washington and New Delhi have since 2004 been pursuing a "strategic partnership" based on shared values such as democracy, pluralism, and rule of law. Numerous economic, security, and global initiatives, including plans for "full civilian nuclear energy cooperation," are underway. This latter initiative, launched by President Bush in July 2005 and provisionally endorsed by the 109th Congress in 2006 (P.L. 109-401, the "Hyde Act"), would reverse three decades of U.S. nonproliferation policy. It requires, among other steps, a Joint Resolution of Approval by Congress. Also in 2005, the United States and

India signed a ten-year defence framework agreement that calls for expanding bilateral security cooperation. Since 2002, the two countries have engaged in numerous and unprecedented combined military exercises. Major U.S. arms sales to India are planned. The influence of a growing and relatively wealthy Indian-American community of more than two million is reflected in Congress's largest countryspecific caucus.

Both leading U.S. presidential candidates express full-throated support for a deepened and expanded U.S.-India partnership. Senator Barak Obama would like to see U.S.-India ties strengthened "across the board," with a particular focus on energy issues. Senator John McCain claims the

United States has a "vested interest in India's success" and he calls for improved military and counterterrorism cooperation, along with mutual efforts to strengthen democracy and energy security. Both Senators are explicit supporters of U.S.-India civil nuclear cooperation as proposed by the Bush Administration.

Cold War Era

India played a key role in establishing the Non-Aligned Movement in 1961. Though India pursued close relations with both USA and USSR, it decided not to join any major power bloc and refrained from joining military alliances. India, however began establishing close military relationship with the Soviet Union.

After the Sino-Indian War and the Indo-Pakistani War of 1965, India made considerable changes to its foreign policy. It developed a close relationship with the Soviet Union and started receiving massive military equipment and financial assistance from the USSR. This had an adverse effect on the Indo-USA relationship. The United States saw Pakistan as a counter-weight to pro-Soviet India and started giving the former military assistance. This created an atmosphere of suspicion between India and USA. The USA-India relationship suffered a considerable setback during the Soviet invasion of Afghanistan when India openly supported the Soviet Union.

Relations between India and the United States came to an all-time low during the early 1970s. Despite reports of atrocities in East Pakistan, and being told, most notably in the *Blood telegram*, of genocidal activities being perpetrated by Pakistani forces, U.S. Secretary of State Henry Kissinger and U.S. President Richard Nixon did nothing to discourage then Pakistani President Yahya Khan and the Pakistan Army. Kissinger was particularly concerned about Soviet expansion into South Asia as a result of a treaty of friendship that had recently been signed between India and the Soviet Union, and sought to demonstrate to the People's Republic of China the value of a tacit alliance with the United States. During the Indo-Pakistani War of 1971, Indian Armed Forces, along with the Mukti Bahini, succeeded in liberating East Pakistan which soon declared independence. Richard Nixon, then USA President, feared that an Indian invasion of West Pakistan would mean total Soviet domination of the region, and that it would seriously undermine the global position of the United States and the regional position of America's new tacit ally, China. In order to demonstrate to China the *bona fides* of the United States as an ally, and in direct violation of the USA Congress-imposed sanctions on Pakistan, Nixon sent military supplies to Pakistan, routing them through Jordan and Iran, while also encouraging China to increase its arms supplies to Pakistan.

When Pakistan's defeat in the eastern sector seemed certain, Nixon sent the USS *Enterprise* to the Bay of Bengal, a move deemed by the Indians as a nuclear threat. The *Enterprise* arrived on station on December 11, 1971. On 6 December and 13 December, the Soviet Navy dispatched two groups of ships, armed with nuclear missiles, from Vladivostok; they trailed U.S. Task Force 74 into the Indian Ocean from 18 December 1971 until 7 January 1972. The Soviets also sent a nuclear submarine to ward off the threat posed by USS *Enterprise* in the Indian Ocean.

Though American efforts had no effect in turning the tide of the war, the incident involving USS *Enterprise* is viewed as the trigger for India's subsequent nuclear program. American policy towards the end of the war was dictated primarily by a need to restrict the escalation of war on the western sector to prevent the 'dismemberment' of West Pakistan. Years after the war, many American writers criticized the White House policies during the war as being badly flawed and ill-serving the interests of the United States. India carried out nuclear tests a few years later resulting in sanctions being imposed by United States, further drifting the two countries apart. In recent years, Kissinger came under fire for comments made during the Indo-Pakistan War in which he described Indians as "bastards." Kissinger has since expressed his regret over the comments.

Until 1971 nonalignment had a dual effect on United States policies in South Asia. On the one hand, Washington considered Indian economic and political stability necessary to prevent that important regional player from succumbing to communism and Soviet influence; hence the United States gave economic assistance and support to India during its 1962 war with China. On the other hand, India's nonalignment had led the United States in 1954 to ally itself with Pakistan, which appeared to support Western security interests. The United States-Pakistan alliance was renewed in 1959, with accompanying assurances from President Dwight D. Eisenhower to Nehru that the arms supplied to Pakistan would not be used in any aggressive war. When Pakistan and India went to war in 1965, the United States government refused to support India and suspended military transfers to both countries.

In 1971 the intertwining of the United States-Soviet, Chinese-Soviet, and Indian-Pakistani conflicts dragged India-United States relations to the nadir. That year, while Washington initiated a new relationship with Beijing, New Delhi signed a friendship treaty with Moscow to counteract United States and Chinese influence in South Asia. As the situation in East Pakistan deteriorated, India was unable to convince the United States to cease arms deliveries to Pakistan and persuade Pakistan's leaders to reach a political settlement with East Pakistan's elected representatives. Indira Gandhi's November 1971 visit to Washington failed to alter President Richard M. Nixon's pro-Pakistan stance. When war formally began after Pakistani strikes on Indian airfields in early December 1971, the United States and China voted for a cease-fire in the UN Security Council, but the Soviet Union's veto prevented any resolution from coming into effect. Washington's subsequent deployment of a naval task force to the Bay of Bengal left many in India convinced that the United States was a major security threat.

Relations between India and the United States verged on the antagonistic throughout the 1970s. After Nixon abruptly terminated US$82 million in economic assistance, India closed down a large United States Agency for International Development program. The Indian government also restricted the flow of American scholars and students to India. India's criticisms of United States policies in Vietnam and Cambodia increased, and it upgraded its representation in Hanoi. When the United States expanded its naval base on the island of Diego Garcia and engaged in naval exercises with Pakistan in the Indian Ocean in 1974, India saw its security further threatened. Both governments, however, attempted to limit the damage to bilateral relations. A 1973 agreement defused a dispute over United States rupee holdings by writing off more than 50 percent of the debt and directing use of the remainder to mutually acceptable programs. In 1974 the Indo-United States Joint Commission was established to insulate bilateral dealings in education and culture, economics, and science and technology from political controversy and to provide mechanisms for regular exchanges at high levels of public life.

Hopes for improved relations were expressed in 1977 when Jimmy Carter became president of the United States and the Janata Party government led by Morarji Desai took over in India. These expectations came to an abrupt end two years later when the Soviet Union invaded Afghanistan. The promulgation of the Carter Doctrine, establishment of the Rapid Deployment Force (later called the United States Central

Command) and an Indian Ocean fleet, planned expansion of the naval base at Diego Garcia, and arrangements to supply Pakistan with US$3.2 billion in military and economic aid over five years all appeared as direct United States intervention in the countries of the Persian Gulf and Indian Ocean. These actions fueled instability in the region and, in India's view, threatened India's security.

The personal rapport between Indira Gandhi and United States president Ronald Reagan, established during a series of meetings in the early 1980s, enabled the two countries gradually to begin improving bilateral relations. The Reagan administration reassessed its policy toward India and decided to expand areas of cooperation, particularly in the economic and scientific realms, as a means of counteracting Soviet influence in the region. Washington also regarded New Delhi's status as the major regional power in South Asia in a more favourable light. For her part, Gandhi realized that India was unable to block United States arms sales to Pakistan, but that improved dialogue with the United States could open other areas of interaction that could benefit Indian interests. Indira Gandhi's highly successful 1982 state visit to the United States was followed by a series of high-level exchanges, including the visits of Vice President George Bush and Secretary of State George Shultz to India. In addition, in 1982 the two sides resolved their dispute concerning supplies of fuel and spare parts for the nuclear power plant at Tarapur. In 1984 the United States decided to expand technology transfers to India.

The warming trend in relations between New Delhi and Washington continued with the 1985 and 1987 visits by Prime Minister Rajiv Gandhi to Washington. Furthermore, as the United States appreciation of India's role as a force for stability in South Asia grew, Washington supported New Delhi's moves in Sri Lanka in 1987 and in Maldives in 1988. In the mid-and late 1980s, visits exchanged by the United States secretary of defence and the Indian minister of defence symbolized a modest but growing program of cooperation in military technology and other defence matters. In 1988 Washington and New Delhi finalized an accord to provide United States technology for India's light combat aircraft program and also agreed to transfer technology for the F-5 fighter. Cooperation between India and the United States in a variety of scientific fields followed the signing of a bilateral agreement on scientific and technological exchanges in 1985. Nonmilitary technology transfers also accelerated, and in 1987 India purchased a Cray supercomputer for agricultural research and weather forecasting and accepted stringent United States safeguards to preclude military uses. Furthermore, economic liberalization measures paved the way for increased trade and United States investment in India. In 1988 the improved economic climate resulted in the conclusion of a deal for a Pepsi-Cola plant and the signing of a bilateral tax treaty. In 1989 United States investment in India reached US$1 billion.

In the 1980s, the Indian and United States governments had divergent views on a wide range of international issues, including Afghanistan, Cambodia, the Middle East, and Central America. Serious differences also remained over United States policy toward Pakistan and the issue of nuclear proliferation. India was repeatedly incensed in the 1980s when the United States provided advanced military technology and other assistance to Pakistan. New Delhi also found objectionable Washington's unwillingness to cut off military assistance to Islamabad despite United States concerns about Pakistan's covert nuclear program.

For its part, Washington continued to urge New Delhi to sign the Treaty on the Non-Proliferation of Nuclear Weapons and, after the successful test launch of the Indian Agni intermediate-range ballistic missile in May 1989, called on New Delhi to refrain from developing a ballistic missile capability by adhering to the restrictions of the Missile Technology Control Regime. India rejected these appeals on the grounds that it had a right to develop such technology and that the Treaty on the Non-Proliferation of Nuclear Weapons and the United States-sponsored Missile Technology Control Regime discriminated against nonnuclear states.

Bureaucratic and private-sector resistance to foreign participation in the economy, infrastructure problems, bureaucratic red tape, and legal problems remained formidable obstacles to significant Indian-United States economic cooperation. In the late 1980s, India had differences with the United States over improving its legal protection of intellectual property rights, opening its markets to American service industries, and liberalizing its foreign investment regulations. In April 1991, the Office of the United States Trade Representative placed India on Washington's watch list over intellectual property rights issues. Six months later, the United States gave India a three-month grace period before imposing retaliatory sanctions against India's pharmaceutical industry for inadequate patent protection. India resisted United States pressure to adopt a less protectionist stance in the Uruguay Round of negotiations to renew the General Agreement on Tariffs and Trade (GATT).

In the early 1990s, economic reforms permitted a qualitative breakthrough in relations between India and the United States. Washington was instrumental in speeding a US$1.8 billion IMF credit that New Delhi obtained in January 1991 to deal with a severe external-debt-payments crisis. In 1990 India and the United States signed a double taxation pact designed to facilitate American investment in India, further breaking a thirty-year deadlock in economic relations. The United States provided only modest bilateral economic assistance in the form of food aid but was India's largest trading partner and an important source of investments and technology. In December 1990, the United States approved the export of a second Cray supercomputer for the Indian Institute of Science in Bangalore, Karnataka, although the deal fell through two years later because of India's unwillingness to accept safeguards to prevent the computer's diversion to military uses.

The Soviet withdrawal from Afghanistan in 1989 had led Washington to reassess its relationship with Pakistan, with positive ramifications for New Delhi. Without containment of the Soviet Union as the driving factor behind close Pakistani-

United States ties, and concerns mounting about Pakistan's nuclear weapons program, the United States suspended military and economic assistance to that country in October 1990. New Delhi appreciated this action and was relieved in summer 1991 when the United States Congress voted not to include India in the Pressler Amendment, which forbade United States assistance to Pakistan if it violated nuclear nonproliferation criteria. Washington also took a more evenhanded approach to the Kashmir problem in 1990, urging both antagonists to resolve their dispute peacefully under the terms of the Simla Accord. Furthermore, the United States began pressuring Pakistan to end its support for Kashmiri and Punjabi Sikh separatists. This pressure was in addition to efforts initiated in the 1980s to prevent assistance to Sikh terrorists from the Sikh expatriate community in the United States. In the wake of terrorist bombings in Bombay in March 1993—widely believed in India to have been instigated by Pakistanis—and stepped-up activities among Kashmiri militants, Indian politicians and the media reveled in the possibility that the United States might declare Pakistan a practitioner of state-sponsored terrorism. Washington's decision in July 1993 not to declare Pakistan a terrorist-supporting state displeased many prominent Indians, and Indian political analysts accused the United States of having a "double standard" in regard to specific states sponsoring terrorism.

Military cooperation also grew. Exchanges of senior military officials became frequent, a high-level bilateral conference on regional security affairs was held, and Minister of Defence Sharad Pawar journeyed to Washington in April 1992 to discuss arms supplies and military technology. Not only did United States navy ships make occasional ports calls in India, but the two navies conducted their first-ever joint exercise in May 1992. Indian officials came to have a greater appreciation of United States interests in maintaining a military presence on Diego Garcia and in the Persian Gulf.

In 1993, India and the United States appeared committed to improve relations and bilateral cooperation despite differences over India's refusal to sign the Treaty on the Non-Proliferation of Nuclear Weapons and to participate in discussions with the United States, Russia, China, and Pakistan on establishing a South Asian nuclear-free zone.

Nevertheless, Washington directed its efforts to creating a climate of restraint between New Delhi and Islamabad in order to freeze or roll back their nuclear weapons programs. However, India and the United States remained wary of each other's long-term strategy regionally and globally. Some Indian political analysts criticize the United States for following a "two-track policy." On the one hand, Washington has supported New Delhi's economic reform and has facilitated international loans to India, but, on the other, it has relentlessly pursued an agenda to force India's accession to United States nonproliferation goals and has used human rights issues to try to force India to meet Washington's political objections.

Moreover, many Indians have expressed worries that, with the emergence of the United States as the sole superpower, and as the leader of a Western-dominated coalition after the Persian Gulf War, Washington might attempt to impose its own standards for democratic values, human rights, and free markets. India fears that a United States vision of a new world order not only would hurt the interests of Third World countries economically and politically, but also would damage India's drive to become a leading power in a multipolar system. Washington's decision not to place Pakistan on its list of nations that sponsor terrorism and its successful efforts in getting Russia to cancel the sale of cryogenic engines to India are seen as detrimental to good Indian-United States relations.

In the midst of increasing anti-United States political rhetoric and newspaper headlines, Indian and United States officials have seemed to agree on only one thing, that bilateral relations had reached their lowest point in two decades. Observers in both countries believe that the administration of President William Clinton places a low priority on relations with India despite the fact that the United States has become India's prime trade partner. Against this backdrop, Prime

Minister Rao visited the United States in May 1994 for an uneventful round of talks with President Clinton, who encouraged India's economic reforms. Six memorandums of understanding were signed with the intent of expanding official contacts, reviewing and updating a 1984 understanding on high-technology transfer, enhancing defence cooperation, stimulating bilateral ties, and establishing a business partnership initiative.

High-level visits to India in early 1995 portended greater stability in India-United States relations. Secretary of Defence William J. Perry visited New Delhi in January to sign a "landmark agreement" on military cooperation that was seen by some local observers as a convergence in India-United States security perceptions after nearly fifty years of divergent viewpoints. Following the Perry visit was a commercial mission led by Secretary of Commerce Ronald H. Brown that also occurred in January. Agreements signed by Indian and United States businesses during the visit resulted in US$7 billion in contracts and investments in the communications, health care, insurance, finance, and automotive sectors. Some of the deals consummated were intended to build the infrastructure needed by foreign firms to do business in India. In March 1995, Hilary Rodham Clinton, the wife of the United States president, toured India as part of an extensive South Asian goodwill tour. In April, Secretary of the Treasury Robert E. Rubin visited New Delhi to sign a bilateral investment protection treaty reflecting the substantial increases in United States investment in India since 1991 and Washington's encouragement to India to apply for Agency for International Development loans.

POWERS OF THE PRESIDENT AND CONGRESS

Subject to the advise and consent role of the U.S. Senate, the President of the United States negotiates treaties with foreign nations, but treaties enter into force only if ratified by two-thirds of the Senate. The President is also Commander in Chief of the United States Armed Forces, and as such has broad authority over the armed forces; however only Congress has authority to declare war, and the civilian and military budget is written by the Congress. The United States Secretary of State is the foreign minister of the United States and is the primary conductor of state-to-state diplomacy. Both the Secretary of State and ambassadors are appointed by the President, with the advice and consent of the Senate. Congress also has power to regulate commerce with foreign nations.

Historical overview

The main trend regarding the history of U.S. foreign policy since the American Revolution is the shift from non-interventionism before and after World War I, to its growth as a world power and global hegemon during and since World War II and the end of the Cold War in the 20th century. Since the 19th century, US foreign policy also has been characterized by a shift from the realist school to the idealistic or Wilsonian school of international relations.

Foreign policy themes were expressed considerably in George Washington's farewell address; these included among other things, observing good faith and justice towards all nations and cultivating peace and harmony with all, excluding both "inveterate antipathies against particular nations, and passionate attachments for others", "steer[ing] clear of permanent alliances with any portion of the foreign world", and advocating trade with all nations. These policies became the basis of the Federalist Party in the 1790s. But the rival Jeffersonians feared Britain and favored France in the 1790s, declaring the War of 1812 on Britain. After the 1778 alliance with France, the U.S. did not sign another permanent treaty until the North Atlantic Treaty in 1949. Over time, other themes, key goals, attitudes, or stances have been variously expressed by Presidential 'doctrines', named for them. Initially these were uncommon events, but since WWII, these have been made by most presidents.

Despite occasional entanglements with European Powers such as the War of 1812 and the 1898 Spanish-American War, U.S. foreign policy was marked by steady expansion of its foreign trade and scope during the 19th century, and it maintained its policy of avoiding wars with and between European powers. Concerning its domestic borders, the 1803 Louisiana Purchase doubled the nation's geographical area; Spain ceded the territory of Florida in 1819; annexation brought Texas in 1845; a war with Mexico in 1848 added California, Arizona and New Mexico. The U.S. bought Alaska from the Russian Empire in 1867, and it annexed the Republic of Hawaii in 1898. Victory over Spain in 1898 brought the Philippines, and Puerto Rico, as well as oversight of Cuba. The short experiment in imperialism ended by 1908, as the U.S. turned its attention to the Panama Canal and the stabilization of regions to its south, including Mexico.

The 20th century was marked by two world wars in which the United States, along with allied powers, defeated its enemies and increased its international reputation. President Wilson's Fourteen Points, developed from his idealistic Wilsonianism program of spreading democracy and fighting militarism so as to end wars. It became the basis of the German Armistice (really a surrender) and the 1919 Paris Peace Conference. The resulting Treaty of Versailles, due to European allies' punitive and territorial designs, showed insufficient conformity with these points and the U.S. signed separate treaties with each of its adversaries; due to Senate objections also, the U.S. never joined the League of Nations, which was established as a result of Wilson's initiative. In the 1920s, the United States followed an independent course, and succeeded in a program of naval disarmament, and refunding the German economy. New York became the financial capital of the world, but the downside was that the Crash of 1929 hurled the entire world into the Great Depression. American trade policy relied on high tariffs under the Republicans, and reciprocal trade agreements under the Democrats, but in any case exports were at very low levels in the 1930s.

The United States adopted a non-interventionist foreign policy from 1932 to 1938, but then President Franklin D. Roosevelt moved toward strong support of the Allies in their wars against Germany and Japan. As a result of intense internal debate, the national policy was one of becoming the Arsenal of Democracy, that is financing and equipping the Allied armies without sending American combat soldiers. Roosevelt mentioned four fundamental freedoms, which ought to be enjoyed by people "everywhere in the world"; these included the freedom of speech and religion, as well as freedom from want and fear. Roosevelt helped establish terms for a post-war world among potential allies at the Atlantic Conference; specific points were included to correct earlier failures, which became a step toward the United Nations. American policy was to threaten Japan, to force it out of China, and to prevent its attacking the Soviet Union. However, Japan reacted by an attack on Pearl Harbor in December 1941, and the United States was at war with Japan, Germany, and Italy. Instead of the loans given to allies in World War I, the United States provided Lend-Lease grants of $50,000,000,000. Working closely with Winston Churchill of Britain, and Joseph Stalin of the Soviet Union, Roosevelt sent his forces into the Pacific against Japan, then into North Africa against Italy and Germany, and finally into Europe starting with France and Italy in 1944 against the Germans. The American economy roared forward, doubling industrial production, and building vast quantities of airplanes, ships, tanks, munitions, and, finally, the atomic bomb. Much of the American war effort went to strategic bombers, which flattened the cities of Japan and Germany.

After the war, the U.S. rose to become the dominant non-colonial economic power with broad influence in much of the world, with the key policies of the Marshall Plan and the Truman Doctrine. Almost immediately however, the world witnessed division into broad two camps during the Cold War; one side was led by the U.S., and the other by the Soviet Union, but this situation also led to the establishment of the Non-Aligned Movement. This period lasted until almost the end of the 20th century, and is thought to be both an ideological and power struggle between the two superpowers. A policy of containment was adopted to limit Soviet expansion, and a series of proxy wars were fought with mixed results. In 1991, the Soviet Union dissolved into separate nations, and the Cold War formally ended as the United States gave separate diplomatic recognition to the Russian Federation and other former Soviet states. With these changes to forty-five years of established diplomacy and military confrontation, new challenges confronted U.S. policymakers. U.S. foreign policy is characterized still by a commitment to free trade, protection of its national interests, and a concern for human rights.

In the 21st century, U.S. influence remains strong but, in relative terms, is declining in terms of economic output compared to rising nations such as China, India, Russia, Brazil, and the newly consolidated European Union. Substantial problems remain, such as climate change, nuclear proliferation, and the specter of nuclear terrorism. Foreign policy analysts Hachigian and Sutphen in their book *The Next American Century* suggest all six powers have similar vested interests in stability and terrorism prevention and trade; if they can find common ground, then the next decades may be marked by peaceful growth and prosperity.

EXPORTING DEMOCRACY

In United States history, critics have charged that presidents have used democracy to justify military intervention abroad. Critics have also charged that the U.S. overthrew democratically elected governments in Iran, Guatemala, and in other instances. Studies have been devoted to the historical success rate of the U.S. in exporting democracy abroad. Some studies of American intervention have been pessimistic about the overall effectiveness of U.S. efforts to encourage democracy in foreign nations.

Until recently, scholars have generally agreed with international relations professor Abraham Lowenthal that U.S. attempts to export democracy have been "negligible, often counterproductive, and only occasionally positive." Other studies find U.S. intervention has had mixed results, and another by

Hermann and Kegley has found that military interventions have improved democracy in other countries.

Opinion that U.S. intervention does not export democracy

Professor Paul W. Drake argued that the U.S. first attempted to export democracy in Latin America through intervention from 1912 to 1932. Drake argued that this was contradictory because international law defines intervention as "dictatorial interference in the affairs of another state for the purpose of altering the condition of things." The study suggested that efforts to promote democracy failed because democracy needs to develop out of internal conditions, and can not be forcibly imposed. There was disagreement about what constituted *democracy*; Drake suggested American leaders sometimes defined democracy in a narrow sense of a nation having elections; Drake suggested a broader understanding was needed. Further, there was disagreement about what constituted a "rebellion"; Drake saw a pattern in which the U.S. State Department disapproved of any type of rebellion, even so-called "revolutions", and in some instances rebellions against dictatorships. Historian Walter LaFeber stated, "The world's leading revolutionary nation (the U.S.) in the eighteenth century became the leading protector of the status quo in the twentieth century."

Mesquita and Downs evaluated 35 U.S. interventions from 1945 to 2004 and concluded that in only one case, Colombia, did a "full fledged, stable democracy" develop within ten years following the intervention. Samia Amin Pei argued that nation building in developed countries usually unravelled four to six years after American intervention ended. Pei, based on study of a database on worldwide democracies called *Polity*, agreed with Mesquita and Downs that U.S. intervention efforts usually don't produce real democracies, and that most cases result in greater authoritarianism after ten years.

Professor Joshua Muravchik argued U.S. occupation was critical for Axis power democratization after World War II, but America's failure to encourage democracy in the third world "prove... that U.S. military occupation is not a sufficient condition to make a country democratic."

The success of democracy in former Axis countries such as Italy were seen as a result of high national per-capita income, although U.S. protection was seen as a key to stabilization and important for encouraging the transition to democracy. Steven Krasner agreed that there was a link between wealth and democracy; when per-capita incomes of $6,000 were achieved in a democracy, there was little chance of that country ever reverting to an autocracy, according to an analysis of his research in the *Los Angeles Times*.

Opinion that U.S. intervention has mixed results

Tures examined 228 cases of American intervention from 1973 to 2005, using Freedom House data. A plurality of interventions, 96, caused no change in the country's democracy. In 69 instances the country became less democratic after the intervention. In the remaining 63 cases, a country became more democratic.

Opinion that U.S. intervention effectively exports democracy

Hermann and Kegley found that American military interventions designed to protect or promote democracy increased freedom in those countries. Penceny argued that the democracies created after military intervention are still closer to an autocracy than a democracy, quoting Przeworski "while some democracies are more democratic than others, unless offices are contested, no regime should be considered democratic." Therefore, Penceny concludes, it is difficult to know from the Hermann and Kegley study whether U.S. intervention has only produced less repressive autocratic governments or genuine democracies.

Penceny stated that the United States attempted to export democracy in 33 of its 93 20th-century military interventions. Penceny argued that proliberal policies after military intervention had a positive impact on democracy.

Covert actions

United States foreign policy also includes covert actions to topple foreign governments that have been opposed to the United States. In 1953 the CIA, working with the British government, endorsed the military in a coup d'état against the anti-British government of Iran led by Prime Minister Mohammad Mossadegh who had attempted to nationalize Iran's oil, threatening the interests of the Anglo-Iranian Oil Company.

Human Rights

The inclusion of Human Rights in U.S. Foreign Policy had a controversial start. For one thing, human rights driven foreign policy did not originate in the Executive branch but was instead enforced upon it by Congress, starting in the 1970s. Following the Vietnam War, the feeling that US Foreign Policy had grown apart from traditional American values was seized upon by Senator Donald M. Fraser (D, MI), leading the Subcommittee on International Organizations and Movements, in criticizing Republican Foreign Policy under the Nixon administration. In the early 1970s, Congress concluded the Vietnam War and passed the War Powers Act. As "part of a growing assertiveness by Congress about many aspects of Foreign Policy," Human Rights concerns became a battleground between the Legislative and the Executive branches in the formulation of foreign policy. David Forsythe points to three specific, early examples of Congress interjecting its own thoughts on foreign policy:

1. Subsection (a) of the International Financial Assistance Act of 1977: ensured assistance through international financial institutions would be limited to countries "other than those whose governments engage in a consistent pattern of gross violations of internationally recognized human rights."
2. Section 116 of the Foreign Assistance Act of 1961, as amended in 1984: reads in part, "o assistance may be provided under this part to the government of any country which engages in a consistent pattern of gross violations of internationally recognized human rights."

3. Section 502B of the Foreign Assistance Act of 1961, as amended in 1978: "No security assistance may be provided to any country the government of which engages in a consistent pattern of gross violations of internationally recognized human rights."

These measures were repeatedly used by Congress, with varying success, to affect US Foreign Policy towards the inclusion of Human Rights concerns. Specific examples include El Salvador, Nicaragua, Guatemala and South Africa. The Executive (from Nixon to Reagan) argued that the Cold War required placing regional security in favour of US interests over any behavioral concerns of national allies. Congress argued the opposite, in favour of distancing the United States from oppressive regimes.

Despite the many advances in US Foreign Policy towards the inclusion of human rights, the substance remains strictly limited to its bilateral relations and only when politically relevant and/or feasible. The end of the Cold War resulted in a dramatic shift towards protecting human rights that lead to the development peacekeeping and peacemaking operations. And while the recent intervention in Libya may show how far the United States has come, the situation in Syria may shows how much ground is left.

War on Drugs

United States foreign policy is influenced by the efforts of the U.S. government to control imports of illicit drugs, including cocaine, heroin, methamphetamine, and cannabis. This is especially true in Latin America, a focus for the U.S. War on Drugs. Those efforts date back to at least 1880, when the U.S. and China completed an agreement that prohibited the shipment of opium between the two countries.

Over a century later, the Foreign Relations Authorization Act requires the President to identify the major drug transit or major illicit drug-producing countries. In September 2005 , the following countries were identified: Bahamas, Bolivia, Brazil, Burma, Colombia, Dominican Republic, Ecuador, Guatemala,

Haiti, India, Jamaica, Laos, Mexico, Nigeria, Pakistan, Panama, Paraguay, Peru and Venezuela.

Two of these, Burma and Venezuela are countries that the U.S. considers to have failed to adhere to their obligations under international counternarcotics agreements during the previous 12 months. Notably absent from the 2005 list were Afghanistan, the People's Republic of China and Vietnam; Canada was also omitted in spite of evidence that criminal groups there are increasingly involved in the production of MDMA destined for the United States and that large-scale cross-border trafficking of Canadian-grown cannabis continues. The U.S. believes that the Netherlands are successfully countering the production and flow of MDMA to the U.S.

Criticism

Critics from the left cite episodes that undercut leftist governments or showed support for Israel. Others cite human rights abuses and violations of international law. Critics have charged that the U.S. presidents have used democracy to justify military intervention abroad. It was also noted that the U.S. overthrew democratically elected governments in Iran, Guatemala, and in other instances. Studies have been devoted to the historical success rate of the U.S. in exporting democracy abroad. Some studies of American intervention have been pessimistic about the overall effectiveness of U.S. efforts to encourage democracy in foreign nations. Until recently, scholars have generally agreed with international relations professor Abraham Lowenthal that U.S. attempts to export democracy have been "negligible, often counterproductive, and only occasionally positive." Other studies find U.S. intervention has had mixed results, and another by Hermann and Kegley has found that military interventions have improved democracy in other countries.

Support

Regarding support for certain anti-Communist dictatorships during the Cold War, a response is that they were seen as a necessary evil, with the alternatives even worse Communist or fundamentalist dictatorships. David Schmitz says this policy did not serve U.S. interests. Friendly tyrants resisted necessary reforms and destroyed the political center (though not in South Korea), while the 'realist' policy of coddling dictators brought a backlash among foreign populations with long memories.

Many democracies have voluntary military ties with United States. Treaty of Mutual Cooperation and Security between the United States and Japan, Mutual Defence Treaty with South Korea, and Major non-NATO ally. Those nations with military alliances with the U.S. can spend less on the military since they can count on U.S. protection. This may give a false impression that the U.S. is less peaceful than those nations.

Research on the democratic peace theory has generally found that democracies, including the United States, have not made war on one another. There have been U.S. support for coups against some democracies, but for example Spencer R. Weart argues that part of the explanation was the perception, correct or not, that these states were turning into Communist dictatorships. Also important was the role of rarely transparent United States government agencies, who sometimes mislead or did not fully implement the decisions of elected civilian leaders.

Empirical studies have found that democracies, including the United States, have killed much fewer civilians than dictatorships. Media may be biased against the U.S. regarding reporting human rights violations. Studies have found that *The New York Times* coverage of worldwide human rights violations predominantly focuses on the human rights violations in nations where there is clear U.S. involvement, while having relatively little coverage of the human rights violations in other nations. For example, the bloodiest war in recent time, involving eight nations and killing millions of civilians, was the Second Congo War, which was almost completely ignored by the media. Finally, those nations with military alliances with the U.S. can spend less on the military and have a less active foreign policy since they can count on U.S. protection. This may give a false impression that the U.S. is less peaceful than those nations.

Niall Ferguson argues that the U.S. is incorrectly blamed for all the human rights violations in nations they have supported. He writes that it is generally agreed that Guatemala was the worst of the US-backed regimes during the Cold War. However, the U.S. cannot credibly be blamed for all the 200,000 deaths during the long Guatemalan Civil War.

The U.S. Intelligence Oversight Board writes that military aid was cut for long periods because of such violations, that the U.S. helped stop a coup in 1993, and that efforts were made to improve the conduct of the security services.

Today the U.S. states that democratic nations best support U.S. national interests. According to the U.S. State Department, "Democracy is the one national interest that helps to secure all the others. Democratically governed nations are more likely to secure the peace, deter aggression, expand open markets, promote economic development, protect American citizens, combat international terrorism and crime, uphold human and worker rights, avoid humanitarian crises and refugee flows, improve the global environment, and protect human health."

According to former U.S. President Bill Clinton, "Ultimately, the best strategy to ensure our security and to build a durable peace is to support the advance of democracy elsewhere. Democracies don't attack each other." In one view mentioned by the U.S. State Department, democracy is also good for business. Countries that embrace political reforms are also more likely to pursue economic reforms that improve the productivity of businesses. Accordingly, since the mid-1980s, under President Ronald Reagan, there has been an increase in levels of foreign direct investment going to emerging market democracies relative to countries that have not undertaken political reforms. Leaked cables in 2010 suggested that the "dark shadow of terrorism still dominates the United States' relations with the world".

The United States officially maintains that it supports democracy and human rights through several tools Examples of these tools are as follows:

- A published yearly report by the State Department entitled "Supporting Human Rights and Democracy: The U.S. Record" in compliance with a 2002 law (enacted and signed by President George W. Bush, which requires the Department to report on actions taken by the U.S. Government to encourage respect for human rights.
- A yearly published "Country Reports on Human Rights Practices."
- In 2006 (under President George W. Bush), the United States created a "Human Rights Defenders Fund" and "Freedom Awards."
- The "Human Rights and Democracy Achievement Award" recognizes the exceptional achievement of officers of foreign affairs agencies posted abroad.
- The "Ambassadorial Roundtable Series", created in 2006, are informal discussions between newly-confirmed U.S. Ambassadors and human rights and democracy non-governmental organizations.
- The National Endowment for Democracy, a private non-profit created by Congress in 1983 (and signed into law by President Ronald Reagan, which is mostly funded by the U.S. Government and gives cash grants to strengthen democratic institutions around the world.

7

The Trump Presidency: Signals for India

India's ties with the United States have been on the upswing, particularly since the beginning of the millennium and a positive factor in the recently concluded and otherwise bitterly contested and vicious electoral campaign was the uniformly bipartisan support for continued improved relations with India. Mr Trump had, in fact, said India and the US would be "best friends." Indian Prime Minister Narendra Modi was among the first to greet the President-elect, calling to congratulate Mr Trump on his election.

"We look forward to working with you closely to take India-US bilateral ties to a new height," Mr Modi said on November 9 in a congratulatory message to the newly elected President on Twitter, hours before the two spoke on the phone. New Delhi has been hopeful that Mr Trump would also be able, as he had forcefully reiterated throughout his campaign, to make Pakistan more accountable towards curbing terrorism emanating from that country. The President-elect's reported phone conversation at the end of November with Pakistan Prime Minister Nawaz Sharif however sent more conflicting signals about what his policies could look like.

Mr Modi also sent Foreign Secretary Dr. Subrahmanyam Jaishankar, a former Indian envoy to the US, to Washington, to establish contact with Congressmen and the transition team, and to set an early date for a meeting between the two leaders as soon as possible after he assumes office on January 20, 2017. "Foreign Secretary did visit the United States as part of regular bilateral consultations," Vikas Swarup, India's External Affairs Ministry spokesman said. "He met with the members of the current administration and had meetings in the US Congress. It is also my understanding that Foreign Secretary interacted with very senior levels of the Trump transition team," Swarup said.

India formally and officially keeps away from the electoral process in other countries, although the effort is to have good relations with the contestants as is diplomatically appropriate. Now that the elections are over, policymakers in New Delhi hope that the new President will commit to protecting the US-led international order, and continue to strengthen the US-India strategic partnership.

India has traditionally always maintained a distance from the American political transition process even while trying to build relationships with an incoming administration. Dr Vivek Lall, a distinguished US industry leader and defence analyst, says that Mr Trump will be a dynamic leader taking into account the realities of the international order, as seen by the naked eyes of an administration and also as enunciated by the Departments of Defense and State."And the fact that there is strong, bipartisan support in both the Houses of the US Congress as well as within the two Departments."

The strategic communities in both Washington and New Delhi are convinced that Mr Trump will be well-disposed towards India. Many countries, India certainly, also hope that positive relations likely to emerge between Washington and Moscow will help Russia maintain an objective distance from China. Some of Mr Trump's campaign pronouncements, like his warmth towards Russian President Vladimir Putin, may have a significant bearing on the international order.

China's aggressive assertions are generating global concern, and its attempt to annex South China Sea and build a strong presence in the Indian Ocean through Gwadar in Pakistan has added fuel to the fire. The US Department of State and Navy officials have periodically expressed voices of protest. Nonetheless, Beijing has warned of war if Washington attempts to disrupt its forays in the South China, of which it claims some 80 percent despite protests from all its littoral neighbours.

As for Indo-US relations, the President-elect has named Indian-origin Nikki Haley as his choice for the next US Permanent Representative at the United Nations. She is both the first woman appointed to the top level of the Trump administration, and the first person of Indian origin ever to hold a cabinet-level post in any US administration. The 44-year old lady, who is currently Governor of South Carolina, will have a crucial responsibility to try and steer the global organisation in a favourable direction (India hopes) on pressing issues, including UN reform and terrorism.

TRUMP TO CALL MODI AND EVERYONE IS ON THEIR TOES

On his fourth day in office, the new president of the United States, Donald J Trump, would be dialling Prime Minister Narendra Modi's number. A call has been scheduled between the two leaders for 1pm EST (11.30pm IST). Modi is the fifth world leader after prime ministers of Canada, Mexico, Israel and the Egyptian president who President Trump is set to call.

The conversation is expected to set the tone for Delhi's engagement with the new administration in Washington DC. Despite recent historic bilateral pacts that elevated India as a major defence partner of the US and bipartisan support in the Congress, India has much to worry about Trump's views on outsourcing.

With his Make America Great Again and America First war cry, the Trump administration is expected to place curbs on H1B and L1 visas, crucial to Indian tech firms and techies in the Silicon Valley. The power corridors in India are yet to get a clear understanding of how the Make In India slogan will resonate with American protectionism. The Republican for Hindus Coalition led by Indian-origin Shalabh Kumar was an important contributor to Trump's campaign fund.

Trump had even announced his love for "Hindus" at the organisation's fundraiser, which the South Block had been cautious about reacting to, given India's secular fabric and because Hillary Clinton was tipped to be the presidential favourite then. A day after Trump's surprise victory that shocked many, Modi had congratulated the then president-elect soon after his win, on November 9.

Addressing the inaugural session of the recently-held second Raisina Dialogue, the prime minister said, "With the United States, our actions have brought speed, substance and strength to the entire spectrum of our engagement."He further added that in his conversation with Trump," we agreed to keep building on these gains in our strategic partnership." With Trump adopting a stern approach with respect to Beijing and talking tough on trade and Chinese manoeuvres in the South China Sea, India will have to cautiously gauge China's reaction in the region and the world.

The tango between Trump and Russian President Vladimir Putin will also be an important lookout for Delhi, to see signs of any changing axis in the neighbourhood with old ally Moscow getting closer with China and working with Pakistan.

Foreign secretary S Jaishankar, addressing the Raisina Dialogue, had said,"We established early contact with the Trump transition team and see a strong convergence of interests and concerns. With Russia, India's relationship has actually grown very substantially in the last two years, as has the bonding between our leaders. An improvement in US-Russia ties is therefore not against Indian interests."

In his inaugural speech, Trump swore to "eradicate radical islamic terrorism completely from the face of the earth". India would like to know if the islamic terrorism encompasses terror outfits targeting India from Pakistani soil as well or will it only be about the Islamic State or ISIS. In Gen Mattis as his secretary of defence, Trump has a retired marine corps commander with 41 years of military experience who has worked closely in the Af-Pak region, but hardly had interactions with India.

In his Senate hearings ahead of his confirmation though, he recognised India's role in region and replied,"Cooperation on defence trade and technology has grown to the benefit of both countries under the Defense Technology and Trade Initiative.I also believe that India's 'Act East' policy allows it to play a greater role in contributing to security in the Asia-Pacific region."

It would be interesting to see how the chemistry between Modi, who rose from a chaiwala to the post of the prime minister, and Trump - the multibillionaire political outsider who now commands the superpower nation, plays out.

Despite their strikingly different personalities, Modi and Trump's predecessor Barack Obama met eight times in a span of two years. And India was crucial in Obama's drive for the Paris Climate Change act as well the Asia pivot strategy. Tuesday will set the ball formally rolling for a new chapter in Indo-US relations.

TRUMP'S VICTORY: WIDENING INDIA'S WINDOW OF OPPORTUNITIES?

Trump's worldview

Trump's impromptu statements and unpredictable nature make it difficult to comprehend his world view. He was a Democrat in the beginning of his political career. Later, he turned into an Independent and now, he is a Republican. As President-elect, he is setting the terms of discourse on how he wants things or what kind of message he wants to convey. World leaders are reacting and adjusting to him rather than the other way around (though it is too soon to predict the rationale behind calls to Taiwan and Pakistan).

His willingness to speak his mind than be deliberate and scripted like his adversary Hillary Clinton and renounce the neo-liberal agenda for racist and nationalist sentiments shows how smartly he engineered his victory. To look at it positively, he is quite adaptable to situations, as he is not committed to a dogma or ideology.

Foreign policy style

There is a lot of uncertainty about what his policies are going to be due to his impulsive nature. He may run his administration like a corporate, largely with a top-down approach. Focus will be more on tactic than strategy. He is for making deals rather than having a deliberative approach or trying to figure out multiple points.

In comparison with the outgoing President Barack Obama, who is a man of thought, Trump is more action and less thought. Trump criticizes Obama's stratagem of leading from behind without having a huge American footprint as a contributing factor to the decline of US leadership. Chances for Trump to make a big mistake or set up a huge crisis for America cannot be ignored either. His initial stride in foreign diplomacy,of irking China, is not a positive development. If it backfires, he will not get the backing of the 'establishment'.

Global priorities and Indian prospects

Nation building abroad will no longer be a priority for the US, as synergies will be directed towards American priorities. Considering the fact that India has often been on the other side of the table on US interventions abroad, this strategy would work to India's benefit.

The stand against anti-terrorism and ISIS can help offset Indian efforts against terrorism. But this does not warrant a hard-line approach towards Pakistan as India expects. The US would want to keep Pakistan on good terms for its geo-political interests, in spite of its failure to bring in stability in the Afghanistan – Pakistan region.

The vibes that Defense Secretary General James N Mattis and National Security Adviser Michael Flynn share with Pakistan will make it hard to speculate the new administration's dynamics with Pakistan. If the former is accommodating of Pakistan, the latter prefers a hard-line stance with allies if US interests are at stake. Trump's focus is expected to be on the Middle East and not on South Asian terrorism.

Protectionism and Indian prospects

Calls for protectionism will run counter to the Republican Party's long established ideals – belief in the free market. Courting the protectionist agenda will be costly for Trump. His call to tax companies (35 per cent) that take jobs outside the country and move out of the US for their operations is not a practical plan of action, as it runs counter to WTO rules and cannot be implemented beyond 150 days.

Post the development of designating India as its defense partner without being formal alliance partner with the US, it maybe difficult for India to negotiate the terms and conditions as it calls for enhanced Indo – US relations in the defense sector. As of now, one needs to wait to understand how the new administration will view upgrading military ties with India. India will have to be wary of Trump's protectionist outlook.

'Make in America' is going to clash with 'Make in India'. Indian services sector, especially the IT industry and exports to the US may hit a rough patch.

Yet, the entry of skilled labors, wherever the US needs it, would be welcomed and Trump is expected to be flexible considering mutual benefits.

Amidst the unease towards major trade deals such as Trans-Pacific Partnership (TPP), Trump will be promoting bilateral treaties. Both India and China will benefit unless Trump takes a hard protectionist stance, which is highly unlikely. With Trump, there will be greater room for Indian autonomy.

The focus on stabilizing Afghanistan upon the acknowledgement of Pakistan failing to bring peace in the region will benefit India, as it can play the role of a stabilizer and further its interests in Central Asian and South Asian regions.

Trump is in favor of strong leaders. In that case, it may be possible for Narendra Modi to influence Trump, who seem adaptable to situations of mutual benefit. However, a clash of interests may turn out bad for both the nations.

Reset of US–Russia ties

With Trump intending to pursue a reset of US–Russian ties,the reversal of ties can help Trump succeed in a critical power manipulation. Nevertheless, the dynamics of contention between Mattis, who is anti-Putin, and Rex Tillerson (Secretary of State), who is pro-Russian, can be expected in the process. If Trump can help stabilize Syria with Russian help, he will be successful in selling to all how good relations with Russia is a wiser strategy. He could use this to reverse the anti-Russia sentiments in the US Congress too. Even the European partners will welcome the reset in Russian relations.

The US and its allies have been trying to isolate Russia politically and economically in the wake of the Ukraine crisis and the annexation of Crimea. India, being a long-standing ally of Russia, has found it hard to keep up the momentum in the relation. The Indian stance to take Russia for granted resulted in the growing proximity between Russia and China and Russian tilt towards Pakistan. A reset of relations between US and Russia would mean that India would not have to choose between the two. Therefore, it will be a benefiting move for India. Added to this, a US–Russia reset would help further ties with Iran, as the latter is a Russian ally in the Middle East.

Asian policies

Trump's call for slapping 45 per cent tariff on Chinese goods is not a feasible option. As a businessperson, Trump would try to get a better deal for the US. A consensus is bound to be arrived at, as the least thing that China would want is a trade war with the US. With his reversal of position vis-à-vis the allies in the Asia Pacific region, post his electoral victory, Trump may consider the interests of the US allies and will continue the pivot to Asia, albeit, under a different name.

Indian strategy

India has to consolidate its development agenda and rise as an economic powerhouse, while maintaining a balance of power in Asia. Rather than being China – centrist, the spotlight need to be on Indian imperatives. Indian approach towards the US can be attuned to that of a transaction mode. This is precisely how Trump is expected to act and what will be the preferred mode by the Indians.

India will be perceived as a strategic partner under the new administration, but not with immediate priority. The Indian approach should be that of maintaining a strategic independence in areas where it has a strategic premium – Indian Ocean Region, South Asia –to play against adversaries. India need not rely on the US for its interests rather it can streamline its strategies towards avenues of mutual convergence. The India caucus in the US can make a difference, depending on the money it can invest. Presently, it makes up one per cent in the US Congress with five representations – Senator Kamala Harris and members of the House of Representatives Ami Bera, Ro Khanna, Pramila Jaypal and Raja Krishnamoorthi.

Future of American politics and Democrats

It is a time for self-reflection for the Democratic Party. Democrats have to revisit their strategies. The decision to field Tim Kaine, a conservative, for the Vice Presidential ticket was a reflection of the party's failure to comprehend the ground realities, even after Bernie Sander's solid inroads during the presidential campaign. The blame game is on Hillary Clinton for the massive electoral defeat on the ground that it was her election to lose. Now, the party is at a loss to find a new leader, who can reverse its fortune. If Trump's protectionist positions affect the US economy and its fortunes, then, in the long run, the Democrats may find their lost ground. Except for Russia, most nations failed to foresee the victory of Donald Trump. With his business acumen, Trump would be willing to be tactical at home and abroad. The world can only wait to see how his policies take shape.

'INDO-US TIES TO STRENGTHEN, WIDEN UNDER TRUMP ADMINISTRATION'

Underlining India's key role in South Asia, a prominent

Indian-American Republican closely associated with vice-president-elect Mike Pence has said that Indo-US ties will further strengthen under the incoming Trump administration. "President-elect Donald Trump and Vice-president-elect Pence are aware that India will play a key role in South Asia for US and a great strategic partner in global development," Raju Chintala, from Pence's home State of Indiana, said.

"The new administration under leadership of President Trump will continue to strengthen and widen relations between India and US, especially defence and commerce," said Chintala who landed in Washington DC from Indianapolis as part of the Republican delegation from Indiana to participate in the presidential inauguration and various related events including the presidential ball on Friday night.

"It will be a rewarding partnership for both India and the US," Chintala said. "Terrorism is another area that Trump administration will collaborate with India," Chintala said hoping that Trump will focus on eradicating ISIS and terrorism during his tenure.

As Indiana Governor, Chintala said, Pence had planned to visit India this year. "Pence wanted to visit India and recognises potential exports for US companies," he said, adding that the vice-president elect is very much keen to enhance business and trade relationship with India.

Born and raised in the Nalgonda District of Telangana, Chintala has known Pence for more than a decade now and is known as a close acquaintance of the vice-president elect ever since he was a member of the US House of Representative and thereafter became Governor of Indiana. Since graduating from the Indiana Leadership Forum in 2004, Chintala has advised federal and state elected officials; actively served in political campaigns at the city, state, and federal levels.

He is one of the only few Asian Americans to seek elected office in the State of Indiana; and worked on behalf of the Republican Party in other capacities. He was an alternate delegate from Indiana at the Republican National Convention in Cleveland last summer.

INDO-US TIES WILL TOUCH NEW HEIGHTS UNDER TRUMP: MIKE PENCE'S CLOSE AIDE

Indo-US ties will touch new heights under the Trump administration as the two countries are "natural partners" and have common interests amid China's assertiveness in the Asia-Pacific region, an Indian-American entrepreneur considered close to Vice President Mike Pence has said. With Indian-Americans playing the role of an umbilical cord between the two counties, India and the United States have common interests in balancing the increasing economic and military influence of China in the Asia-Pacific region and fighting together the menace of terrorism in South and Central Asia, said Indiana-based Gurinder Singh Khalsa.

Founder and chairman of Sikhs Political Action Committee or SikhsPAC, Khalsa has emerged as one of the vocal leader of the Indian-American Sikhs in particular in the Midwest region.

"India and the United States are natural partners at this time. Both have an interest in balancing growing Chinese economic and military influence in southeast Asian. Both have an interest in fighting terrorism originating in central Asian areas like Pakistan and Afghanistan," Khalsa told PTI in an interview. "It is to India's long-term benefit to continue improving relations with the US. We also have many shared business priorities, particularly in IT and tech industries," he said.

China has been assertive in the disputed South China Sea region, building artificial islands which could potentially be used for military purposes. It is also building a number of ports in South Asian countries. The US has called for freedom of navigation to be respected amid the South China Sea actions by Beijing.

Khalsa, an accomplished businessman from Indiana, is a friend of Pence from the days the US vice president was not even elected the Governor of Indiana. Khalsa says he wants to focus on strengthening India-US relationship and be the voice of Indian-Americans and other such ethnic communities in the US.

"(Pence) has been very outspoken about the need for more economic cooperation between India and Indiana. Prior to his selection as Vice President, he spoke to us about his intention to travel to India after the election. He wanted to be the first Indiana Governor to visit India after the election," Khalsa said recollecting his meetings with Pence.

"To be clear, his interests are very definitely in the United States. He is an American and he will be advocating for Americans. But, I don't think that necessarily conflicts with his desire to improve economic and political ties with India. It simply means, he'll be a tough, but fair negotiator," he said sharing his impression about Pence.

TRUMP ADMINISTRATION TO EXPAND INDIA-US MILITARY-STRATEGIC ALLIANCE

The Trump administration has served notice that it intends to expand the Indo-US military strategic alliance. This is not surprising, but nonetheless highly significant: first, because it underscores the new administration's intention to pursue confrontation with China; and second, because Washington's drive to harness India to its military-strategic offensive against China has dangerously destabilized the region, fueling tensions between India and both China and Pakistan.

US Secretary of Defense, General James "Mad Dog" Mattis, telephoned his Indian counterpart, Manohar Parrikar last week. Mattis, according to the Pentagon readout of their Feb. 8 conversation, hailed the "tremendous progress" made in "recent years" in Indo-US "defense cooperation" and said the new administration is eager to "sustain the momentum" and "build upon it."

The readout made specific mention of the bilateral Defense Technology and Trade Initiative (DTTI) under which the US and India are codeveloping and coproducing advanced weapon systems.

Mattis placed his call to Parrikar shortly after returning from a trip to East Asia, during which he reaffirmed Washington's longstanding strategic alliances with Japan and South Korea. He also reiterated the Obama administration's commitment to go to war with China if Beijing were ever to threaten East China Sea islets (known in Japan as the Senkaku and in China as the Diaoyu) that are currently held by Japan, but claimed by China.

Mattis's call came the day after officials in Washington had said that all the legal changes necessary to give effect to India's recent designation as a "Major (US) Defense Partner" have now been completed. As a quid pro quo for New Delhi agreeing to allow the Pentagon to use Indian military bases to service its warplanes and battleships, the Obama administration last year conferred "Major Defense Partner" status on India. This gives New Delhi access to US weapons on a par with Washington's most trusted treaty allies and Indian companies "a presumption of approval" when they seek to buy most US Commerce Department-controlled military and "dual use" goods.

Since the turn of the 21st century, Republican and Democratic administrations alike have prioritized strengthening strategic ties with India, viewing it as critical to US efforts to contain and, if need be, thwart China's rise. India's size, large nuclear-armed military, and strategic location are all reasons India has been touted by the Pentagon, CIA, and US foreign policy think tanks as a "strategic prize." From the standpoint of the strategists of US imperialism, India is China's western underbelly. Moreover, it juts far out into the Indian Ocean, providing a prime vantage point for controlling the sea-lanes that convey much of China's oil and other natural resource imports, and almost all its exports to Europe, Africa and the Middle East.

Since the Obama administration launched its "Pivot to Asia" in 2011, and especially since the Indian elite propelled Narendra Modi and his Hindu supremacist Bharatiya Janata Party (BJP) to power in May 2014, India has been integrated ever more completely into Washington's military-strategic offensive against China. In their parting addresses, both Defense Secretary Ashton Carter and Secretary of State John Kerry characterized the enhanced Indo-US military-strategic ties as one of the major achievements of Obama's eight-year presidency.

Under Modi, India has been transformed into a veritable frontline state in Washington's anti- China offensive.

In addition to opening its military bases for routine US use, India—as revealed by the head of the US Pacific Command, Admiral Harry Harris, last month—is now exchanging intelligence with the US Navy on Chinese submarine and ship movements in the Indian Ocean.

New Delhi has also dramatically expanded its bilateral and trilateral military-security cooperation with America's closest Asia-Pacific allies, Japan and Australia.

Beginning with the January 2015 "India-US Joint Strategic Vision for the Asia-Pacific and Indian Ocean Region," the Modi government has consistently parroted Washington's provocative position on the South China Sea dispute, painting China as the "aggressor." This stance is encouraging the US to act ever more recklessly. The Trump administration has gone so far as to threaten to block China's access to the South China Sea islets it currently controls, an act that would be tantamount to a declaration of war.

The extent to which India is being integrated into the US war build-up against China has been further underscored by this week's announcement that the Pentagon has decided to make India a hub for servicing and repairing battleships and other vessels attached to its Seven Fleet—the force that would play the lead role in implementing the US military's Air-Sea Battle plan against China.

The ever-tighter Indo-US alliance has overturned the balance of power in the South Asian region, leading to the dangerous intensification of geopolitical tensions between India and its principal rivals, China and Pakistan. One expression of this is a nuclear and ballistic missile arms race, involving all three states.

Emboldened by the many strategic "favors" Washington has showered upon it, New Delhi has launched a campaign of diplomatic, economic and military pressure aimed at forcing Islamabad to stamp out all logistical support from Pakistan for the anti-Indian insurgency in Jammu and Kashmir. Last fall, South Asia was plunged into its gravest war crisis in over a decade, when India mounted commando raids inside Pakistan in retaliation for an attack on an Indian military base carried out by Islamist Kashmiri separatists.

For more than four decades, India did not publicly admit to attacks inside Pakistan for fear of triggering a dynamic of escalating strikes and counterstrikes that could quickly lead to all-out war. The Modi government has dashed this policy. It has celebrated the commando raids as the throwing off of the shackles of "strategic restraint" and has vowed that it will continue to punish Pakistan until it "renounces" terrorism even if that leads to the first-ever war between nuclear-armed states.

The Modi government has been encouraged in this provocative stance by Washington. Eager to demonstrate to New Delhi the value Washington places on their strategic partnership, the Obama administration supported India's illegal and highly provocative "surgical strikes" inside Pakistan, first implicitly and then explicitly.

Even before Mattis's phone call to his Indian counterpart, Parrikar, New Delhi was calculating how it could exploit the harder line the Trump administration is expected to adopt with Pakistan, which Washington has repeatedly criticized for not doing more to stamp out Taliban safe havens inside Pakistan. In reality, if Islamabad, or at least sections of Pakistan's military-intelligence apparatus, have maintained ties with some Taliban factions it is because they are hedging against the impact of the Indo-US alliance, which has drastically increased the strategic imbalance between Pakistan and India, a country with a six times larger population and an eight times larger economy.

Pakistan's principal military-strategic response to the burgeoning Indo-US ties had been to deepen its longstanding alliance with Beijing. This in turn has further exacerbated tensions between Beijing and New Delhi.

In a statement to the Indian parliament last week, External Affairs Minister Sushma Swaraj reiterated the Modi government's hardline policy of refusing all substantive contacts with Pakistan until it abandons any material support for the Kashmir insurgency. Swaraj proclaimed India's policy was "no dialogue, until peace" and boasted about Islamabad's growing diplomatic isolation.

Up until 2015, China adopted a cautious approach to the Indo-US military-strategic alliance, based on the calculation that a strong reaction might backfire and push New Delhi further into Washington's embrace. But over the past two years, Beijing has taken an increasingly confrontational stance, as exemplified by its decision to make the $50 billion China-Pakistan Economic Corridor a cornerstone of its One Belt, One Road initiative.

Significantly India figures large on the list of key strategic concerns Beijing has reportedly given to the Trump administration. According to Michael Pillsbury, a Trump advisor and China expert, Beijing listed six top "sensitivities": Taiwan; the One China policy; the antiballistic missile system Washington is building in South Korea (THAAD); US arms sales to India; the Sino-Indian border dispute; and the Dali Lama and the Tibetan government-in-exile, which is located in India.

At Modi's invitation, the US Ambassador to India, Richard Verma, made a high-profile visit last October to Arunachal Pradesh, territory China claims as South Tibet. On a similar visit earlier last year a lower-level US diplomat said Washington considers Arunachal Pradesh an indisputable part of India.

INDIA'S PLACE IN AN UNCERTAIN TRUMP PRESIDENCY

With Donald Trump inaugurated as president of the US, the world is contemplating how international relations will play out with the global leader, including for those watching in India. Questions arise on whether to take Trump's nationalist rhetoric seriously or to believe his businessman persona will make him a practical president to deal with, or that the judicial system in the US will not allow him to implement some of his calls, such as the restrictions on the temporary movement of IT workers.

Taking into account such uncertainty and what we've seen of Trump and his team thus far, the path forward for India in key geo-economic and geopolitical areas could be more challenging than ever. However, from this India has an opportunity to expand and deepen its trade relations in new markets, uplift its domestic capacity, reduce the harmful effects of climate change and become a leading actor in the Asia-Pacific.

Regardless of shake-ups in the global order, India's true focus must remain in designing and implementing a clear, internally-based strategy through a transparent and inclusive process to promote open and fair trade and cooperation bilaterally, regionally and multilaterally. Participation and input from civil society, the business community and other external experts will be critical.

For those Indian policy-makers, negotiators, diplomats and businesses wondering what to do with such uncertainty and destructive anti-globalisation likely to come from the US, let's be clear that Trump must be taken seriously for his 'transactionalist' and zero-sum worldview that will guide his 'America First' administration.

That administration has been filled with business characters and political insiders who, while chosen for their loyalty to the president, will undoubtedly vie for Trump's attention, especially on the top priority of trade. This could be like what we saw in the campaign where Trump played his staff against each other, creating rivalries. Although generally connected in their criticism of China and, as Mr Trump puts it, the "raw deal" given to the US, the hierarchy is unclear between nominated commerce secretary Wilbur Ross and others like Peter Navarro,

Robert Lighthizer, Jason Greenblatt and Steven Mnuchin, all with their foot in the door on international trade. India will have to wait and see how the dynamics of the administration evolves.

From overall observations, we'd expect relations between the US and India to remain constant for some time; hopefully even continue the positive movement made in the past two presidencies. A Trump presidency will have less of a direct impact on India, barring a few specific areas like movement of Indian professionals to the US or impediments to FDI to India.

Although no less important, more impact may be indirect in terms of trade, climate change and security, that Indian decision-makers should be closely monitoring with input from external experts. Importantly, the relationship may be dictated chiefly by business considerations and less of shared values or cultural connections; something to consider when trying to maintain forward moving Indo-US relations.

With regard to trade as a tool for its economic and development goals, India will have to broaden its gaze to weather this storm of uncertainty. The anti-globalisation and nationalist fervour from so-called 'losers' of globalisation are so palpable that a country like India that has gained much from its open trade stance will have to make even greater effort to listen to its people at all levels and particularly from the most vulnerable to open trade. This will also require clear and targeted domestic provisions for retraining, relocation and unemployment support.

Trump's rhetoric on immigration turned into action swiftly through executive orders. His 'America First' stance focused on American workers is expected to restrict temporary work visas that could severely impact India's employment and remittances as well as hamper diplomatic ties between the two nations. Strengthening that threat further is Trump's attorney general pick, Senator Jeff Sessions, a long-time critic of such visas. India and its impacted industries must unequivocally show the administration that its skilled and unskilled domestic labour, the kinds of jobs Trump has called to return home, will not fill the gap if Indian professionals are blocked out of the US labour market.

As a potential conflict between the US and China heightens, India will have to play the balancing act, not unlike its recent US and Russian relations. India should not expect that the potential rise in tension between the US and China will draw Washington closer to Delhi, considering Trump's zero-sum worldview. Likewise, India shouldn't become complacent in thinking that its friendship will blossom due to Trump's global tirades against what he sees as his enemies. Rather, India must cultivate both countries' relationships based on its own principles and strategic vision.

Considering the advancements and accessibility of renewable technology, India has the opportunity to be a driver in the industry to address the serious challenges of climate change. India must plan immediately to acquire sources of funding and investment, considering the US may renege on its financial commitment, less it actually removes itself from the Paris Agreement. To start gaining a foothold on becoming a leader in renewable technology, India can first promote its intrinsic aggregator industry to develop solar technology. Such groups of aggregators, with established supply links in compatible sectors such as electronics, can procure components domestically and internationally more efficiently than multinational brick and mortar solar companies. In the long-run, India must invest in renewable company start-ups.

As regional leadership gaps arise with potential US withdrawal, whether in economic integration or climate change, India should place itself as a safe alternative to China that will be a non-intrusive partner in the Asia-Pacific, with a history of understanding and promoting the needs of developing countries in the region and beyond. Countries that leaned more toward the US and less toward China, like Vietnam, South Korea and Japan, can look to India as a strong partner in the region on trade and security cooperation; both bilaterally and in regional arrangements.

To whatever extent a Trump presidency creates a neo-protectionist 'America First' regime and whether that challenges the Indo-US relations or not, India's core focus must remain on promoting mutually beneficial trade arrangements and cooperation bilaterally, regionally and multilaterally. The likely swell in unpredictability out of the US should not invite reactionary approaches from the Indian government, businesses or citizenry. If India is guided by grounded principles based in its development and economic needs, it surely can weather any storm of uncertainty that may come its way.

INDIA-US TIES STRONGER, LOOKING FORWARD TO WORKING WITH TRUMP GOVT: JAITLEY

Finance minister Arun Jaitley, speaking at a reception hosted by India's ambassador to the US Navtej Sarna, said the Indian government is looking forward to working with the Trump administration to strengthen the various dimensions of the bilateral ties.

Finance Minister Arun Jaitley said on Friday India-US relations have grown "far stronger and far matured" over decades and in the spirit of bipartisan support it enjoys in both countries, it would be a "great privilege" for New Delhi to continue working with the new Donald Trump administration.

Jaitley, who is here for the annual spring meetings of the World Bank group, met US commerce secretary Wilbur Ross on Thursday, in the first cabinet-level meeting with the Trump administration. He will meet treasury secretary Steven Mnuchin on Saturday. "The India-US relationship over the last few decades has significantly improved. It is far stronger, it is far matured," Jaitley said at a dinner hosted by ambassador Navtej Sarna. "It has defied changes in the government whether in the US or in India."

He added: "In one sense it is a bipartisan relationship. I am sure it will be a great privilege for us to continue to work with the new administration to strengthen the various dimensions of this relationship."

There have been a series of meetings between Indian officials and Trump administration officials and cabinet members since the new president took office — including phone calls between Prime Minister Narendra Modi and Trump. In addition, national security adviser H R McMaster became the first high-ranking Trump official to visit India earlier this week at the end of his three-nation tour of South Asia, after he visited Afghanistan and Pakistan. He met Modi.

In his meeting with Ross, Jaitley raised the issue of the Trump administration's review of the H-1B temporary visa programme for high-skilled foreigners that is expected to adversely impact Indians and Indian tech firms operating in the US.

New Delhi has said it will be watching the review closely. The finance minister used the opportunity to give an update on the India economic growth saying, "In the last three years even in the midst of a slowdown across the world, India has been able to grow in the range of seven to eight per cent."

And that, he added, could get a "significant boost", as economists are expecting when the new Goods and Services Tax legislation will be implemented around the middle of the year.

U.S.-INDIA RELATIONS: DOMESTIC ISSUES, STRATEGIC DYNAMICS

With the lifting of Cold War geopolitical constraints and the near-simultaneous opening of India's economy in early 1990s, the world's largest democracy has emerged as an increasingly important player on the global stage. India dominates the geography of the now strategically vital South Asia region, and its vibrant economy, pluralist society, cultural influence, and growing military power have made the country a key focus of U.S. foreign policy attention in the 21st century. This attention is to some degree motivated by China's longer-standing and more rapid rise, with many analysts viewing U.S. and Indian geopolitical interests as convergent on many fronts, perhaps especially in the area of Asian power balances. President George W. Bush is credited with building on the breakthrough visit by President Bill Clinton in 2000, which ended the estrangement of the post-1998 Indian nuclear weapons tests. Under President Bush and continuing with President Barack Obama the U.S. and Indian governments have been seeking to sustain a substantive "strategic partnership," even as bilateral commercial and people-to-people contacts flourish of their own accord.

The U.S.-India partnership is based on shared values such as democracy, pluralism, and rule of law. Numerous economic, security, and global initiatives, including unprecedented plans for civilian nuclear cooperation, are underway.

The two countries inked a ten-year defence framework agreement in 2005 to facilitate expanded bilateral security cooperation.

In the new century, large-scale combined military exercises have become commonplace, and bilateral cooperation on intelligence and counterterrorism is increasing. Unprecedented major U.S. arms sales to India are underway; more are anticipated. The influence of a geographically dispersed and relatively wealthy Indian-American community of some 2.7 million is reflected in Congress's largest country-specific caucus. More than 100,000 Indian students are attending American universities. Notably, a number of Indian-Americans now occupy senior positions in the Obama Administration, Agency for International Development Administrator Rajiv Shah among them.

Further U.S. interest in South Asia focuses on ongoing tensions between India and Pakistan rooted largely in competing claims to the Kashmir region and in "cross-border terrorism" in both Kashmir and major Indian cities. In the interests of regional stability, in particular as a means of forwarding U.S. interests in nearby Afghanistan, the United States strongly endorses an existing, but until recently moribund India-Pakistan peace initiative, and remains concerned about the potential for conflict over Kashmiri sovereignty to cause open hostilities between these two nuclear-armed countries. The United States also seeks to curtail the proliferation of nuclear weapons and missiles in South Asia.

President Obama desires to continue expanded engagement and cooperation with India. His May 2010 National Security Strategy noted that, "The United States and India are building a strategic partnership that is underpinned by our shared interests, our shared values as the world's two largest democracies, and close connections among our people." Yet there are concerns among observers in both countries that momentum has waned (by some accounts due to U.S. inattention), that outstanding areas of friction continue to hinder optimal levels of cooperation, and that India's geostrategic, economic, and security circumstances combine with New Delhi's lingering skepticism over America's global and regional role to preclude the kind of "special relationship" that many boosters of U.S.-India ties envisage. While U.S.-India engagement under the Obama Administration has not (to date) realized any groundbreaking initiatives as was the case under the Bush Administration, it may be that the apparently growing "dominance of ordinariness" in the relationship is a hidden strength that demonstrates its maturing into diplomatic normalcy.

Indeed, there is a pervasive sense in policy circles that dramatic new breakthroughs in U.S.-India relations are not on the horizon, and that President Obama's November 2010 travel to India may have brought the two countries to a plateau of sorts whereupon routinized, but still meaningful interactions take place in the near term. Both national governments have been dealing with serious domestic issues in 2011 (the United States with federal budget issues, India with major corruption scandals), as well as with more pressing foreign policy concerns.

Given a setting in which the private sectors of both countries are impatient with the pace of economic reform in India and with rampant corruption there, some analysts call on the two governments to concentrate on limited goals with clear chances for success, such as in defence trade and with the development of multilateral and Asian architectures, in both the economic and security realms. One leading Indian commentator urges American patience and recognition that New Delhi views engagement with the United States as its highest foreign policy priority. The contention here is that India's four purported top long-term foreign policy objectives—a stable Afghanistan-Pakistan region; exerting influence across the Indian Ocean region; obtaining status as a "rule-maker" in the international system; and strengthening "global power" factors such as sustained economic growth and military modernization—all require strategic cooperation with the United States.

Yet a more pessimistic view has the bilateral relationship constrained in large part by differences over the U.S.-Pakistan alliance and by India's apparent reluctance to exert power in its own region, resulting in years of "a lot of rhetoric but very little substantive movement" in U.S.-India ties.

The sweeping scope of the bilateral relationship, as well as the perceived lack of focus within it, may be found in the various and usually large number of issue-areas listed in joint statements. However, in May 2011, the lead U.S. diplomat for the region helpfully summarized U.S.-India relations under the rubric of four major "agendas":

- an *innovation* agenda that includes collaboration on energy security, civil nuclear cooperation, agriculture, space, climate, and other sciences;
- a *security* agenda that includes military-to-military relations, arms sales, and nonproliferation;
- a *people-to-people* agenda that encourages civic engagement, and open governance and democracy initiatives; and
- a *growth* agenda focused on increasing bilateral trade and investment by removing barriers to both.

Tangible progress is being made in each of these areas despite ongoing U.S. government irritants, in particular obstacles to full implementation of civil nuclear cooperation; overly restrictive limits on foreign investment; lingering barriers to trade; and insufficient protection of intellectual property rights, among others. Even leading American boosters of expanded U.S.-India ties insistently call on New Delhi to take more rapid action in these areas.

Notable Developments in 2011

- U.S.-India cooperation in the area of nuclear energy—an initiative launched in 2005 and approved by Congress in 2008—continues to be delayed by the lack of both a liability arrangement and an agreement on monitoring arrangements for U.S. nuclear exports to certain Indian entities.
- In April, New Delhi announced that it had narrowed the list of competitors for a roughly $11 billion contract for 126 new medium multi-role combat aircraft (MMRCA) to two finalists, both European vendors. U.S. government officials expressed being "deeply disappointed" by news of the "deselection" of U.S.-based Boeing and Lockheed Martin from consideration, and what seemed a choice with major geostrategic implications elicited much debate over its meaning.
- Major corruption scandals that broke in New Delhi in late 2010 have snowballed into a crisis not only for the sitting Congress Party-led United Progressive Alliance national coalition government, but also for India's political system writ large. Summer months have seen the emergence of a massive people's movement protesting the country's pervasive corruption, a movement lead in particular by social activist Anne Hazare.
- U.S. Ambassador to India Tim Roemer tendered his resignation on April 28, 2011, the same day that New Delhi announced the MMRCA deselection, and departed the New Delhi post on June 30. Roemer explained his departure as arising for personal, professional, and family reasons. The interim Chief of Mission, Peter Burleigh, is a highly competent veteran American diplomat with significant regional experience, but

observers warn that U.S.-India relations could suffer if the Obama Administration does not move quickly to appoint a new permanent Ambassador.

- In June, Ranjan Mathai, a career foreign service office and former ambassador to France, was appointed to replace Nirupama Rao as Indian foreign secretary beginning in August. Rao retired from the Indian Foreign Service and was appointed to succeed Meera Shankar as Ambassador to the United States.

EARLY OBAMA ADMINISTRATION ENGAGEMENT

Just days into President Obama's term, Secretary of State Hillary Clinton and Indian External Affairs Minister S.M. Krishna agreed to "further strengthen the excellent bilateral relationship" between the United States and India. Soon after, President Obama issued a statement asserting that, "Our rapidly growing and deepening friendship with India offers benefits to all the world's citizens" and that the people of India "should know they have no better friend and partner than the people of the United States." As part of her confirmation hearing to become Secretary of State, Clinton told Senators she would work to fulfill President Obama's commitment to "establish a true strategic partnership with India, increase our military cooperation, trade, and support democracies around the world."

Despite such top-level assurances from the new U.S. Administration, during 2009 and into 2010, many in India became concerned that Washington was not focusing on the bilateral relationship with the same vigour as did the Bush Administration, which was viewed in India as having pursued both broader and stronger ties in an unprecedented manner. Many concerns arose in New Delhi, among them that the Obama Administration was overly focused on U.S. relations with China in ways that would reduce India's influence and visibility; that it was intent on deepening relations with India's main rival, Pakistan, in ways that could be harmful to Indian security and perhaps lead to a more interventionist approach to the Kashmir problem; that a new U.S. emphasis on nonproliferation and arms control would lead to pressure on India join such multilateral initiatives as the Comprehensive Test Ban Treaty and the Fissile Material Cutoff Treaty; and that the Administration might pursue so-called protectionist economic policies that could adversely affect bilateral commerce in goods and services.

While some of these concerns persist, robust, positive, high-level U.S. attention to relations with India has continued. Secretary Clinton was widely seen to have concluded a successful visit to India in July 2009, inking several agreements, and also making important symbolic points by staying at Mumbai's Taj Mahal hotel (site of a major Islamist terrorist attack in 2008) and having a high-profile meeting with women's groups.

In November 2009, President Obama hosted his inaugural state visit when Indian Prime Minister Manmohan Singh dined at the White House. Despite the important symbolism, the resulting diplomacy was seen by many proponents of closer ties as disappointing (if not an outright failure) in its outcome, at least to the extent that no "breakthroughs" in the bilateral relationship were announced. Yet from other perspectives there were visible ideational gains: the relationship was shown to transcend the preferences of any single leader or government; the two leaders demonstrated that their countries' strategic goals were increasingly well aligned; and plans were made to continue taking advantage of complementarities while differences are well managed. Perhaps most significantly, the visit itself contributed to ameliorating concerns in India that the Obama Administration was insufficiently attuned to India's potential role as a U.S. partner.

Still, in the wake of Prime Minister Singh's U.S. travel, some observers continued voicing concerns at the Obama Administration's perceived "air of ambivalence" toward India, with one going so far as to accuse the U.S. Administration of "diplomatic negligence" in its allegedly insufficient attention to New Delhi's key concerns, and for policies that could "put India into its subcontinental box" by relegating it to a regional role through the Asia-wide elevation of China.

June 2010 Strategic Dialogue

The United States and India formally reengaged the U.S.-India Strategic Dialogue initiated under President G.W. Bush when a large delegation of high-ranking Indian officials led by External Affairs Minister Krishna visited Washington, DC, in June 2010. As leader of the U.S. delegation, Secretary Clinton lauded India as "an indispensable partner and a trusted friend." At a State Department reception, President Obama declared his firm belief that "the relationship between the United States and India will be a defining partnership in the 21st century."

In anticipation of the Dialogue, Undersecretary of State for Political Affairs William Burns had given a policy speech on "India's rise and the future of the U.S.-India relationship" in which he asserted, "The simple truth that India's strength and progress on the world stage is deeply in the strategic interest of the United States."

Burns acknowledged that progress in the partnership is not automatic and would require sustained efforts on both sides, and also that some Indians worry the United States sees India through the prism of ties with Pakistan and/or was overly focused on China. He sought to ameliorate these concerns by assuring his audience that the United States does not view relations in Asia as a zero-sum game and that its relations with Pakistan did not come at the expense of India. Two days later, the Strategic Dialogue produced a joint statement in which the two countries pledged to "deepen people-to-people, business-to-business, and government-to-government linkages ... for the mutual benefit of both countries and for the promotion of global peace, stability, and prosperity."

President Obama's November 2010 Visit to India

As the U.S. President planned his November 2010 visit to India, an array of prickly bilateral issues confronted him, including differences over the proper regional roles to be played by China and Pakistan; the status of conflict in Afghanistan; international efforts to address Iran's controversial nuclear program; restrictions on high-technology exports to India, outsourcing, and sticking points on the conclusion of arrangements for both civil nuclear and defence cooperation, among others. Moreover, while Indian officials will present a long list of demands to their American interlocutors, they come under fire for paying insufficient attention to American interests and concerns, and for not recognizing the sometimes serious costs of appearing insensitive to same.

Upon arriving in the Indian financial hub of Mumbai on November 7, 2010, President Obama laid a white rose at a memorial to the victims of the November 2008 terrorist attack and spoke at the Taj Mahal Palace hotel, a main target of that attack. While in that city, the President announced $10 billion in new trade deals, among them a $7.7 billion contract for Boeing to supply 30 737 commercial aircraft to India's SpiceJet airline.

The new deals were projected to create some 50,000 U.S. jobs. Many Indian observers were irked by the President's failure to mention Pakistan in his initial remarks, fueling for some a persistent Indian belief that the United States remains too devoted to its alliance with Islamabad. When asked about this in a meeting with a group of Mumbai college students, President Obama sought to impress upon the audience a belief that no country has a bigger stake in Pakistan's success than does India, commenting, "I think that if Pakistan is unstable, that's bad for India. If Pakistan is stable and prosperous, that's good."

In New Delhi, President Obama's historic speech to a joint session of the Indian Parliament characterized the U.S.-India partnership as serving three broad purposes: (1) promoting prosperity on both countries, especially through greater trade and two-way investment, and food security and health-related initiatives; (2) enhancing shared security by working together to prevent terrorist attacks, and; (3) strengthening democratic governance and human rights. In the context of this last issue-area, President Obama chided India for often "shying away" from taking clear public stands in the face of gross human rights violations and the suppression of democratic movements, as was recently seen to be the case in Burma.

While appearing a joint news conference, Prime Minister Singh called the American President "a sincere and valued friend" of India, and he welcomed an acceleration of the deepening of bilateral ties with an aim of working "as equal partners" in the relationship.

For his part, President Obama reiterated his view that the U.S.-India relationship will be one of the defining partnerships of the 21 century, and he reviewed the litany of varied bilateral initiatives both underway and planned. Both leaders expressed satisfaction with adjustments in U.S. export control regulations that are expected to facilitate greater joint cooperation in high-technology fields.

8

Target China, US Further Enhances Military-Strategic Alliance with India

Because of its size, proximity to China, commanding geographic position within the Indian Ocean region, and rapidly expanding military power and ambitions, India has long been viewed by the strategists of US imperialism as a key element in Washington's military-strategic offensive against China. Under Obama—particularly in the two-and-a-half years since Narendra Modi and his Hindu-supremacist Bharatiya Janata Party (BJP) came to power in New Delhi—Washington has gone a long way to transforming India into a "frontline" state in its confrontation with China.

In August, India allowed US warplanes and battleships to begin making routine use of its military bases and ports for resupply, repair, and rest. The Modi government has adopted the US stance on the South China Sea, parroting Washington's claims that China is threatening "freedom of the seas and overflight," and it has dramatically increased Indian bilateral and trilateral cooperation with Japan and Australia, the principal US allies in the Asia-Pacific.

Both the Obama administration and Congress have taken important steps in recent days to ensure that the "momentum" in the Indo-US alliance continues under the incoming Donald Trump administration. US Defense Secretary Ashton Carter traveled to New Delhi late last week to finalize details of an agreement designating India a "Major Defense Partner" of the US. This will reportedly give India the same right to buy advanced US weapons and weapons systems as Washington's treaty allies, including NATO countries, and Japan, Australia and South Korea.

A joint statement issued by Carter and his Indian counterpart, Manohar Parrikar, at the end of their December 8 meeting said, "The designation as a 'Major Defence Partner' is a status unique to India and institutionalizes the progress made to facilitate defense trade and technology sharing with India to a level at par with that of the United States' closest allies and partners, and ensures enduring cooperation into the future."

Carter and Parrikar exchanged memorandum governing the "end use" of any advanced weapons and technology the US transfers to India. According to news reports, there had been disagreements between Washington and New Delhi in recent months about the "level of technology transfer and cooperation," with India pressing for benefits akin to those granted the most trusted of US allies like Britain and Australia.

Thursday's joint statement did not address this issue. But the agreement clearly marks a further important step in making "non-aligned" India a de facto treaty ally of the US. Underscoring the strength of US-Indian military ties, Carter noted that this was seventh time he had met with Parrikar and that "defense relations" have become a "major driver" in Indo-US "bilateral relations."

The joint statement also emphasized the "tremendous progress" made in implementing the Indo-US Defence Technology and Trade Initiative (DTTI), under which the US is working to co-produce and even co-develop advanced weapons and weapon systems in India. The Modi government, which has ambitions for India to become a major arms exporter, has promoted the DTTI as an important part of its "Make in India" initiative, which aims to rapidly grow India's manufacturing sector.

The Obama administration views arms sales to India as a key means of harnessing India to its predatory strategic objectives by making it dependent on US weaponry, promoting Indo-US military inter-operability, and weaning New Delhi away from its traditional ally and principal arms-supplier, Russia. It is also eager to boost the bottom line of American weapons manufacturers. As Carter was visiting New Delhi, the US Senate was passing legislation, already adopted by the House of Representatives, to promote Indo-US military-strategic ties.

The "2017 National Defence Authorization Act," that is the Pentagon's $618 billion budget allocation, contains a section titled "Enhancing defence and security cooperation with India." It calls on the US secretaries of state and defense to take the necessary steps to designate India a Major Defense Partner, instructs the administration to designate a high-ranking official to ensure the success of the DTTI, and highlights "defence and security cooperation" with India as a means of advancing US "interests in South Asia" and the "greater Indo-Asia-Pacific regions."

Speaking following the Senate vote, Mark Warner, the senior Democratic senator from Virginia and co-chair of Senate India Caucus, applauded the "inclusion of forward-leaning provisions designed to strengthen bilateral defense cooperation with India, including expanded military-to-military engagement, increased defence trade, and greater cooperation on technological development." The bipartisan push to strengthen the US strategic-military alliance with India comes in the midst of a war crisis between India and Pakistan that has brought South Asia's rival nuclear-armed states to the brink of war.

October and November saw the fiercest cross-border artillery and gunfire exchanges since a ceasefire was put in place in 2003. In recent days the firing appears to have abated, however, the countries' political and military leaders continue to exchange bellicose threats. On Sunday Indian Home Minister Rajnath Singh said that if Pakistan "does not mend its ways, it will get splintered into ten pieces." In August, the Modi government, as part of a new hardline policy towards Pakistan, signaled it is ready to support the ethno-nationalist separatist insurgency in Pakistan's southwest province, Balochistan.

A huge factor fueling the Indo-Pakistani frictions is the US drive to harness India to its anti-China "Pivot to Asia." It has overturned the "balance of terror" between India and Pakistan, emboldening New Delhi and heightening the crisis of the Pakistani ruling elite, which for decades sought to offset Pakistan's strategic imbalance with India by serving as Washington's principal South Asian ally and mercenary.

Buoyed by Washington's strategic favors and eager to pursue the Indian bourgeoisie's great power ambitions, the Modi government has served notice that it is intent on changing the "rules of the game" with Pakistan. In late September it publicly boasted that Indian Special Forces had carried out raids inside Pakistan, ostensibly in retaliation for an Islamist attack on a military base in Indian-held Kashmir. The BJP government has vowed it will continue to shun diplomatic contact with Pakistan and conduct such strikes until Islamabad demonstrably cut offs all logistical support for the anti-Indian insurgency in Kashmir from inside Pakistan. Eager to demonstrate to New Delhi the benefits of its alliance with Washington, the Obama administration backed the illegal and highly provocative Indian military strikes inside Pakistan, first implicitly, then explicitly.

Even before the current war crisis, Pakistan and China had responded to the ever-burgeoning Indo-US partnership by strengthening their longstanding strategic ties. Recent developments, including a major campaign jointly mounted by the BJP government and the Indian media to trash Beijing for its support for Pakistan, have only caused them to draw closer together.

The explosive and reactionary rivalry between the Indian and Pakistani bourgeoisies is thus increasingly enmeshed with the US-China conflict, adding to each a further highly combustible element.

Pakistan's enhanced ties with Beijing are causing its ties with Washington to further fray. The same US defense appropriations bill that enhances Indo-US military ties, stipulates that unless the US defense secretary certifies that Pakistan has taken action to suppress the Haqqani Network—a Taliban faction with ties to section of the Pakistani military-intelligence apparatus—Washington must slash the payments it makes to Pakistan for supporting the US war in Afghanistan in 2017 in half, from $900 million to $450 million.

DONALD TRUMP AMERICA'S PROBLEM, BUT INDIA'S OPPORTUNITY

On many issues, Indian opinion makers habitually imitate their American counterparts with a missionary zeal. It's obvious that the effect will be magnified in the case of Donald Trump. As American media declared war against its 45th President, the battle cry inevitably reverberated from the ramparts of New Delhi. It isn't clear what stakes they had in this clash, but Indian liberals have greeted Trump with long LitFest sessions and defiant Facebook walls — both expressing apocalyptic fears. Something tells me Trump won't be losing his sleep over it.

Ever since the 70-year-old started converting his electoral promises into action through a spate of executive orders, Indian media went into a tailspin. Amid widespread cries of armageddon and daily dart-throwing on the Trump dartboard, not a single attempt has been made to contextualise Trump's ascension and evaluate whether he poses the same threat for Indo-US bilateral relations as he does, seemingly, for American domestic policies and politics.

This isn't to condone or criticise Trump's actions since he stepped into the White House. His executive orders on Obamacare, refugee or immigration policies are part of a separate debate. As Indians, what should be of immediate concern to us is to what extent are we impacted by Trump's policies and whether or not India will have leverage over him.

Strange as it may seem, relationships between nations are not governed by liberal principles or social justice.

While to a certain extent solidarity with American brethren over Trump is understandable and even inevitable, it makes little sense for Indians to roam about with a hurt look and 'Not My President' placard on shoulders. Not only because our President is Pranab Mukherjee, but also because bilateral relationship depends on shared interests and realpolitik. On these counts, India is actually better placed than most nations with Trump in the Oval Office. If we follow the Trump trajectory closely — right from the extraordinarily long election campaign to early signs from his cabinet — the consistently positive rhetoric on India and areas of mutual concern become evident.

Trump had all along maintained that he will be India's 'big friend' and on more than one occasion had praised Prime Minister Narendra Modi for his 'decisive leadership' and ability to do away with bureaucratic deadwood. That set the tempo for good chemistry between the leaders.

During a charity event last October, the then-Republican presidential nominee had called himself "a big fan of India" and promised to "stand shoulder to shoulder with India in sharing intelligence and keeping our people safe mutually". The significance of his visiting a non-battleground state during peak campaign season to attend a Republican Hindu Coalition wasn't lost on anyone.

In his book *The Field of Fight: How We Can Win the Global War Against Radical Islam and Its Allies* that hit the stands last August, Lieutenant General (rtd) Michael T Flynn has written: "Countries like Pakistan need to be told that we will not tolerate the existence of training camps and safe havens for Taliban, Haqqani, and al-Qaeda forces on their territory, nor will we permit their banks and other financial institutions to move illicit funds for the terror network." Trump has since appointed him as the National Security Adviser, raising hopes that US will act on Flynn's threat that Pakistan will be treated "harshly" and the aid will be "cut off" if Islamabad doesn't mend ways.

Another key Trump aide, US Defence Secretary James Mattis, made no bones about the need for a closer strategic partnership with India. During his confirmation procedure at the US Senate, the retired Marine Corps General had called Indo-US relationship one of "utmost importance" and advocated much closer, long-term ties based on security and defence in Asia Pacific region.

Modi had called Trump just hours after his victory and the POTUS returned the favour on 24 January. Albeit a courtesy call, the implication of it being placed ahead of Trump's phone calls to European heads of states, Beijing or even Moscow was hard to miss. A White House release stated that "United States considers India a true friend and partner in addressing challenges around the world" and that the duo "discussed opportunities to strengthen the partnership in broad areas such as the economy and defense". The statement also made it clear that "United States and India stand shoulder to shoulder in the global fight against terrorism. President Trump looked forward to hosting Prime Minister Modi in the United States later this year."

Reading between the lines, it is quite clear that Trump administration considers India a natural counterbalance to China, whose rise as a mercantile power bent on throwing around its economic and diplomatic heft carries disconcerting side-effects for both India and the US. It is entirely possible that having withdrawn from the Trans-Pacific Partnership, Washington now may rely on India greater than ever to restore some sort of a balance in Asia. Already, Chinese president Xi Jinping has indicated at Davos that Beijing isn't avert to taking up global economic leadership if America cedes that spot.

Speaking to *CNBC*, Manpreet Anand, former US deputy assistant secretary in the Bureau of South and Central Asian Affairs, said that Trump may accelerate the dovetailing of US-India security interests in Asia. "Through successive administrations and strong congressional support, the US has made tremendous investments to expand its relationship with India over the past several years... The Trump administration has an opportunity to double down on those efforts as the strategic interests of our two countries continue to align," Anand said. With Trump at the White House, India's biggest geopolitical gain could be the expected improvement of US-Russia ties that hit the nadir under Barack Obama. During this time, Russia had gravitated towards the China-Pakistan axis putting at direct risk the long-standing relationship with India. It is unlikely that Moscow and Washington would be exchanging love letters soon but a transactional relationship between two deal-makers in Vladimir Putin and Trump may stop a total breakdown of ties and prevent a bankrupt Moscow from seeking Chinese aid. Beijing has shown it would only be too happy to bankroll Russia and increase its influence in Eurasia.

The tetchy questions over US immigration program — H1B visa — remain. According to Ananth Kumar, Union minister for chemicals and fertilizers, there is no reason to think that Indian IT and pharma industry will be hit severely by Trump's policies. "Prime Minister has already had a telephonic conversation with the US President (Trump). I don't think there will be any change in the attitude of the US in terms of commerce-related issues," he said on Saturday.

There could be initial pressure on IT firms to hire locally, but consequently, opportunities for Indian tech industry will increase manifold. The overall net result should be positive.

Also, as an Indian-American Republican leader pointed out on Monday, Trump's "Buy American" and Modi's "Make In India" need not be mutually exclusive policies and indeed, could be even complementary, given the fact that Trump is worried about an yawning trade deficit with China and may impose some tariffs that could pave the way for better bilateral trade between the two nations. Shalabh Kumar, a big donor to Trump fund, expects trade to rise from over $100 billion now to rise to at least $300 billion by the end of Trump's current term.

Of course, leadership can't be put into grand theories and rarely do relationships follow the rules of logic. There could be many variables. But if mutual interest is the basis of stable Indo-US relation, we Indians need not be despondent about Trump. He is America's problem but our opportunity.

CHINA'S SECURITY ENVIRONMENT: OPPORTUNITIES AND CHALLENGES

There are two defining characteristics of the security environment in the Asia-Pacific region after the end of Cold War: (1) The United States has become the only superpower in the world today. It is also the most important external power in Asia, and plays a key role in South Asian security; (2) China and India are emerging Asian powers. Each has a population of over a billion, possess nuclear weapons and numbers among the fastest growing economies in the world. Relations among these three countries will undoubtedly dominate the course of events within the Asia-Pacific region in the 21st century. Their interactions, and how they deal with the triangle will, to a large extent, influence future peace and stability in the region.

China and India, the two largest developing countries in the world, have a commonality of history, culture, economy and social characteristics, and profiles of development. Each applies itself to internal economic development, carries out an independent foreign policy and strives for a peaceful international environment. China and India are among what Brzezinski described as "five geo-strategic players", what Henry Kissinger listed as the "six big powers", and what Samuel Huntington pointed out are "core states of seven civilizations."

China is a big power in East Asia while India is a big power in South Asia. Each has advantages and influence in their respective regions. However, they are not world powers that have global influence. In terms of institution and comprehensive strength, they cannot even be ranked as strong powers.

For America, China and India, at one end, are two emerging markets offering economic benefits and developing opportunities. At the other end, China and India are also two transitional countries demonstrating uncertainty, from the United States' strategic point of view. What Washington fears most is the possibility of China and India, with Russia, forming an alliance based on a common understanding and interests of a new international political and economical order and a multipolar world.The United States and India, the largest democracies in the world, share common political values and strategic interests. Their common geo-political, economic and socio-political interests are advancing a co-operative agenda (which their differences over nuclear proliferation may not be able to halt). With the US–India relationship moving forward over the past two years, the two countries have developed a comprehensive co-operative framework covering democracy, economy and security.

The United States now pays more attention to India's role as the largest democracy than it did before. India's continuous and fast-growing economy, especially its information technology industry, attracts great investment from transnational corporations based in America. In the security arena, the U.S. leadership has gradually begun to 'forget' India's nuclear tests and has come to recognize India as a *de facto* nuclear power, as also its preponderant position in South Asia. With India's support for America's unilateral action in missile defence, the US and India moved from divergence to co-operation in the field of non-proliferation. After 9/11, counter-terrorism has been a new field of strategic co-operation for U.S. and India. In a related development, Pakistan turns out to be less of an 'obstacle' for the US–India framework of relationships.

China and the United States, the largest developing and developed countries respectively, also have comprehensive common strategic interests. Besides large potential economic cooperation, they also share broad interests in other fields such as regional stability and the role and reform of the United Nations.

What is more likely is the emergence of a "soft balance of power" system among the three countries. Alternately, at one end, a vicious competitive relationship among the three countries may emerge, and the "soft balance of power" may be changed into a "hard balance of power" similar to that in the Cold War era, if one of them regards the development of relations between the two other countries as a challenge to its national interests, or if any two in this triad forge a relationship as a means to contain the third country. At the other end, it is possible for China, the US and India to establish a relatively harmonious relationship if they can seek out common views and interests, and push their differences aside to deal with bilateral and trilateral relations within a strategic perspective.

China's Security Environment

South Asia is one of the most unstable regions in world today. Focusing on the Kashmir issue, the conflict between India and Pakistan has lasted for more than half a century, during which three wars have been fought. The Kashmir issue includes many conflicting factors: territorial dispute, ethnic and religious divergence, political opposition and nuclear confrontation. One can also find in the Kashmir issue three threats for today's world: national separatism, religious extremism and cross-border terrorism. India and, immediately thereafter, Pakistan tested their nuclear weapons and then became *de facto* nuclear powers in the year 1998. The United States has initiated a counter-terrorism campaign after 9/11, which focuses substantially on this region. These various elements are new factors in the conflict over Kashmir between India and Pakistan.

Nuclear proliferation in South Asia makes the Kashmir issue more dangerous. According to the assessment of the Institute for Science and International Security, if all of the plutonium available to it is made into nuclear weapons, India can produce 45-95 warheads; while if all of the plutonium and weapon-grade uranium available to Pakistan is converted to nuclear weapons, this could produce 30-50 warheads.

A May 2002 report published in *The New Scientist* pointed out that, if a limited nuclear war were to break out between India and Pakistan, 10 small warheads used in the five biggest cities of each of these countries, respectively, would kill three million people and injure even more. The international community at large fears that a war between the two nuclear countries could open a Pandora's box and lead to the world's first nuclear war.

The struggle against terrorism makes the Kashmir issue even more complicated. After 9/11, India has sought increasingly and far more vigorously to establish the connections between terrorism and Pakistan. India has condemned the two Pakistan-based groups, the Lashkar-e-Toiba and Jaish-e-Mohammed, that led the terrorist attack on India's Parliament on December 13, 2001, and that are also responsible for cross-border terrorist activities.

Pakistan, on the other hand, actively works with the United States in the military campaign against terrorism in Afghanistan and claims that it is opposed to any fundamentalist organization or individuals who engage in terrorist activity in the name of Kashmir at home or abroad. However, President Musharraf has also declared that Pakistan would continue to support the Kashmiri struggle for independence 'morally, politically and diplomatically'.

In conclusion, nuclear tests and counter-terrorism make South Asia an international hotspot and a focus of global attention. In terms of non-proliferation and anti-terrorism, China and the South Asian countries share common interests and a potential for co-operation. China borders most South Asian countries. Regional stability in South Asia is, consequently, an important guarantee for China's west and southwest security environment. China hopes that both India and Pakistan will try to solve their problems by political and diplomatic means. China's President, Jiang Zemin, recently made mention of an old Chinese saying, 'peace favours both and conflict injures either', when he attended the First Summit of the Member States of the Conference on Interaction and Confidence Building Measures in Asia (CICA) which was convened in Almaty, Kazakhstan, on June 3-5, 2002.

America Factor in Sino-India Relationships

India, in the assessment of one Indian scholar, has always viewed close US-China relations with misgivings and feared that they might adversely affect her interests. Three factors dominate this evaluation: (1) During the 1971 India-Pakistan war, the US and China jointly supported Pakistan. The US had sent its Seventh Fleet into the Bay of Bengal to threaten India. (2) In India's perception, the United States was guilty by omission of ignoring China's actions in actively building up Pakistan's nuclear deterrence against India through the nineteen eighties, because both China and Pakistan were US allies in fighting the Soviet Union in Afghanistan. (3) Soon after India's nuclear tests in 1998, the United States and China issued a Joint Communiqué to condemn these.

In comparison to the up-and-down Sino-U.S. relationship framework, the US-India relationship has witnessed an upswing after the end of the Cold War. The perception that regards an 'emerging China' as a threat is beginning to dominate policy-making circles in both the US and India. This will be harmful for both Sino-US and Sino-India relations. For America, China and India are two major powers that can influence security affairs in the Asia-Pacific, especially in East Asia and South Asia. China and India are also populous, transitional and emerging big powers. Both China and India regards their relations with the US as their most important external relationship.

The economic development of China and India needs America's cooperation and support. At the same time, America needs the huge markets of the two big Asian countries. The United States could be a positive factor for Sino-India relationships – if it tries to promote regional stability in South Asia and help China and India's economic modernization. It could, as well, cast itself in a negative role – when it plays the 'India card' in its dealings with China; or plays the 'China card' in developing its relations with India.

Within China, in recent years, there has been a fundamental reassessment of South Asia and its importance in geo-politics, as well as of India and its role in regional affairs. The nature of Sino-Indian relationships should be "good neighbours in geo-politics, good friends in economic cooperation, and good partners in international affairs." Such a relationship must be established on the basis of their common sense and understanding of mutual interests. Through economic co-operation and regional stability, China, the US and India should and would be able to reach a 'win-win-win' situation.

INDIA-U.S. RELATIONS: A VISION FOR THE 21ST CENTURY

At the dawn of a new century, President Clinton and Prime Minister Vajpayee resolve to create a closer and qualitatively new relationship between the United States and India. We are two of the world's largest democracies. We are nations forged from many traditions and faiths, proving year after year that diversity is our strength. From vastly different origins and experiences, we have come to the same conclusions: that freedom and democracy are the strongest bases for both peace and prosperity, and that they are universal aspirations, constrained neither by culture nor levels of economic development. There have been times in the past when our relationship drifted without a steady course. As we now look towards the future, we are convinced that it is time to chart a new and purposeful direction in our relationship. Globalization is erasing boundaries and building networks between nations and peoples, economies and cultures. The world is increasingly coming together around the democratic ideals India and the United States have long championed and lived by.

Together, we represent a fifth of the world's people, more than a quarter of the world's economy. We have built creative, entrepreneurial societies. We are leaders in the information age. The currents of commerce and culture that link our societies run strong and deep. In many ways, the character of the 21st century world will depend on the success of our cooperation for peace, prosperity, democracy and freedom. That presents us with an opportunity, but also a profound responsibility to work together. Our partnership of shared ideals leads us to seek a natural partnership of shared endeavors.

In the new century, India and the United States will be partners in peace, with a common interest in and complementary responsibility for ensuring regional and international security.

We will engage in regular consultations on, and work together for, strategic stability in Asia and beyond. We will bolster joint efforts to counter terrorism and meet other challenges to regional peace. We will strengthen the international security system, including in the United Nations, and support the United Nations in its peacekeeping efforts. We acknowledge that tensions in South Asia can only be resolved by the nations of South Asia. India is committed to enhancing cooperation, peace and stability in the region.

India and the United States share a commitment to reducing and ultimately eliminating nuclear weapons, but we have not always agreed on how to reach this common goal. The United States believes India should forgo nuclear weapons. India believes that it needs to maintain a credible minimum nuclear deterrent in keeping with its own assessment of its security needs. Nonetheless, India and the U.S. are prepared to work together to prevent the proliferation of nuclear weapons and their means of delivery. To this end, we will persist with and build upon the productive bilateral dialogue already underway.

We reaffirm our respective voluntary commitments to forgo further nuclear explosive tests. We will work together and with others for an early commencement of negotiations on a treaty to end the production of fissile materials for nuclear weapons. We have both shown strong commitments to export controls, and will continue to strengthen them. We will work together to prevent the spread of dangerous technologies. We are committed to build confidence and reduce the chances of miscalculation. We will pursue our security needs in a restrained and responsible manner, and will not engage in nuclear and missile arms races. We will seek to narrow our differences and increase mutual understanding on non-proliferation and security issues. This will help us to realize the full potential of Indo-U.S. relations and contribute significantly to regional and global security.

The true measure of our strength lies in the ability of our people to shape their destiny and to realize their aspirations for a better life. That is why the United States and India are and will be allies in the cause of democracy. We will share our experience in nurturing and strengthening democratic institutions the world over and fighting the challenge to democratic order from forces such as terrorism. We will cooperate with others to launch an international Community of Democracies this year.

The United States applauds India's success in opening its economy, its achievements in science and technology, its commitment to a new wave of economic expansion and reform, and its determination to bring the benefits of economic growth to all its people. Our nations pledge to reduce impediments to bilateral trade and investment and to expand commerce between us, especially in the emerging knowledge-based industries and high-technology areas.

We will work together to preserve stability and growth in the global economy as well. And we will join in an unrelenting battle against poverty in the world, so that the promise of a new economy is felt everywhere and no nation is left behind. That is among the fundamental challenges of our time. Opening trade and resisting protectionism are the best means for meeting it. We support an open, equitable and transparent rule-based multilateral trading system, and we will work together to strengthen it. We agree that developed countries should embrace policies that offer developing countries the opportunity to grow, because growth is the key to rising incomes and rising standards. At the same time, we share the conviction that human development also requires empowerment of people and availability of basic freedoms.

As leaders in the forefront of the new high-technology economy, we recognize that countries can achieve robust economic growth while protecting the environment and taking action to combat climate change. We will do our part to meet the global environmental challenges, including climate change and the impacts of air and water pollution on human health. We also pledge a common effort to battle the infectious diseases that kill people and retard progress in so many countries. India is at the forefront of the global effort that has brought us to the threshold of the eradication of polio. With leadership, joint research, and application of modern science, we can and will do the same for the leading killers of our time, including AIDS, malaria and tuberculosis. We are proud of the cooperation between Indians and Americans in advancing frontiers of knowledge.

But even as we unravel the mysteries of time and space, we must continue to apply our knowledge to older challenges: eradicating human suffering, disease and poverty. In the past, our cooperation helped ease mass hunger in the world. In the future, it will focus as well on the development of clean energy, health, and education.

Our partnership is not an end in itself, but a means to all these ends. And it is reinforced by the ties of scholarship, commerce, and increasingly of kinship among our people. The industry, enterprise and cultural contributions of Americans of Indian heritage have enriched and enlivened both our societies. Today, we pledge to deepen the Indian-American partnership in tangible ways, always seeking to reconcile our differences through dialogue and engagement, always seizing opportunities to advance the countless interests we have in common.

As a first step, President Clinton has invited Prime Minister Vajpayee to visit Washington at a mutually convenient opportunity, and the Prime Minister has accepted that invitation. Henceforth, the President of the United States and the Prime Minister of India should meet regularly to institutionalize our dialogue. We have also agreed on and separately outlined an architecture of additional high-level consultations, and of joint working groups, across the broad spectrum of areas in which we are determined to institutionalize our enhanced cooperation. And we will encourage even stronger people-to-people ties.

For India and the United States, this is a day of new beginnings. We have before us for the first time in 50 years the possibility to realize the full potential of our relationship. We will work to seize that chance, for our benefit and all those with whom we share this increasingly interdependent world.

Institutional Dialogue Between the United States and India

1. During the visit of President Clinton to Delhi in March 2000, President Clinton and Prime Minister Vajpayee agreed as part of their vision for the future relationship that a regular, wide-ranging dialogue is important for achieving the goal of establishing closer and multifaceted relations between India and the United States and for the two countries to work jointly for promotion of peace and prosperity in the 21st century. The two leaders agreed on a number of steps to intensify and institutionalize the dialogue between India and the United States.
2. The President of the United States and Prime Minister of India will hold regular bilateral 'Summits' in alternating capitals or elsewhere, including on the occasions of multilateral meetings, to review bilateral relations and consult on international developments and issues. They will remain in frequent contact by telephone and through letters.
3. The two countries will also hold an Annual Foreign Policy Dialogue at the level of the Secretary of State of the United States and External Affairs Minister of India. This dialogue will be broad-based and touch upon all aspects of US-India relations, including considering the work of other groups as appropriate.
4. The two countries also consider the ongoing Dialogue on Security and Non-proliferation between the Deputy Secretary of State of the United States and External Affairs Minister of India important for improving mutual understanding on bilateral, regional and international security matters. They agreed that this dialogue should continue and take place semi-annually or as often as considered desirable by both sides. The Principals of this dialogue will establish Expert Groups on specific issues as considered desirable and appropriate.

5. Foreign Office Consultations between the Under Secretary of State for Political Affairs of the United States and Foreign Secretary of India will continue. The two leaders believe that close cooperation between the two countries is a factor of stability in the politically and culturally diverse and rapidly transforming Asia. A Dialogue on Asian Security will also be conducted as part of the Foreign Office Consultations. The two sides will also stay in close touch and consult on international democracy initiatives.
6. The two leaders consider combating international terrorism as one of the most important global challenges. They expressed satisfaction at the establishment of the Joint Working Group on Counter-terrorism and its productive first meeting in February 2000. They agree that the Joint Working Group should continue to meet regularly and become an effective mechanism for the two countries to share information and intensify their cooperation in combating terrorism.
7. The two leaders see an enormous potential for enhancement of economic and business relations between the two countries in the Knowledge Age. They decided to institutionalize bilateral economic dialogue. They will keep themselves informed and follow developments in the bilateral economic dialogue closely through a high-level coordinating group. The coordinating group will be led on the US side by the White House with the support of the State Department, and on the Indian side by the Prime Minister's Office with the support of the Ministry of External Affairs.

The Coordinating Group will develop a common economic agenda for and undertake preparations for the Heads of Government meetings. With broad inter-agency and inter-ministerial representations at senior official levels, it would convene regularly to facilitate close coordination on the various issues raised in the ministerial dialogues and ensure that discussions therein complement and reinforce broad economic and foreign policy objectives, including the deepening of bilateral cooperation on high technology and information technology issues.

US-India Financial and Economic Forum: The US Secretary of the Treasury and the Indian Minister of Finance will host a forum on finance and investment issues, macroeconomic policy and international economic developments at regular intervals. Their meetings at the ministerial level would be supplemented by sub-Cabinet meetings and involve, as appropriate, the participation of the Securities and Exchange Commission, Federal Reserve, Council of Economic Advisors, and other officials of the US Government and the Securities and Exchange Board of India, Reserve Bank of India, and other officials of the Government of India.

US-India Commercial Dialogue: The US Secretary of Commerce and Minister of Commerce and Industry of India will lead a dialogue to deepen ties between the Indian and American Business communities. The dialogue will encompass regular government-to-government meetings to be held in conjunction with private sector meetings. Its aim will be to (a) facilitate trade, and (b) maximize investment opportunities across a broad range of economic sectors, including information technology, infrastructure, biotechnology, and services. Participation will include, as appropriate, representatives of other Cabinet agencies and ministries on both sides. Close contact will be maintained with business associations, and activities will be planned with the benefit of such private sector input, including the establishment of subcommittees to pursue specific projects or sectoral issues of mutual interest.

US-India Working Group on Trade: The United States Trade Representative and the Ministry of Commerce and other concerned Ministries/Departments of the Government of India will engage in regular discussion to enhance cooperation on trade policy. As appropriate, individual trade issues could be examined in greater depth with the participation of other agencies with corresponding responsibilities and through creation of sub-groups. The Group will serve as a locus of consultation on a broad range of trade-related issues, including those pertaining to the World Trade Organization. The Group will receive inputs from the private sector (including trade policy issues identified in the US-India Commercial Dialogue) as appropriate.

The two leaders consider cooperation between the two countries in energy and environment an important part of their vision for the future. They have agreed to set up a Joint Consultative Group on Clean Energy and Environment. The Group will hold periodic ministerial/high level meetings as desirable and appropriate and will lay emphasis on collaborative projects, developing and deploying clean energy technologies, public and private sector investment and cooperation, and climate change and other environmental issues. The Co-conveners of the Group will be the Department of State of the United States and the Ministry of External Affairs of India.

The two leaders believe that the strong scientific resources of the two countries provide excellent opportunities for scientific collaboration between them. They agree to set up a US-India Science and Technology Forum. The Forum shall promote research and development, the transfer of technology, the creation of a comprehensive electronic reference source for US-India science and technology cooperation, and the electronic exchange and dissemination of information on US-India science and technology cooperation, and other programs consistent with the previous practice of the US-India Foundation.

9

Trump Presidency and Future of India-US Relations

It is more than three months since Donald Trump won the US presidential election and more than three weeks since he was inaugurated to that high office.

Analysts and observers had hoped that Trump would mellow his pronouncements on various national and international issues after his victory in the election. They had expected that President-elect Trump would be more responsible and measured in his declarations than candidate Trump. This did not happen. They anticipated that President Trump would conduct himself with greater decorum than before. Their hopes were again belied.

With the benefit of hindsight, it is possible to make some realistic assumptions on the future course of India-US relations under Trump. India-US partnership has been one of the few areas that has been non-controversial and a bright spot for the USA on the foreign policy front in recent years. It can be confidently asserted that India-US relations enjoy bipartisan support in the US Congress and across the board among the US citizens. Starting with Bill Clinton's visit to India in March, 2000, the state of partnership today is the highest ever between the two countries.

The three most recent Presidents viz Clinton, Obama (Democrats) and Bush (Republican) have all worked assiduously to take the relationship to ever newer heights. On the Indian side also, if Prime Minister Vajpayee had characterised the two countries as "natural allies" and Prime Minister Modi termed the connect as an "indispensable partnership," Prime Minister Manmohan Singh had staked the survival of his government on the India-US civil nuclear deal and termed this as the biggest achievement of his 10-year rule. President Obama termed India-US ties as the "defining partnership of the 21st century."

Over the last decade, India-US bilateral relations have developed into a "global strategic partnership" based on shared democratic values and increasing convergence of interests on bilateral, regional and global issues. Regular exchange of high level political visits has provided sustained momentum to bilateral cooperation while the wide-ranging and ever-expanding dialogue architecture has established a long-term framework for India-U.S. engagement. Today, the India-US bilateral cooperation is broad-based and multi-sectoral, covering trade and investment, defence and security, education, science and technology, cyber security, high-technology, civil nuclear energy, space technology and applications, clean energy, environment, agriculture and health.

Donald Trump has hence inherited a vigorous and vibrant relationship between India and the USA. It is expected that Trump will do all that is necessary to take the bilateral partnership to newer heights. This was clearly evident from the fact that Prime Minister Narendra Modi was the fifth world leader, after Presidents of Mexico and Egypt and Prime Ministers of Canada and Israel, whom Trump called after his inauguration on January 20, 2017. The Modi-Trump conversation on January 24 was marked by cordiality and warmth which cannot be said about some other conversations that Trump had with some other leaders. Official statements issued by the two sides did not go into specifics but Trump's early phone call is evidence of the priority that Trump attaches to Indo-US ties. According to a White House statement, Trump emphasised that Washington considers India a "true friend and partner in addressing challenges around the world." Both leaders were said to have discussed opportunities to strengthen their partnership on the economy and defence. They also discussed security in south and central Asia and resolved to "stand shoulder to shoulder in the global fight against terrorism." Modi tweeted that he had a "warm conversation" with the President and said the pair had "agreed to work closely in the coming days to further strengthen our bilateral ties." Both Modi and Trump invited each other for state visits. This telephonic conversation could set the tone for the future of Indo-US relationship under a Republican administration.

Although no specifics or details were provided after the telephonic conversation, it is clear that there was convergence between the two leaders on further strengthening relations in strategic, political, economic and defence areas, particularly in confronting the scourge of terrorism.

In addition to the Modi-Trump telephonic conversation, Indian government and incoming Trump Administration had already established several contacts after Trump's victory on November 8, 2016.

The first was the congratulatory message and call by PM Modi on November 9, just hours after the election results declaring Trump as the winner were announced. The second was by Foreign Secretary S Jaishankar during his visit to New York in end November, where he is reported to have met a number of advisors and officials in the Trump Transition Team. These were followed by interaction between NSA Ajit Doval and his counterpart Gen Mike Flynn on December 19 in Washington DC. Discussions on "regional and global issues" were reported to have taken place. With Flynn's resignation on February 14, contact at NSA level would have to be re-established with the new incumbent in due course.

PM Modi is himself reported to have said at a meeting just after the elections that he is looking forward to working with US president-elect Donald Trump with whom he has good relations and feels that the incoming Republican administration will be well inclined towards India.

A perusal of statements made by Trump during his campaigning would demonstrate that he did not make any sharply critical comments about India as he did for many other countries. On the contrary, he by and large made positive and laudatory references to India. He said that if he got elected, India will have a true friend in the White House. He showered encomiums on Prime Minister Modi saying that he is very energetic and that he (Trump) was looking forward to working with him.

The issue of job losses in the United States consistently surfaced as a contentious and divisive issue in this as well as previous US Presidential elections. In the current elections, factory closures and "stealing" of American jobs has featured extensively. Trump has mostly targeted China and Mexico for taking away American manufacturing jobs and blamed them for shutdown of industries. Only on a few occasions has he criticised the off-shoring of software and IT jobs to India. Indian companies, particularly in the IT sector like Infosys, WIPRO, TCS etc which are active in the USA, have already started taking corrective measures by increasingly hiring local professionals in view of some comments by Trump, as also Attorney General Jeff Sessions during his confirmation hearings. Irrespective of any immediate action that the US Administration might take to streamline the H1B visa regime, I feel reasonably confident that in the near future, the US government will be persuaded by its industry and will realise that the competitiveness of the US industry is critically dependent on the specialised and technically sophisticated work performed by Indian software engineers etc.

If Trump acts on his promise of bringing down the corporate tax in the USA from 35% to 15%, it could encourage and tempt some US companies currently based in India to relocate to USA. This could have an adverse impact on the Make in India initiative of the Indian government if some companies leave the country.

Trump's relations with Pakistan are also likely to have a significant impact on India. Trump's strong statements against terrorism make it likely that he applies added pressure on Pakistan to stop supporting and providing sanctuary to terrorists. This could be beneficial for India. Trump's temporary ban on admitting nationals from seven Muslim majority nations has worried Pakistan that it could also be included in this category. This apprehension became even more pronounced when in a White House press briefing, the spokesperson stated in response to a question that entry of Pakistani nationals could also be banned. This prompted Pakistan to quickly put Lashkar-e-Taibe chief Hafiz Saeed under house arrest on January 31 this year to burnish its counter-terrorism credentials in front of the Trump administration. Over the last many years, Trump has made several statements that were highly condemnatory of Pakistan saying that it is no friend of USA as it takes billions of dollars from America while it continued to help its enemies and got US soldiers killed. Trump has also commented adversely against nuclear weapons in Pakistan. He stated at one of his election rallies that he would like to get the help and support of India to deal with the problem of a "semi-stable, nuclear armed Pakistan."

In conclusion, it appears highly likely that in strategic, political, security, defence and economic terms, relations between India and the USA will continue their upward trajectory under President Trump. Impact of USA's relations with Pakistan on India is likely to be beneficial and positive. As far as implications for India with respect to USA's evolving relations with China and Russia are concerned, it will be better to wait for further denouements to unfold. Relations between these countries with the USA are complex and multi-faceted. It is too early to speculate how they will evolve and what ramifications they might entail for India.

THE TRUMP PRESIDENCY AND THE FUTURE OF INDO-US RELATIONS

Less than three months into Donald Trump's tenure as President of the United States, Indian observers are contemplating the future of bilateral relations with the global leader, not to mention the regional implications of the new administration. Questions arise whether to take Mr Trump's "America First" rhetoric seriously, or to believe that dealing with a businessman persona will ultimately benefit India's diplomats, businesses, and citizens.

Taking into account such uncertainty and what we've seen of Mr. Trump and his team thus far, the path forward for India in key geo-economics and geopolitical areas is fraught with challenges. Nevertheless, India has an opportunity to expand and deepen its trade relations, upgrade its domestic capacity, move forward with climate change action, and become a leader in the Asia-Pacific region.

Therefore, India must design and implement a clear, internally-based strategy through an inclusive process to promote open and fair trade and cooperation bilaterally, regionally, and multilaterally.

Relations between the US and India will likely remain constant for some time, and hopefully even continue the positive movement made under the past two presidencies. The Trump Presidency will have less of a direct impact on India, barring a few critical areas like movement of Indian professionals to the United States or impediments to foreign direct investment (FDI) into India.

Although no less important, the Trump administration - guided by an 'America First' strategy that emphasizes transactionalism - is likely to create more indirect impact in terms of trade, climate change, and regional integration. Importantly, the bilateral relationship is expected to be dictated chiefly by business considerations and less by shared values or cultural connections; something for Indian representatives to consider when trying to maintain progress in Indo-US relations.

Despite the Trump administration positioning itself for greater bilateral trade agreements - of which India must certainly take advantage - India should broaden its gaze with regard to trade as a tool for meeting economic and development goals in order to weather this storm of uncertainty. The UK, Canada, and Peru as well as economic communities in Latin

America, Sub-Saharan Africa, and Central Asia are top potential trading partners. Also, completing current negotiations with the EU, Australia, and especially the Regional Comprehensive Economic Partnership agreement will be vital for India to broaden its market access while upgrading its trading standards and capacity. India's recent accession to the Customs Convention on International Transport of Goods is a welcomed step toward efficient multi-modal movement of goods.

Considering the fervent populism seen in many parts of the world, a country like India that has gained much from its stance on open trade will have to make even greater efforts to listen to its people at all levels when implementing trade policy - particularly from those most vulnerable to trade liberalization. This will also require clear and targeted domestic provisions for retraining, relocation, and unemployment support.

As Mr. Trump's 'America First' position moves into action at the executive and legislative level, restrictions on temporary work visas could severely impact India's employment and remittances as well as hamper diplomatic ties between the two countries. Increasing that threat is Attorney General Jeff Sessions, a long-time critic of such visas. Immigration restrictions could also negatively affect the US economy, as Indian IT companies contributed $22.5 billion in US taxes annually and $6.6 billion in Social Security from 2011-2015. They also invested $2 billion into the United States from 2011-2013, and continue to provide thousands of US-based jobs. The United States will sorely need such contributions from India considering that by 2022 it is projected to have a skilled labor shortfall of 17 million, whereas India will have a surplus.

India and its industries must unequivocally show the US administration that its skilled and unskilled jobs - the kinds of jobs Mr. Trump has called to return home - cannot be filled with domestic labor alone; blocking Indian professionals out of the US labor market will only exacerbate the labor shortage. India's numerous allies in Congress will be essential in this effort. Concomitantly, Indian skilled labor must elevate itself from dependency on the US by connecting with other markets to provide services in IT, banking, and finance, as well as growing retail and healthcare services.

As relations between the United States and China remain unpredictable, India will have to play the balancing act, not unlike with recent US and Russian relations. India should not expect that the potential rise in tension between the U.S. and China will draw Washington closer to Delhi, considering Mr. Trump's transactional worldview. Likewise, India should not become complacent in thinking that its friendship will blossom due to Mr. Trump's global tirades against what he sees as his enemies. Rather, India must cultivate relationships with both countries based on its own principles and strategic vision.

With the potential of US disengagement in the global movement to tackle climate change looming, India has the opportunity to be a driver in the green industry, considering the advancements and accessibility of renewable technology. While financing will be a challenge if the US breaks from its commitments, India can gain a foothold on becoming a leader in renewable technology by first promoting its intrinsic aggregator industry to develop solar technology. Such groups of aggregators, with established supply links in compatible sectors such as electronics, can procure components domestically and internationally more efficiently than multinational brick and mortar solar companies. In the long-run, of course, India must invest in start-ups of the renewables industry.

As regional leadership gaps arise with the potential US withdrawal, whether in economic integration or climate change, India should advance itself diplomatically as a cooperative partner with a history of understanding and promoting the needs of developing countries in the region. Historical US allies such as South Korea, Japan, and more recently Vietnam can look to India as a strong partner in the region on trade and economic integration; both bilaterally and in regional arrangements.

To whatever extent the Trump Administration's 'America First' policy regime may or may not challenge Indo-US relations, India's core focus must remain on promoting mutually beneficial trade arrangements and cooperation bilaterally, regionally, and multilaterally. The unnerving lack of predictability from the United States should not invite reactionary approaches from the Indian government, businesses, or citizenry. If India is guided by grounded principles based in its development and economic needs, it can surely weather any storm of uncertainty that may come its way.

TRUMP AND THE FUTURE OF INDO-US RELATIONS

Less than three months into Donald Trump's term as President, those watching in India are intensely anticipating how bilateral relations will proceed with the United States.

Given the many uncertainties posed by Trump's 'America First' foreign policy rhetoric and what we have seen of the administration's actions, the way forward for India's diplomats, businesses and citizens in key geo-economic and geopolitical areas is filled with challenges. But India can seize this as an opportunity to advance its domestic capacity, expand and strengthen its trade relations, progress climate change action and take a leading role in the Asia Pacific region.

India's focus must be to design and operationalise a clear strategy through a transparent and inclusive process to engage in open and fair trade and cooperation bilaterally, regionally and multilaterally.

Bilateral relations between the United States and India are expected to remain cordial in the short-to-medium term. But the Trump administration's 'America First' strategy, which emphasises firm reciprocity, is likely to create indirect effects on trade, climate change and regional connectivity.

While Trump's trade strategy is still emerging, the recent 2017 Trade Policy Agenda seems to confirm the administration's transactionalist approach to trade negotiations. Despite the administration's focus on bilateral trade agreements, of which India must take advantage, India will need to widen its reach on trade to hedge against such uncertainty.

Top potential trading partners that India should pursue include the United Kingdom, Canada, Mexico and Peru, as well as economic groups in Latin America, Sub-Saharan Africa and Central Asia. Also, ensuring an ambitious Regional Comprehensive Economic Partnership agreement will be vital for India to gain greater market access while upgrading its trading standards.

Taking into account the backlash against globalisation witnessed in many parts of the world, a country like India that has gained much from open trade and multilateralism will have to work more inclusively with its marginalised population at all levels to bring those communities into the fold to fairly distribute the benefits of global economic growth. Comprehensive consultations on trade policy as well as effective domestic assistance programmes for retraining, relocation and unemployment will be required to ease inevitable transition challenges for workers and families.

The free movement of professionals from India to the United States, which accounts for half of US permanent work migration, has been a bilateral contention for some time. Despite a seemingly positive meeting by Indian Foreign Secretary Subrahmanyam Jaishankar with Trump's Cabinet in early March, the administration and Congress are taking action to slow or block entrance of skilled workers into the United States. This could severely impact India's employment and remittances as well as impede diplomatic ties between the two nations.

India's impacted industries, along with diplomats, must clearly demonstrate to the Trump administration that US skilled and unskilled domestic labour, the kinds of jobs that Trump promised to bring back, will not fill the gap that Indian professionals currently fill in the US labour market.

Considering its advances in and access to renewable technology, India has the opportunity to be a champion in the industry and to address the serious challenges of climate change. To start gaining a foothold, India can first push its domestic industry to develop solar technology and open up to attract greater FDI, while planning long-term investments in start-ups. Small scale aggregators can ensure cost-effective procurement for solar products. Thus, this approach may be a viable option financially to fend off the challenge of limited funding commitments from the United States.

With the potential challenges from Trump's proposed budget cuts, possibly leading to a withdrawal of US leadership in the region, a clearly designed strategy will provide the necessary and beneficial policy predictability for India and its neighbours. In the Asia Pacific, India should advance itself as a cooperative partner with an acute understanding of the needs of developing countries. Historical US allies can look to India as a strong partner in the region on economic integration, climate change action and trade — both bilaterally and in regional arrangements.

Change seems to be inevitable. Given the current churning in the international order, the responsibility of promoting norms for equitable economic growth and development at home and abroad will now fall on countries like India. Thus, India's attention must remain on promoting mutually beneficial trade agreements and cooperation bilaterally, regionally and multilaterally. Guided by a transparent internally-based strategy, India can brave through and indeed thrive in a changing world.

WHAT DONALD TRUMP'S PRESIDENCY MEANS FOR INDIA

On a recent visit in India to lecture at the prestigious Indian Law Institute in New Delhi, I was struck by the widespread sense of uncertainty and anxiety about the new U.S. administration's foreign policy. Notwithstanding that my topic was "International Human Rights and the Environment," questions from the audience — students, lawyers and judges — were mostly about President Donald Trump and his first several weeks in the White House.

These questions included: What is the future of India-U.S. relations under the Trump presidency? Will Trump value a strong, independent India? How will his economic, trade and immigration policies – especially the "America First" promise, visa changes, and tightening immigration rules — affect the Indian IT industry and the number of Indian students pursuing education in American universities?

The Trump administration did inherit strong relations with India, nurtured by three former presidents – Bill Clinton, George W. Bush and Barack Obama. The countries' bilateral relations cover a wide range of sectors, including trade and investment, defense, energy and environment, education, space technology, health, cybersecurity, and agriculture. I was told that for Indian political leaders, uncertainty about the direction of U.S. foreign policy under Trump was somewhat tempered by the confirmation of Rex Tillerson as secretary of state and James Mattis as defense secretary.

Four days after his inauguration, President Trump called Indian Prime Minister Narendra Modi and, while the official statements issued after the conversation mentioned no specifics, according to a White House statement Trump considers India a "true friend and partner in addressing challenges around the world." And Modi tweeted that he had a "warm conversation" with Trump and they had "agreed to work closely in the coming days to further strengthen our bilateral ties." They both invited each other for state visits. Trump and Modi reportedly discussed security in South and Central Asia and resolved to "stand shoulder to shoulder in the global fight against terrorism," in addition to opportunities to strengthen their partnership on defense and the economy.

Discussions are also taking place between Indian government officials and their counterparts in the Trump administration, aimed at exploring measures to further strengthen political, economic and defense relations between the two countries.

However, the Trump administration's proposed restrictions on the H-1B visa program has rattled the $150 billion technology sector, which is vital for the country's economy. Despite the assertions by tech companies that they are re-positioning their business models, the change is likely to adversely affect major

Indian tech players, such as Infosys, Tata Consulting, Wipro, and Cognizant. H-1B is a non-immigrant visa for skilled workers in specialty occupations such as IT and medicine, and is limited for a maximum of six years. Indians get a large percentage of these visas each year. The prevailing sentiment is that H-1B visas are "abused" as many U.S. companies contract out jobs to consulting firms in India that bring in lower-paid workers and it often becomes a path to U.S. citizenship. Thus, there is bipartisan support in the U.S. for H-1B reform.

But when two congressional delegations visiting India during the congressional break met Modi this past Tuesday, he indicated India's discomfort with the administration's intent to curb H-1B visas, urging the U.S. to take a "reflective, balanced and far-sighted" perspective on the movement of skilled professionals.

I met two Indian students who were accepted for graduate studies, one in engineering at Purdue and the other for an MBA at Carnegie Melon. Both are now applying to European universities instead, wary of possible restrictions by the Trump administration on job opportunities for outsiders. "The situation is unpredictable and I can't take chances," said the engineering student.

Strengthening of economic relations between India and the U.S. is obviously in our common interest. Perhaps even more important is our strategic partnership to ensure regional stability, especially in light of India's tough neighbors, China, Pakistan and Afghanistan. The relationship should be treated with respect.

INDO-US RELATIONS: A BIG CHILL DESCENDS

The Barack Obama administration seems to be losing the plot on India. Otherwise why would it burn India-US relations over a nanny's wages? But that in a nutshell is the current state of play. It threatens to destroy years of hard work behind this important relationship, one that was meant to reconfigure the geopolitics of Asia.

The unexpected and entirely avoidable crisis was triggered by the humiliating treatment of an Indian diplomat at the hands of the US law enforcement officers. It provoked massive outrage in New Delhi but Washington doesn't understand why.

The American surprise and bafflement at the extent of the Indian anger shows a curious lack of political insight. It also shows a failure to understand the basic governing principles of good relations.

The Barack Obama administration seems to be losing the plot on India. Otherwise why would it burn India-US relations over a nanny's wages? But that in a nutshell is the current state of play. It threatens to destroy years of hard work behind this important relationship, one that was meant to reconfigure the geopolitics of Asia.

The unexpected and entirely avoidable crisis was triggered by the humiliating treatment of an Indian diplomat at the hands of the US law enforcement officers. It provoked massive outrage in New Delhi but Washington doesn't understand why. The American surprise and bafflement at the extent of the Indian anger shows a curious lack of political insight. It also shows a failure to understand the basic governing principles of good relations.

The public arrest and strip-search of Devyani Khobragade, India's deputy consul general in New York, on December 12 last year has the Indian establishment fuming. And for good reason. A diplomat embodies the sovereignty of a country and must be treated with dignity. More so because the US diplomats in India and other countries enjoy benefits far in excess of what they grant in return.

But their complete disregard for diplomatic conventions, norms and courtesies in Khobragade's case has put a knife through bilateral relations. They have ensured that 2014 will be spent mostly fixing what should never have been broken.

A defining partnership

President Obama, who has called India-US relations the "defining partnership of the 21st century", has kept his distance.

The White House political managers too are missing in action. Surely, they understand the need to box the problem before it spreads through the entire system. Hard work and political acumen are required in American-style extra-large helpings.

Washington must consider the long-term implications: India-US relations are important for regional stability in South Asia, for the security of Afghanistan as US troops depart and for the long fight against the forces of religious conservatism. Above all they are important for ensuring a fair balance of power in Asia and China's peaceful rise.

Questions have been raised whether the Khobragade episode was a symptom of a deeper disease afflicting Indo-US relations. It is true that the relationship has been losing traction under the Obama administration. The Democrat came to office with the 2008 economic crisis darkening almost everything on the American horizon.

His focus was on improving the domestic economy but the fallout was an economically beleaguered America beating up on India on a variety of issues – market access, taxation, intellectual property protection and limits on foreign investment in insurance and retail sectors. Meanwhile, the cornerstone of transformed relations - the civil nuclear deal - was unravelling because of a nuclear liability law passed by India which US suppliers could not work with.

The remarkable breakthrough achieved by the US administration under the former President George W Bush was dying a slow death, mainly because of New Delhi . The nuclear deal was supposed to lead to commercial contracts for the US companies, but the Indian liability law was deemed unacceptable by Washington.

Disappointment with the UPA government grew in the US establishment for the opportunities missed and the roads not travelled. Prime Minister Manmohan Singh, who championed the nuclear deal, watched quietly as the Congress Party old guard set about undermining relations with the US. They pursued economic and trade policies that were deemed "unfriendly" by the Obama administration.

Before the Khobragade affair lit the big fire, Washington was keenly awaiting India's national election for a new leadership to emerge to bring the relationship out of its funk.

Shifting equations

If Narendra Modi from the nationalist Bharatiya Janata Party becomes India's new prime minister, the Obama administration may have another problem on its hand. Washington blacklisted Modi in 2005 and revoked his US visa because of the anti-Muslim violence in Gujarat, which claimed more than 1,000 lives. Even though he has been cleared by Indian courts of complicity in the riots, Washington has made no overtures to Modi.

US officials cannot hope that Modi will forgive and forget the insult. But no matter who is at the helm in India, 2014 will be a difficult year for Indo-US relations. The departure of US troops from Afghanistan will loom large over South Asia. Their absence will likely boost armed groups, affecting India's strategic calculations.

New Delhi's chagrin will multiply in direct proportion to Washington's dependence on Pakistan to facilitate the troop withdrawal. The current impasse between Kabul and Washington on a Bilateral Security Agreement to allow for a continuing US presence beyond 2014 is a further complication. The guessing game on the US exit strategy in Afghanistan can muddy India's own outlook.

Contradictions between the interests of Washington, Kabul, New Delhi, which broadly want to contain armed groups and those of Islamabad, which creates influence through those very forces, are real and challenging. Managing these requires more engagement between the US and India not less.

Challenges ahead in 2014

A bigger and more abiding challenge is China and its restless quest for supremacy. India, itself at the receiving end of China's aggressive moves, has quietly watched the US take one step forward and two back in dealing with Beijing's provocations in

South and East China Seas. China's recent declaration of an air-defence identification zone prompted Washington to first fly B-52s through it only to reel back days later. The Obama administration's cautious response to China's slow but sure territorial creep in Asia doesn't raise confidence levels in New Delhi. This in turn lowers enthusiasm for an American embrace.

Thus the perennial question: can performance match the promise of Indo-US relations? The short answer is yes because the fundamentals are solid. The inherent logic for stronger ties remains unchanged. The US sees India as an anchor in Asia, a lynchpin of stability against the threat of armed groups from Pakistan and Afghanistan. India's population and size, its democratic system and legal tradition present a welcome alternative to the Chinese model. Americans have no fears about the "rise" of India – in fact, they eagerly await its true unleashing on the world stage.

Strengthening ties

A recent survey showed that more members of the Council on Foreign Relations, a prestigious think tank, named India (37 percent) as an important US ally of the future than any other country. Also worth noting is that far fewer see India as a key partner than did four years ago when 55 percent named it as the partner of choice.

India sees the US as a guarantor of peace against an unpredictable China and a stabilising force in Afghanistan. Bluntly put, the US is the preferred hegemon. The links between the three-million-strong Indian American community and the mother country add another layer of texture to the relationship. A new Indian government can start by first addressing the hostility of the American business community triggered by India's policies. Renewing the confidence of the Wall Street and the Main Street about India's economic prospects is key to regaining lost ground.

The US too must attend to India's concerns, including the targeting of Indian IT companies by the US Congress in various immigration reform bills under consideration. It must also conclude a "totalization agreement" with India and stop pocketing $1bn annually in social security taxes from temporary Indian workers – a blatant American power play if there was any. The agreement would end double taxation on income of Indian professionals who pay US social security taxes but return to India without enjoying any benefits in return. The year of living dangerously must give way to a year of fence mending and re-engaging. Given the larger interests of both countries, that is the best option.

CONTEXT OF THE U.S.-INDIA RELATIONSHIP

U.S. and congressional interests in India cover a wide spectrum of issues, ranging from the militarized dispute with Pakistan and weapons proliferation to concerns about regional security, terrorism, human rights, health, energy, and trade and investment opportunities. In the 1990s, India-U.S. relations were particularly affected by the demise of the Soviet Union — India's main trading partner and most reliable source of economic and military assistance for most of the Cold War — and New Delhi's resulting need to diversify its international relationships. Also significant were India's adoption of significant economic policy reforms beginning in 1991, a deepening bitterness between India and Pakistan over Kashmir, and signs of a growing Indian preoccupation with China as a potential long-term strategic rival. With the fading of Cold War constraints, the United States and India began exploring the possibilities for a more normalized relationship between the world's two largest democracies. Throughout the 1990s, however, regional rivalries, separatist tendencies, and sectarian tensions continued to divert India's attention and resources from economic and social development. Fallout from these unresolved problems — particularly nuclear proliferation and human rights issues — presented major irritants in bilateral relations.

India's May 1998 nuclear tests were an unwelcome surprise and seen to be a policy failure in Washington, and they spurred then-Deputy Secretary of State Strobe Talbott to launch a series of meetings with Indian External Affairs Minister Jaswant

Singh in an effort to bring New Delhi more in line with U.S. arms control and nonproliferation goals. While this proximate purpose went unfulfilled, the two officials soon engaged a broader agenda on the entire scope of U.S.-India relations, eventually meeting fourteen times in seven different countries over a two-year period. The Talbott-Singh talks were considered the most extensive U.S.-India engagement up to that time and likely enabled circumstances in which the United States could play a key role in defusing the 1999 Kargil crisis, as well as laying the groundwork for a landmark U.S. presidential visit in 2000.

President Bill Clinton's March 2000 visit to South Asia seemed a major U.S. initiative to improve relations with India. One outcome was a Joint Statement in which the two countries pledged to "deepen the India-American partnership in tangible ways." A U.S.-India Joint Working Group on Counterterrorism was established that year and continues to meet regularly. During his subsequent visit to the United States later in 2000, Prime Minister Atal Bihari Vajpayee addressed a joint session of Congress and issued a second Joint Statement with President Clinton agreeing to cooperate on arms control, terrorism, and HIV/AIDS.

In the wake of the September 2001 terrorist attacks on the United States, India took the immediate and unprecedented step of offering to the United States full cooperation and the use of India's bases for counterterrorism operations. Engagement was accelerated after a November 2001 meeting between President Bush and Prime Minister Vajpayee, when the two leaders agreed to greatly expand U.S.-India cooperation on a wide range of issues, including regional security, space and scientific collaboration, civilian nuclear safety, and broadened economic ties.

Notable progress has come in the area of security cooperation, with an increasing focus on counterterrorism, joint military exercises, and arms sales. In late 2001, the U.S.-India Defence Policy Group met in New Delhi for the first time since India's 1998 nuclear tests and outlined a defence partnership based on regular and high-level policy dialogue.

Prime Minister Manmohan Singh paid a landmark July 2005 visit to Washington, where what may be the most significant joint U.S.-India statement to date was issued. In March 2006, President Bush spent three days in India, discussed further strengthening a bilateral "global partnership," and issued another Joint Statement. The Bush Administration has vowed to "help India become a major world power in the 21st century," and U.S.-India relations are today conducted under the rubric of three major "dialogue" areas: strategic (including global issues and defence), economic (including trade, finance, commerce, and environment), and energy. President Bush's 2002 *National Security Strategy of the United States* stated that "U.S. interests require a strong relationship with India." The 2006 version claims that "India now is poised to shoulder global obligations in cooperation with the United States in a way befitting a major power." In the course of an annual assessment of global threats, Director of National Intelligence Mike McConnell said, We expect India's growing confidence on the world stage as a result of its sustained high rates of economic growth will make New Delhi a more effective partner of the United States but also a more formidable interlocutor in areas of disagreement, particularly in the WTO.

In late 2007, Under Secretary of State Burns, who traveled to New Delhi at least eight times over a two-year period, penned an article lauding stronger U.S.-India relations while also identifying "considerable hurdles" to achieving an effective "global partnership." Foremost among these are terrorism, narcotics trafficking, and nuclear proliferation, which he avers must be dealt with through stronger bilateral security ties that will include defence sales. At a 2007 U.S.-India business conference in Washington, Secretary of State Rice laid out the perspective that, We in America look to the rise of India as an opportunity, a chance to work with a great fellow democracy to share not only the benefits of the international system, but indeed, the burdens and the responsibilities of maintaining it, of strengthening it, and defending it. We are eager to continue charting a global partnership with India, one that addresses the global challenges upon which the safety and success of every nation now depends: stemming nuclear proliferation, fighting terrorism, combating disease, protecting the environment, supporting education and upward mobility, expanding economic development, and promoting freedom under the rule of law.

Some analysts, however, see great potential but little likelihood of India becoming a major global power in the foreseeable future. Despite possession of a large, youthful, entrepreneurial population, a booming national economy, and growing power projection capabilities in the military realm, there remains much doubt about the capacity of India's leaders to engage in effective long-term strategic thinking and policy making. One senior Washington-based India-watcher has opined that, "The Indian strategic community is hopelessly unstrategic," and that its political community is "too domestically focused," thus precluding India's emergence as a substantive major power. Some Indian analysts agree that their national leaders lack a "coherent national grand strategy." Recognition of India's increasing stature and importance — and of the growing political influence some 2.3 million Indian-Americans — is found in the U.S. Congress, where the India and Indian-American Caucus is now the largest of all country-specific caucuses. Over the past seven years, legal Indian immigrants have come to the United States at a more rapid rate than any other group. In 2005 and 2006, the Indian-American community, relatively wealthy, geographically dispersed, and well-entrenched in several U.S. business sectors, conducted a major (and apparently successful) lobbying effort to encourage congressional passage of legislation to enable U.S.-India civil nuclear cooperation.

Bibliography

Ahmad, Imtiaz: *State and Foreign Policy: India's Role in USA*, New Delhi, Vikas, 1993.

Alam, Aftab : *US Policy Towards South Asia: Special Reference to Indo-Pak Relations*, Raj, Delhi, 1998.

Arend, A.: *International Law and the Use of Force,* London, Routledge, 1993.

Chandra, R.: *Judicial System in Mechanical Warfare*, Lucknow, Print House (India), 1992.

Chitkara, M.G. : *Indo-Pak Relations Challenges Before New Millennium*, APH, Delhi, 2001.

Deepak, B R : *India and China : 1904-2004 : A Century of Peace and Conflict*, Manak, Delhi, 2005.

Ghose, S.K.: *Politics of Violence: Dawn of a Dangerous Era*, Springfield, Nataraj, 1992.

Ghosh, Ajoy : *Indo-Pak Conflict : Threat to South Asian Security*, Reference Press, Delhi, 2003.

Hollihan, Thomas A. : *Uncivil Wars, Political Campaigns in a Media Age*, Boston: St. Martins, Delhi, 2001.

Huntington, S.P.: *The Soldier and the State,* N.Y., Vintage Books, 1964.

Janowitz, M.: *The Professional Soldier: A Social and Political Portrait*, N.Y., The Free Press, 1960.

Jha, Prem Shankar : *India, America and China : The Battle Between Soft and Hard Power*, Penguin Books India, Delhi, 2010.

John L. Esposito: *Islam: The Straight Path*, Oxford : Oxford University, England, 1991,

Kaplan, David, *The Cult At the End of the World*, New York: Crown Publishers, 1996.

Kegley, C. W.: *The new global terrorism: Characteristics, causes, and controls,* Upper Saddle Creek, NJ: Prentice Hall, 2003.

Kelly, John B.: *Britain and the Persian Gulf 1795-1880*, Oxford, Clarendon Press, 1968.

Kunju, N. : *Indo-Pak : Nuclear Cold War*, Reliance, Delhi, 2002.

Laquer, Walter: *Terrorism Attack from Computer Hacking,* Oxford: Oxford University Press, 1999.

Leo Tansky, *US and USSR Aid to Developing Countries: A Comparative Study of India, Turkey, and the UAR,* New York, 1967.

Paletz, David L. : *The Media in American Politics,* Addison-Wesley, New York, 2001.

Peter Kunstadter. : *Southeast Asian Tribes, Minorities and Nations.* Princeton: Princeton University Press, 1967.

Posen, B.R.: *The Sources of Military Doctrine*, Ithaca, 1984, Cornell Univ. Press.

Qureshi, A. Iqbal : *Islam and the Theory of Interest,* Kitab Bhavan, New Delhi, 1994.

Rhodes, Richard, *The Making of the Atomic Bomb*, New York: Simon and Schuster, 1988.

Rishiraj Singh: *Arms Control : The Politics of Disarmament*, Dominant, Delhi, 2004.

Schroeer, Dietrich, *Science, Technology, and the Nuclear Arms Race*, Ontario: John Wiley & Sons, 1984.

Schudson, Michael : *Watergate in American Memory, How We Remember, Forget and Reconstruct the Past,* Basic Books, New York, 1992.

Stephen E. Ambrose and James Alden Barber: *The Military and American Society,* New York, 1972.

Sunil Sondhi : *International Relations : Search for Security and Development*, South Asian Pub, Delhi, 2007.

Whitaker, D. J.: *The Terrorism Reader,* New York: Routledge, 2001.

White, J. R.: *Terrorism: An introduction: 2002 update,* Belmont, CA: Wadsworth, 2002.

Index

O

P

S

T

W

❑❑❑